YOUR CHINESE
HOROSCOPE 2000

ABOUT THE AUTHOR

Neil Somerville is one of the leading writers in the West on Chinese horoscopes. He has been interested in Eastern forms of divination for many years and believes that much can be learnt from the ancient wisdom of the East. His annual book on Chinese horoscopes has built up an international following and he is also the author of *Chinese Love Signs* (Thorsons, 1995).

Neil Somerville was born in the year of the Water Snake. His wife was born under the sign of the Monkey, his son is an Ox and daughter a Horse.

YOUR CHINESE HOROSCOPE 2000

NEIL SOMERVILLE

What the Year of the Dragon holds in store for you

Thorsons
An Imprint of HarperCollinsPublishers

TO ROS, RICHARD AND EMILY

Thorsons
An Imprint of HarperCollins*Publishers*
77–85 Fulham Palace Road
Hammersmith, London W6 8JB
The Thorsons website address is:
www.thorsons.com

Published by Thorsons 1999
10 9 8 7 6 5 4 3 2 1

© Neil Somerville 1999

Neil Somerville asserts the moral right to
be identified as the author of this work

A catalogue record for this book
is available from the British Library

ISBN 0 7225 3787 5

Printed and bound in Great Britain by
Caledonian International Book Manufacturing Ltd, Glasgow, G64

There are times in our lives when everything goes so right,
as if fortune has given us her blessing.
And there are times when everything goes so wrong,
as if we are under fortune's curse.
But at all times, good and bad,
it is we who can so influence what happens.
And it is those who act with fortitude,
with belief in themselves and their abilities,
whom fortune can help the most.
Neil Somerville

CONTENTS

ACKNOWLEDGEMENTS

———•———

In writing *Your Chinese Horoscope 2000* I am grateful for the assistance and support that those around me have given.

I wish to acknowledge Theodora Lau's *The Handbook of Chinese Horoscopes* (Harper & Row, 1979; Arrow, 1981), which was particularly useful to me in my research.

In addition to Ms Lau's work, I commend the following books to those who wish to find out more about Chinese horoscopes: Kristyna Arcarti, *Chinese Horoscopes for Beginners* (Headway, 1995); Catherine Aubier, *Chinese Zodiac Signs* (Arrow, 1984), a series of 12 books; Paula Delsol, *Chinese Horoscopes* (Pan, 1973); E. A. Crawford and Teresa Kennedy, *Chinese Elemental Astrology* (Piatkus, 1992); Barry Fantoni, *Barry Fantoni's Chinese Horoscopes* (Warner, 1994); Bridget Giles and the Diagram Group, *Chinese Astrology* (Collins Gem, HarperCollins*Publishers*, 1996); Kwok Man-Ho, *Authentic Chinese Horoscopes* (Arrow, 1987), a series of 12 books; Lori Reid, *The Complete Book of Chinese Horoscopes* (Element Books, 1997); Paul Rigby and Harvey Bean, *Chinese Astrologics* (Publications Division, South China Morning Post Ltd, 1981); Derek Walters, *Ming Shu* (Pagoda Books, 1987) and *The Chinese Astrology Workbook* (The Aquarian Press, 1988); Suzanne White,

ACKNOWLEDGEMENTS

Suzanne White's Book of Chinese Chance
(Fontana/Collins, 1978), *The New Astrology* (Pan, 1987)
and *The New Chinese Astrology* (Pan, 1994).

INTRODUCTION

The origins of Chinese horoscopes have been lost in the mists of time. It is known that Oriental astrologers practised their art many thousands of years ago and even today Chinese astrology continues to fascinate and intrigue.

In Chinese astrology there are 12 signs named after 12 different animals. No one quite knows how the signs acquired their names, but there is one legend that offers an explanation.

According to this legend, one Chinese New Year the Buddha invited all the animals in his kingdom to come before him. Unfortunately – for reasons best known to the animals – only 12 turned up. The first to arrive was the Rat, followed by the Ox, Tiger, Rabbit, Dragon, Snake, Horse, Goat, Monkey, Rooster, Dog and finally Pig.

In gratitude, the Buddha decided to name a year after each of the animals and that those born during that year would inherit some of the personality of that animal. Therefore those born in the Year of the Ox would be hardworking, resolute and stubborn, just like the Ox, while those born in the Year of the Dog would be loyal and faithful, just like the Dog. While not everyone can possibly share all the characteristics of a sign, it is incredible what similarities do occur and this is partly where the fascination of Chinese horoscopes lies.

In addition to the 12 signs of the Chinese zodiac there are also five elements and these have a strengthening or moderating influence upon the sign. Details about the effects of the elements are given in each of the chapters on the 12 signs.

To find out which sign you were born under, refer to the tables on pages xii–xv. As the Chinese year is based on the lunar year and does not start until late January or early February, it is particularly important for anyone born in those two months to check carefully the dates of the Chinese year in which they were born.

Also included, in the Appendix, are two charts showing the compatibility between the signs for both personal and business relationships, and details about the signs ruling the different hours of the day. From this it is possible to locate your ascendant and, as in Western astrology, this has a significant influence on your personality.

In writing this book, I have taken the unusual step of combining the intriguing nature of Chinese horoscopes with the Western desire to know what the future holds and have based my interpretations upon various factors relating to each of the signs. I have been pleased that over the years in which *Your Chinese Horoscope* has been published so many have found the sections on the forthcoming year of interest, and hope that the horoscope has been constructive and of help. Remember, though, that at all times you are the master of your own destiny. I sincerely hope that *Your Chinese Horoscope 2000* will prove interesting and helpful for the year ahead.

THE CHINESE YEARS

Rat	18 February	1912	to	5 February	1913
Ox	6 February	1913	to	25 January	1914
Tiger	26 January	1914	to	13 February	1915
Rabbit	14 February	1915	to	2 February	1916
Dragon	3 February	1916	to	22 January	1917
Snake	23 January	1917	to	10 February	1918
Horse	11 February	1918	to	31 January	1919
Goat	1 February	1919	to	19 February	1920
Monkey	20 February	1920	to	7 February	1921
Rooster	8 February	1921	to	27 January	1922
Dog	28 January	1922	to	15 February	1923
Pig	16 February	1923	to	4 February	1924
Rat	5 February	1924	to	23 January	1925
Ox	24 January	1925	to	12 February	1926
Tiger	13 February	1926	to	1 February	1927
Rabbit	2 February	1927	to	22 January	1928
Dragon	23 January	1928	to	9 February	1929
Snake	10 February	1929	to	29 January	1930
Horse	30 January	1930	to	16 February	1931
Goat	17 February	1931	to	5 February	1932
Monkey	6 February	1932	to	25 January	1933
Rooster	26 January	1933	to	13 February	1934
Dog	14 February	1934	to	3 February	1935
Pig	4 February	1935	to	23 January	1936

Rat	24 January	1936	to	10 February	1937
Ox	11 February	1937	to	30 January	1938
Tiger	31 January	1938	to	18 February	1939
Rabbit	19 February	1939	to	7 February	1940
Dragon	8 February	1940	to	26 January	1941
Snake	27 January	1941	to	14 February	1942
Horse	15 February	1942	to	4 February	1943
Goat	5 February	1943	to	24 January	1944
Monkey	25 January	1944	to	12 February	1945
Rooster	13 February	1945	to	1 February	1946
Dog	2 February	1946	to	21 January	1947
Pig	22 January	1947	to	9 February	1948
Rat	10 February	1948	to	28 January	1949
Ox	29 January	1949	to	16 February	1950
Tiger	17 February	1950	to	5 February	1951
Rabbit	6 February	1951	to	26 January	1952
Dragon	27 January	1952	to	13 February	1953
Snake	14 February	1953	to	2 February	1954
Horse	3 February	1954	to	23 January	1955
Goat	24 January	1955	to	11 February	1956
Monkey	12 February	1956	to	30 January	1957
Rooster	31 January	1957	to	17 February	1958
Dog	18 February	1958	to	7 February	1959
Pig	8 February	1959	to	27 January	1960
Rat	28 January	1960	to	14 February	1961
Ox	15 February	1961	to	4 February	1962
Tiger	5 February	1962	to	24 January	1963
Rabbit	25 January	1963	to	12 February	1964
Dragon	13 February	1964	to	1 February	1965
Snake	2 February	1965	to	20 January	1966
Horse	21 January	1966	to	8 February	1967

Goat	9 February	1967	to	29 January	1968
Monkey	30 January	1968	to	16 February	1969
Rooster	17 February	1969	to	5 February	1970
Dog	6 February	1970	to	26 January	1971
Pig	27 January	1971	to	14 February	1972
Rat	15 February	1972	to	2 February	1973
Ox	3 February	1973	to	22 January	1974
Tiger	23 January	1974	to	10 February	1975
Rabbit	11 February	1975	to	30 January	1976
Dragon	31 January	1976	to	17 February	1977
Snake	18 February	1977	to	6 February	1978
Horse	7 February	1978	to	27 January	1979
Goat	28 January	1979	to	15 February	1980
Monkey	16 February	1980	to	4 February	1981
Rooster	5 February	1981	to	24 January	1982
Dog	25 January	1982	to	12 February	1983
Pig	13 February	1983	to	1 February	1984
Rat	2 February	1984	to	19 February	1985
Ox	20 February	1985	to	8 February	1986
Tiger	9 February	1986	to	28 January	1987
Rabbit	29 January	1987	to	16 February	1988
Dragon	17 February	1988	to	5 February	1989
Snake	6 February	1989	to	26 January	1990
Horse	27 January	1990	to	14 February	1991
Goat	15 February	1991	to	3 February	1992
Monkey	4 February	1992	to	22 January	1993
Rooster	23 January	1993	to	9 February	1994
Dog	10 February	1994	to	30 January	1995
Pig	31 January	1995	to	18 February	1996
Rat	19 February	1996	to	6 February	1997
Ox	7 February	1997	to	27 January	1998

Tiger	28 January	1998	to	15 February	1999
Rabbit	16 February	1999	to	4 February	2000
Dragon	5 February	2000	to	23 January	2001

Note: The names of the signs in the Chinese zodiac occasionally differ in the various books on Chinese astrology, although the characteristics of the signs remain the same. In some books the Ox is referred to as the Buffalo or Bull, the Rabbit as the Hare or Cat, the Goat as the Sheep and the Pig as the Boar.

For the sake of convenience, the male gender is used throughout this book. Unless otherwise stated, the characteristics of the signs apply to both sexes.

WELCOME TO
THE YEAR OF THE DRAGON

Whether on a national flag, a coat of arms or as leader of the carnival, the Dragon likes to be at the forefront. With its aura, mystique and fire-breathing abilities, it is a powerful symbol and has come to signify a great deal. Among the 12 Chinese signs the Dragon stands unique as the only one based upon myth and legend, but its influence is strong. Its year is one of drama, excitement and golden opportunity.

The Year of the Dragon starts on 5 February 2000 and, coming after the celebrations of the new millennium, will bring a feeling of expectancy and hope. The Dragon will certainly try to deliver – sometimes succeeding, but also firing some salutary warnings to mankind.

On the political stage the Dragon year will bring significant change. This is election year in the United States and the campaign will be fiercely contested, with the candidates offering a new sense of direction as well as placing great emphasis on personal values and standards for those in high office. Indeed, the campaign will see much soul searching and some dramatic swings in fortune, both in the primary and final stages. The United States will not be alone in seeing change, for the Dragon year will also bring significant transfers of power in other nations. It was, for example, in a previous Dragon year that Nasser seized power, overthrowing the Egyptian monarchy, that Khrushchev was ousted, to be replaced by Brezhnev, and that the British Prime Minister Harold Wilson stunned the nation by his unexpected resignation. This pattern will continue in 2000, with some new and influential figures emerging on the world stage.

Another feature of the year will be the vigorous campaigning by certain groups for causes in which they passionately believe. In some instances, the events that occur will have far-reaching effects, sometimes even crossing national borders. The student rebellion at Berkeley campus in California, the Harlem race riots and the Soweto African township riots all took place in Dragon years, with each having long-term consequences, while, just 12 years ago, support for the Polish Solidarity group was gathering momentum and was about to radically change events in Poland and Eastern Europe. It was also at this time that while on a visit to Poland Mrs Thatcher boldly called for the dismantling of the Berlin Wall, the raising of the Iron Curtain and the Soviet Union's East European satellites to be allowed to join the European mainstream, events which were to come about surprisingly quickly. Other Dragon years have also seen winds of change build up and then unleash their powerful force over subsequent years. The year 2000 will be no exception – and political change is but one of the legacies of the Dragon year.

After the celebrations for the new millennium many politicians and business leaders will feel this is an epoch-making year and a time to commemorate in some lasting way. As a result some lavish and often grandiose schemes will be announced, including major building projects and new attractions and cultural centres for the benefit of present and future generations. Dragon years certainly favour the launch of schemes, often very ambitious ones!

As far as economic matters are concerned, stock markets around the world will be prone to considerable swings of fortune during the year. Positive news stories and economic developments will considerably boost investments, but when more adverse rumours or statistics appear, those rises may soon evaporate. Some of the positive features of Dragon years do tend to be more illusory than substantial and investors will need to keep their wits about them throughout the year.

However, Dragon years are still considered positive for enterprise and starting new businesses and for those who really desire progress over the year, it certainly would be worth making that extra effort. Dragon years do tend to favour the bold and pioneering.

There also tends to be a buzz of excitement in Dragon years, which particularly affects the arts. Brash new designs could well appear, while in the world of music, some exciting bands and artists will emerge to great acclaim with new sounds, styles and memorable performances. It was, for example, in the last Dragon year that Jean-Michel Jarre put on his laser spectacular in London's Docklands and that Beethoven's Unfinished Tenth Symphony was premiered by the Royal Philharmonic Society of London. The theatre and cinema too will offer audiences exciting and innovative treats, while the home entertainment industry, including the world of television, will see yet more major developments, offering audiences even greater choice and gadgetry.

Similarly, sports followers can look forward to an exciting year, with the Sydney Olympics seeing numerous records smashed as well as inspiring performances by certain individuals and teams. Again the Dragon year will encourage a spirit of endeavour and will lift mankind's achievements to new heights.

However, while there will be much excitement in 2000, unfortunately there will also be tragedy. Any year will have its catastrophes and natural disasters, but Dragon years do tend to be characterized by some dreadful earthquakes. Corinth was destroyed in a Dragon year and 12 years ago Armenia was devastated by another quake. When tragedy does strike, world reaction will be swift and several times throughout the year nations will unite in offering resources and help to those suffering and in need. It was also in the last Dragon year that 50 million worldwide took part in the Race against Time, a charity event to help underprivileged children. Again, this Dragon year will see much support for charitable and humanitarian causes.

Environmental issues too could cause concern, with scientists warning of further consequences of global warming and of the effect that pollution and man's actions are having on the planet. It was in a previous Dragon year (1976) that the National Academy of Science warned that gases from spray cans could damage the atmosphere's ozone layer and in the year 2000 further warnings and evidence will lead to new initiatives to protect our planet.

With the Dragon's influence, this will undoubtedly be an active year and one which will see far-reaching developments. However, it is also a year of great opportunity and for those who are prepared to seize the moment and make the most of it, it can be a time for progress and personal achievement. In addition to starting businesses, the Chinese consider this a favourable year in which to get married or have a child and with so many having been inspired by the start of the new millennium, there is no doubt that a great many will aim to make something of the year. This is a time which does offer considerable potential and I hope it will be one that will bring you good fortune and the realization of your ideas, hopes and plans.

31 JANUARY 1900 ～ 18 FEBRUARY 1901   *Metal Rat*

18 FEBRUARY 1912 ～ 5 FEBRUARY 1913   *Water Rat*

5 FEBRUARY 1924 ～ 23 JANUARY 1925   *Wood Rat*

24 JANUARY 1936 ～ 10 FEBRUARY 1937   *Fire Rat*

10 FEBRUARY 1948 ～ 28 JANUARY 1949   *Earth Rat*

28 JANUARY 1960 ～ 14 FEBRUARY 1961   *Metal Rat*

15 FEBRUARY 1972 ～ 2 FEBRUARY 1973   *Water Rat*

2 FEBRUARY 1984 ～ 19 FEBRUARY 1985   *Wood Rat*

19 FEBRUARY 1996 ～ 6 FEBRUARY 1997   *Fire Rat*

THE
RAT

THE PERSONALITY OF THE RAT

> The world is before you and you need not take it or leave
> it as it was when you came in.
>
> *James Baldwin: a Rat*

The Rat is born under the sign of charm. He is intelligent,
popular and loves attending parties and large social gatherings. He is able to establish friendships with remarkable ease
and people generally feel relaxed in his company. He is a very
social creature and is genuinely interested in the welfare and
activities of others. He has a good understanding of human
nature and his advice and opinions are often sought.

The Rat is a hard and diligent worker. He is also very
imaginative and is never short of ideas. However, he does
sometimes lack the confidence to promote his ideas as
much as he should and this can often prevent him from
securing the recognition and credit he so often deserves.

The Rat is very observant and many Rats have made
excellent writers and journalists. The Rat also excels at
personnel and PR work and any job which brings him into
contact with people and the media. His skills are particularly appreciated in times of crisis, for he has an incredibly
strong sense of self-preservation. When it comes to finding
a way out of an awkward situation, the Rat is certain to be
the one who comes up with a solution.

The Rat loves to be where there is a lot of action, but
should he ever find himself in a very bureaucratic or
restrictive environment he can become a stickler for discipline and routine.

He is also something of an opportunist and is constantly on the look-out for ways in which he can improve his wealth and lifestyle. He rarely lets an opportunity go by and can become involved in so many plans and schemes that he sometimes squanders his energies and achieves very little as a result. He is also rather gullible and can be taken in by those less scrupulous than himself.

Another characteristic of the Rat is his attitude to money. He is very thrifty and to some he may appear a little mean. The reason for this is purely that he likes to keep his money within his family. He can be most generous to his partner, his children and close friends and relatives. He can also be generous to himself, for he often finds it impossible to deprive himself of any luxury or object he fancies. The Rat is also very acquisitive and can be a notorious hoarder. He hates waste and is rarely prepared to throw anything away. He can also be rather greedy and will rarely refuse an invitation for a free meal or a complimentary ticket to some lavish function.

The Rat is a good conversationalist, although he can occasionally be a little indiscreet. He can be highly critical of others – for an honest and unbiased opinion, the Rat is a superb critic – and sometimes will use confidential information to his own advantage. However, as the Rat has such a bright and irresistible nature, most are prepared to forgive him for his slight indiscretions.

Throughout his long and eventful life, the Rat will make many friends and will find that he is especially well suited to those born under his own sign and those of the Ox, Dragon and Monkey. He can also get on well with those born under the signs of the Tiger, Snake, Rooster, Dog and

Pig, but the rather sensitive Rabbit and Goat will find the Rat a little too critical and blunt for their liking. The Horse and Rat will also find it difficult to get on with each other – the Rat craves security and will find the Horse's changeable moods and rather independent nature a little unsettling.

The Rat is very family orientated and will do anything to please his nearest and dearest. He is exceptionally loyal to his parents and can himself be a very caring and loving parent. He will take an interest in all his children's activities and will see that they want for nothing. The Rat usually has a large family.

The female Rat has a kindly, outgoing nature and involves herself in a multitude of different activities. She has a wide circle of friends, enjoys entertaining and is an attentive hostess. She is also conscientious about the upkeep of her home and has superb taste in home furnishings. She is most supportive to the other members of her family and, due to her resourceful, friendly and persevering nature, can do well in practically any career she enters.

Although the Rat is essentially outgoing and something of an extrovert, he is also a very private individual. He tends to keep his feelings to himself and while he is not averse to learning what other people are doing, he resents anyone prying too closely into his own affairs. He also does not like solitude and if he is alone for any length of time he can easily get depressed.

The Rat is undoubtedly very talented, but he does sometimes fail to capitalize on his many abilities. He has a tendency to become involved in too many schemes and chase after too many opportunities all at one time. If he were to slow down and concentrate on one thing at a time he could become very successful. If not, success and wealth could elude him. But the Rat, with his tremendous ability to charm, will rarely, if ever, be without friends.

THE FIVE DIFFERENT TYPES OF RAT

In addition to the 12 signs of the Chinese zodiac, there are five elements and these have a strengthening or moderating influence on the sign. The effects of the five elements on the Rat are described below, together with the years in which the elements were exercising their influence. Therefore all Rats born in 1900 and 1960 are Metal Rats, those born in 1912 and 1972 are Water Rats, and so on.

Metal Rat: 1900, 1960
This Rat has excellent taste and certainly knows how to appreciate the finer things in life. His home is comfortable and nicely decorated and he is forever entertaining or mixing in fashionable circles. He has considerable financial acumen and invests his money well. On the surface the Metal Rat appears cheerful and confident, but deep down he can be troubled by worries that are quite often of his own making. He is exceptionally loyal to his family and friends.

Water Rat: 1912, 1972

The Water Rat is intelligent and very astute. He is a deep thinker and can express his thoughts clearly and persuasively. He is always eager to learn and is talented in many different areas. The Water Rat is usually very popular, but his fear of loneliness can sometimes lead him into mixing with the wrong sort of company. He is a particularly skilful writer, but he can get side-tracked very easily and should try to concentrate on just one thing at a time.

Wood Rat: 1924, 1984

The Wood Rat has a friendly, outgoing personality and is most popular with his colleagues and friends. He has a quick, agile brain and likes to turn his hand to anything he thinks may be useful. His one fear is insecurity, but given his intelligence and capabilities, this fear is usually unfounded. He has a good sense of humour, enjoys travel and, due to his highly imaginative nature, can be a gifted writer or artist.

Fire Rat: 1936, 1996

The Fire Rat is rarely still and seems to have a never-ending supply of energy and enthusiasm. He loves being involved in the action – be it travel, following up new ideas or campaigning for a cause in which he fervently believes. He is an original thinker and hates being bound by petty restrictions or the dictates of others. He can be forthright in his views, but can sometimes get carried away in the excitement of the moment and commit himself to various undertakings without checking what all the implications might be. Yet he has a resilient nature and, with the right support, can often go far in life.

Earth Rat: 1948

This Rat is astute and very level-headed. He rarely takes unnecessary chances and while he is constantly trying to improve his financial status, he is prepared to proceed slowly and leave nothing to chance. The Earth Rat is probably not as adventurous as the other types of Rat and prefers to remain in familiar areas rather than rush headlong into something he knows little about. He is talented, conscientious and caring towards his loved ones, but at the same time can be self-conscious and worry a little too much about the image he is trying to project.

PROSPECTS FOR THE RAT IN THE YEAR 2000

The Chinese New Year starts on 5 February 2000. Until then, the old year, the Year of the Rabbit, is still making its presence felt.

The Year of the Rabbit (16 February 1999 to 4 February 2000) will have been an interesting one for the Rat and while not everything will have gone in his favour, he will still have learnt much and gained valuable experience. In the next Chinese year he will be able to draw on this and make even more substantial headway.

From November 1999 the aspects will start to swing back in the Rat's favour and this will mark the beginning of a very positive time in his fortunes. In view of this, the Rat should use the closing months of the Rabbit year wisely and regard it as a good time to complete outstanding projects, overdue correspondence or any tasks he might have been putting off. With a concerted effort he will be delighted with what he is able to accomplish and once these matters are out of the way, he will find himself better able to look forward to the celebrations at the end of 1999.

Indeed, with his outgoing and sociable nature, the Rat will thoroughly enjoy the events that take place in the latter part of the Rabbit year, with his diary quickly filling up with things to do, people to see and places to go. However, although he is usually so masterful in handling his relations with others, some care is needed. The Rat cannot, for instance, expect to have things all his own way or have his plans accepted without some demur; neither should he become intransigent over relatively small matters. Additional care and forethought in his relationships will certainly not come amiss, otherwise tensions and differences of opinion could take the edge off what could be a truly agreeable and memorable time.

As far as the Rat's work is concerned, the closing stages of the Rabbit year will be a constructive time and he should take advantage of any chances to add to his experience. If he sees any opportunities to advance or openings to pursue, he should follow these up. What he is able to accomplish now could develop in a significant manner over the next 12 months.

Financially, this will, though, be an expensive time. In view of this, the Rat should keep a watchful eye on his spending and think long and hard before making large and costly purchases. To succumb to too many temptations over a short period of time could deplete his funds and force him to make economies later. The Rabbit year is not really a time for overspending, for taking risks or for undue complacency.

However, while the Rat will need to proceed with some care in what remains of the Rabbit year, he will detect a change in his fortunes at this time and will become more upbeat about his prospects. This will give him an added reason to enjoy the celebrations for the new millennium and to welcome in, a little later, the next and, for him, much improved Chinese year.

The Year of the Dragon starts on 5 February and will be a splendid one for the Rat. With his amiable and resourceful nature, he is set to do well in most areas of his life, making this a successful and fulfilling year. Indeed, the Rat will often be inspired by the spirit of enterprise that will prevail over the year and this too will help him to give of his best.

The Rat's work prospects are particularly promising and during the year he will benefit from several strokes of good fortune. These could come from learning about an opening or opportunity by chance or simply by being in the right place at the right time. However such fortunate opportunities arise, by remaining alert and his resourceful self, the Rat will be able to pursue and profit from them. This really is a superb year for making progress and all Rats should make every effort to improve upon their present situation. The months of March, April, July and September could see some particularly interesting developments but, given the auspicious aspects, almost all months could bring opportunities.

For those Rats who have been in the same position for some while and would like new challenges, this really is the year to make the effort to bring about change. Again, by remaining alert and being adventurous in their outlook, these Rats will be able to identify some excellent possibilities. Similarly, many of those Rats seeking work will find their quest rewarded, sometimes again in a rather fortuitous way, perhaps by the Rat hearing about an opportunity by chance or through someone's recommendation. In some cases the position offered will be unlike anything the Rat has done before but will have the potential for development and will enable the Rat to discover skills he did not know he had. Indeed, the Dragon year will mark the turning-point in the careers and lives of quite a few Rats.

With the progressive trends that prevail, this is also an excellent time for the Rat to investigate any training opportunities that might be available or to look at ways in which he can extend or refresh his skills, or even learn some new ones. Anything positive he can do to enhance his prospects would be to his advantage as well as be a satisfying use of his time.

The Rat should also be forthcoming with any ideas he has, especially any connected with his work. He is, after all, an original and innovative thinker and could find some of his proposals well received. He should remember that the Dragon year favours the enterprising, and the ever-resourceful Rat is certainly that!

The Rat will also enjoy an improvement in his financial situation over the year. With this upturn many Rats will be tempted to spend their money on themselves, their homes and on travel. However, while much of the Rat's spending will bring him considerable pleasure, he would still be advised to set about his larger purchases with care and forethought. To act too hastily could leave him regretting his action or finding he could have got better elsewhere at a more attractive price. Financially, this will be a good year, but the Rat could be tempted to spend all too easily and he should watch this. Also, with this financial upturn, the Rat would do well to consider making some savings, particularly with a view to the longer term. Over time what he puts aside now could become a useful asset. On a cautionary note, he should be careful if lending to others – if he does not put the loan on a proper basis he could find it later gives rise to misunderstanding and he could experience difficulty in getting repaid. Rats, be warned!

The Rat's domestic and social life is, though, well aspected and will bring him many happy and fulfilling times. He will find those around him supportive towards his various activities as well as interested in his undertakings. Accordingly, the Rat should listen carefully to any advice he is given, particularly from those closest to him. They do speak with his best interests at heart and sometimes will have thought of points the Rat himself may have overlooked or will make suggestions that he can profit from. Over the year the Rat can truly benefit from the input of others as well as be heartened by the considerable affection shown towards him.

The Rat will also take pleasure in following the activities of family members, with their achievements and progress often being a source of much satisfaction to him. There will be good cause for a family celebration over the year and the Rat can look forward to playing a central role.

The Rat is also a keen socializer and again in the year 2000 his social life will not disappoint. There will be parties, get-togethers and social events to attend, and for those Rats seeking romance or new friends, the year will contain some splendid opportunities. The months of April and May and the late summer will be particularly active and a friendship started at this time could well blossom over the year and become significant. Romance will certainly figure strongly in the lives of many Rats over the year. Any Rat who may be discontented with his present situation, be feeling lonely or have had some recent sadness to bear should try to set his sights firmly on the present and future. Admittedly, for some this may be difficult, but with the year holding so much promise, this really is the time to focus on the present and to enjoy it.

The Rat will also enjoy the travelling that he undertakes over the year and he should take advantage of any travel opportunities that arise as well as aim to go away for a holiday or break. He will greatly benefit from the change and rest that a holiday brings as well as have the chance to visit some interesting locations. It is also important that, no matter how busy he may be, the Rat sets time aside for his own hobbies and interests. These will be a valuable source of relaxation for him and any which involve creative or outdoor activities are likely to prove especially satisfying.

In almost all respects this will be a fine year for the Rat. However, to make the most of the favourable aspects, he should set about his activities in a positive manner and take action to secure his aims, ambitions and objectives. For the determined and enterprising Rat, this will be a year of rich and fulfilling rewards – and personal happiness too!

As far as the different types of Rat are concerned, this will be an important year for the *Metal Rat*. In recent years he will have accomplished much and impressed others as well as have formed ideas about how he would like his life and career to develop. In the year 2000 he will be given the opportunity to follow some of these through, in many cases with positive results. In his work the Metal Rat can look forward to making pleasing progress. Often this will come in an unexpected but welcome form. For those Metal Rats who have been in the same position for some time, there will be opportunities for promotion or the chance to transfer to newer and more challenging responsibilities. Such is the positive nature of the year that one step forward can sometimes become two or three. Similarly, for those Metal Rats who are dissatisfied with their present position or seeking work the Year of the Dragon will hold some interesting possibilities. These Rats should actively follow up any openings they see but also look at different ways in which they can use their experience. Some enterprising thinking will not only widen the scope of the positions they could try for but, once successful, will provide them with a real incentive to do well. Also, pleasingly for the Metal Rat, the progressive trends that prevail in the Dragon year will continue into 2001, enabling the development of any progress made now. In addition to making headway in his work, the Metal Rat can also look forward to an improvement in his financial situation during the year. This could be through an increase in income, a gift or the fruition of a policy, but however it manifests, it will enable the Metal Rat to go ahead with some purchases and improvements he has been considering for his accommodation, as well as buying some items for himself and his loved ones. However, when making any sizeable purchase, the Metal Rat would do well to take his time, compare what is on offer and talk his purchase over with those around him rather than proceed too hastily. Also, while he will feel that he deserves some rewards for his efforts, he should not let this turn to overindulgence. Sometimes he may find it hard to resist tempting purchases or treats, but on some occasions a little more forethought would be in his interests. With travel well aspected, the Metal Rat should try to ensure he goes away for a holiday over the year. He will not only benefit from the rest a holiday gives but will also have the chance of visiting some interesting locations. As far as his relations with others are concerned, the Metal Rat will be in fine form. As always, he will take a keen and caring interest in the activities of those around him and several times during the year others will look to him for guidance and support, which he will be pleased to give. He will also find that any interests and household projects in which he can involve his loved ones will lead to some meaningful occasions as well as help preserve the closeness he so values. On a social level, too, the year will go well and the Metal Rat can look forward to attending a variety of social events, with the late summer being a particularly active time. There will be opportunities to add to his circle of friends and acquaintances, and for those Metal Rats who may find themselves lonely, the year will see a distinct improvement in their situation. However, to assist with this, these Metal Rats really should make the effort to go out more, especially to places where they are likely to meet others. Overall, this is a year which holds considerable potential for the Metal Rat, but to benefit from the aspects he does need to make a determined effort to secure his aims and objectives. By taking positive action, however, he will not only obtain pleasing results but sometimes surpass his expectations. The Dragon year is one of the best for the Metal Rat and it rests with him to enjoy it and to make the most of the auspicious trends that prevail.

This will be an exciting year for the *Water Rat*, with some interesting and memorable events taking place. His personal life in particular is splendidly aspected and over the year he will have great cause for celebration. This could be due to an engagement or marriage, a birth in his family or the fulfilment of an ambition, but whatever the event, it will be an important boost for the Water Rat and will give him even greater reason to make the most of the year. However, to maximize his prospects, the Water Rat should give some thought to just what he would like to achieve over the year. This could concern almost any sphere of his life, from work to accommodation to a personal goal, but by deciding upon and working towards specific aims the Water Rat will obtain some truly worthwhile results. Accommodation matters will figure prominently for many Water Rats, with some deciding to move while others will decide to carry out alterations and improvements. In either case, the Water Rat's plans will work out well. Those Water Rats who do move will be delighted with their new home, while the practical projects the Water Rat carries out will bring him much satisfaction, especially those related to the look and comfort of his accommodation. The Water Rat's fine taste and eye for detail will lead to some pleasing results and will be much appreciated by those around him. There will also be considerable activity concerning the Water Rat's work in the year 2000 and while there will be moments of uncertainty, events will generally move in his favour. Many Water Rats will be able to make substantial strides over the year. In some cases, the Water Rat will find that new and changing situations will bring opportunities that had not been available before, and with his experience and resourcefulness, he will be ideally placed to benefit from them. There will also be chances to take on a new duties, try a different type of work or, for those Water Rats already established in a career, for promotion. This is a year for positive advance and the aspects will support the Water Rat well. Financial matters, too, will go well and any problems the Water Rat may have been experiencing of late will ease during the year. However, despite this upturn, the Water Rat should still plan his expenditure with care and budget for any large expenses he may face. Also, if he enters into any major or long-term commitment, he should check the terms and obligations carefully. Financially, this may be a good year, but the Water Rat should not allow himself to become complacent or careless. He will, however, greatly enjoy the travelling that he undertakes and a holiday in the second half of the year could exceed expectations, especially if it is to a destination a little off the usual tourist map. As far as the Water Rat's personal life is concerned, this will be a gratifying year. He will find himself much in demand and will delight in following the activities of those around him. He will also be thankful for the encouragement he receives and be heartened by the affection, interest and support shown towards him. Indeed, the Water Rat may not always realize just how much he means to so many, but his important and valued role will certainly become evident over the course of the year. Both domestically and socially the Water Rat can look forward to some truly meaningful times with those around him. For any Water Rats who may have started the year in low spirits, the Dragon year will certainly bring a noticeable upturn, with the prospects of a busier and more fulfilling social life and some new friendships. The spring months will be a particularly auspicious time. Overall, the Dragon year will see some pleasing developments for the Water Rat. While some of these will not be what he anticipated, they will nevertheless work out in his favour, and generally the year will be one of progress, achievement and personal happiness.

This year holds considerable promise for the *Wood Rat*, although just how much he accomplishes depends a lot upon his own attitude. With willingness, determination and good use of his time this can be a rewarding and satisfying year for the Wood Rat, but if he drifts along without any particular aim in mind, then opportunities could be missed and his activities will not bring him the satisfaction they otherwise could. To make the most of the year the Wood Rat would do well to decide early on just what he wants to accomplish and then set about it in earnest. One particularly rewarding area will be his leisure time. If there is a hobby or pursuit that the Wood Rat has been thinking of taking up, this would be an excellent year in which to do so. Similarly, if there is a skill, sport or craft that he would like to learn or become more proficient in, he should investigate how to set about it. As the saying goes, 'There is no time like the present' and positive action on the Wood Rat's part will be well rewarded. This really is an ideal time for the Wood Rat to improve and enrich his life and give himself some interesting challenges. For those Wood Rats in education, this will be an important year. They should set about their studies in an organized way, leaving plenty of revision time before examinations. What these Wood Rats accomplish now will often have far-reaching implications. They would also do well to consider the type of career they would like to follow and what qualifications they might need. Although for many this may be several years off, by knowing what is required the young Wood Rat will be able to channel his energies in the right direction and this will be useful when he is called upon to choose specialist subjects. In making decisions concerning his education and future, the Wood Rat would find it helpful to discuss his options with those around him. With the support of others, he can make some wise decisions. As far as his social life is concerned, this will be an active and enjoyable year, with a variety of parties and functions to attend and many chances to meet others. There will be opportunities for romance and new friendships, with the summer being an especially lively time. However, while the Wood Rat will thoroughly enjoy himself and likes to be 'one of the crowd', he should not allow his pursuit of pleasure or friendship tempt him into anything which he does not feel comfortable with or get into the 'wrong crowd'. This will only apply to a few Wood Rats, but those concerned, do take note. The Wood Rat will also thoroughly enjoy the travelling that he undertakes over the year and any breaks or holidays involving his interests (particularly sport or outdoor activities) will go well. The Wood Rat also places great store on his family life and those born in 1924 will take particular satisfaction in following the interests of family members. While they may not wish to be viewed as interfering, any advice or help they feel able to pass on will be warmly appreciated. For the more senior Wood Rat, family matters will bring pleasure and joy. However, for the younger Wood Rat, there may be occasions when interests conflict. At these times, the Wood Rat should show some willingness to discuss matters rather than remain inflexible. This is just too good a year to let certain issues sour the atmosphere or become an unwelcome distraction. Young Wood Rats, do take note and try to preserve domestic harmony! Overall, this will be a positive year for the Wood Rat, and by making the most of himself and the chances that arise, he can make great progress as well as gain much satisfaction from his activities.

The *Fire Rat* will enjoy the Year of the Dragon, with most aspects of his life bringing pleasure and satisfaction. In particular he can look forward to some pleasing times with those around him, with both his domestic and social life being active and rewarding. As usual he will play a full part in family activities and will do much to support those around him. His interest in their undertakings, as well as any advice he feels able to pass on, will be much appreciated. The Fire Rat will also delight in some of the family events that take place over the year. These could include a wedding, the birth of a grandchild or some other pleasing event. The Fire Rat will also be encouraged by the support he receives for his own activities, and if ever he feels in need of advice or assistance, he should ask. This includes asking for help with any practical tasks or strenuous activities he wishes to carry out. Similarly, if the Fire Rat has any matters giving him concern, including any important forms and documents to complete, he should again seek advice. Throughout the year he will find it better to ask than to worry himself unnecessarily or struggle on unaided, particularly as the help he requires is available. The Fire Rat will also take much pleasure from his hobbies, and for those Fire Rats who enjoy outdoor activities such as gardening, travelling or following sport, the year will produce some rewarding occasions. The Fire Rat will also enjoy his social life and can look forward to spending many agreeable times in the company of his friends and to attending some interesting social events. For any Fire Rat who would like additional company, the early part of the year 2000 will be an excellent time for meeting others. Indeed, for the lonely and unattached Fire Rat, a friendship started in the Dragon year could blossom and bring much happiness in the future. The Fire Rat will also enjoy some pleasing financial developments over the year, which could include receiving a gift or payment for some work he has done in the past. However, while he will naturally be delighted by this financial upturn, he should still be careful with his money and should avoid too much impulse buying. Where possible, he should plan major purchases and take his time over them rather than acting on a whim. One area which will strongly tempt the Fire Rat this year will be travel and the journeys and any holidays he is able to take will bring him considerable pleasure. He could find this an especially good year to visit destinations he has long wanted to see, to revisit favourite places or to arrange to see relations and friends living some distance away. Generally, this will be an active but fulfilling year for the Fire Rat. However, while he will have much to occupy him, if ever he finds himself with some free time at his disposal, he should consider learning a new skill or starting a different hobby. He could find this becoming a stimulating challenge and one which will bring pleasure in both this and subsequent years. This is something all Fire Rats would do well to give serious thought to and it would help to make this already auspicious year even more rewarding.

This will be an important year for the *Earth Rat*, with some significant changes in store. The Earth Rat does not enter into change lightly, preferring to act only after much deliberation, but for a long time now he will have been considering making some new plans. These could concern almost any sphere of his life – a personal matter, accommodation or work – and with the start of the millennium, there will be many Earth Rats who will decide that now is the right time to set some of their ideas and plans in motion. In doing this the Earth Rat will realize that some of his plans will have far-reaching consequences and could cause some disruption, but will feel this is a small price to pay for the longer term benefits. The Earth Rat will also be helped by the supportive attitude of those around him and should listen carefully to any advice he is given. For many Earth Rats, some of the major changes that occur will involve their work. Some will feel the time has come for fresh challenges and will aim to move from their present position, whether by promotion, taking on different responsibilities or making a career change. Similarly, some of the Earth Rats who are seeking work will decide to break away from their former type of work and try for a position of a different nature or obtain training in a new area. By making such decisions and working towards them, many will start to make the headway that was not possible before. This is a positively aspected year for the Earth Rat and all Earth Rats really should make a concerted effort to better themselves and work towards their goals. Some Earth Rats will also decide to move house over the year, and while it may take some time for them to decide upon their new location, once they find something that meets their requirements, they could find their plans will move surprisingly swiftly. It will also be a positive year for financial matters, with many Earth Rats enjoying an increase in income as well as receiving some money from an additional source. This upturn will be another factor which will prompt the Earth Rat into carrying out some of his plans, particularly those related to his accommodation. Whether he moves or stays where he is, however, the Earth Rat will probably devote some time to changing the decor and adding to the comfort of his home. What he achieves now will bring him and his loved ones considerable satisfaction. The Earth Rat always places great store on his family life and this too will bring him much pleasure. However, as some of the year will be very busy – especially for those Earth Rats who do move – the Earth Rat should try to avoid becoming so preoccupied with his own activities that he does not pay as much attention to others as he should.

At demanding times, to relieve some of the pressure he would do well to encourage activities all can enjoy, such as a trip out or some other pleasurable and relaxing pursuit. The Earth Rat will find such a suggestion will work wonders! Generally, despite the sometimes hectic activity, the Earth Rat's home life will bring him much satisfaction and he will also be thankful for the support he receives. Although the Dragon year will be full and active, it is also important that the Earth Rat devotes time to his own hobbies and interests as well as to his social life. These will not only bring him pleasure but can do much to help him unwind and relax. Any Earth Rat who may be wanting new friends or seeking additional company would find it well worth making the extra effort to go out more and meet others. As he will find throughout the year, positive action will certainly prove effective. Overall, this will be a favourable year for the Earth Rat. By deciding what he wants to achieve and then working purposefully towards it, he will obtain some truly pleasing results, with many being to his long-term advantage.

FAMOUS RATS

Alan Alda, Dave Allen, Ursula Andress, Louis Armstrong, Charles Aznavour, Lauren Bacall, Shirley Bassey, Jeremy Beadle, Irving Berlin, Kenneth Branagh, Marlon Brando, Charlotte Brontë, Jackson Browne, Chris de Burgh, George Bush, Lord Callaghan, Glen Campbell, David Carradine, Jimmy Carter, Maurice Chevalier, Barbara Dickson, Benjamin Disraeli, David Duchovny, Noel Edmonds, T. S. Eliot, Albert Finney, Clark Gable, Liam Gallagher, Al Gore,

Hugh Grant, Geri Halliwell, Thomas Hardy, Prince Harry, Vaclav Havel, Haydn, Charlton Heston, Damon Hill, Ian Hislop, Buddy Holly, Mick Hucknall, Engelbert Humperdinck, Henrik Ibsen, Jeremy Irons, Glenda Jackson, Jean-Michel Jarre, Gene Kelly, Kris Kristofferson, Lawrence of Arabia, Gary Lineker, Sir Andrew Lloyd Webber, Claude Monet, Richard Nixon, Robert Palmer, Sean Penn, Terry Pratchett, the Queen Mother, Patrick Rafter, Vanessa Redgrave, Burt Reynolds, Rossini, William Shakespeare, Yves St Laurent, Tommy Steele, Donna Summer, James Taylor, Leo Tolstoy, Henri Toulouse-Lautrec, Spencer Tracy, Anthea Turner, the Prince of Wales, George Washington, Dennis Weaver, Roger Whittaker, Richard Wilson, Bill Wyman, the Duke of York, Emile Zola.

19 FEBRUARY 1901 ∼ 7 FEBRUARY 1902   *Metal Ox*

6 FEBRUARY 1913 ∼ 25 JANUARY 1914   *Water Ox*

24 JANUARY 1925 ∼ 12 FEBRUARY 1926   *Wood Ox*

11 FEBRUARY 1937 ∼ 30 JANUARY 1938   *Fire Ox*

29 JANUARY 1949 ∼ 16 FEBRUARY 1950   *Earth Ox*

15 FEBRUARY 1961 ∼ 4 FEBRUARY 1962   *Metal Ox*

3 FEBRUARY 1973 ∼ 22 JANUARY 1974   *Water Ox*

20 FEBRUARY 1985 ∼ 8 FEBRUARY 1986   *Wood Ox*

7 FEBRUARY 1997 ∼ 27 JANUARY 1998   *Fire Ox*

THE
OX

THE PERSONALITY OF THE OX

Victory belongs to the most persevering.
Napoleon Bonaparte: an Ox

The Ox is born under the signs of equilibrium and tenacity. He is a hard and conscientious worker and sets about everything he does in a resolute, methodical and determined manner. He has considerable leadership qualities and is often admired for his tough and uncompromising nature. He knows what he wants to achieve in life and, as far as possible, will not be deflected from his ultimate objective.

The Ox takes his responsibilities and duties very seriously. He is decisive and quick to take advantage of any opportunity that comes his way. He is also sincere and places a great deal of trust in his friends and colleagues. He is, nevertheless, something of a loner. He is a quiet and private individual and often keeps his thoughts to himself. He also cherishes his independence and prefers to set about things in his own way rather than be bound by the dictates of others or be influenced by outside pressures.

The Ox tends to have a calm and tranquil nature, but if something angers him or he feels that someone has let him down, he can have a fearsome temper. He can also be stubborn and obstinate and this can lead him into conflict with others. Usually the Ox will succeed in getting his own way, but should things go against him, he is a poor loser and will take any defeat or setback extremely badly.

The Ox is often a deep thinker and rather studious. He is not particularly renowned for his sense of humour and does not take kindly to new gimmicks or anything too innovative. The Ox is too solid and traditional for that and he prefers to stick to the more conventional norm.

His home is very important to him and in some respects he treats it as a private sanctuary. His family tends to be closely knit and the Ox will make sure that each member does their fair share around the house. The Ox tends to be a hoarder, but he is always well organized and neat. He also places great importance on punctuality and there is nothing that infuriates him more than to be kept waiting – particularly if it is due to someone's inefficiency. The Ox can be a hard taskmaster!

Once settled in a job or house the Ox will quite happily remain there for many years. He does not like change and he is also not particularly keen on travel. He does, however, enjoy gardening and other outdoor pursuits and he will often spend much of his spare time out of doors. The Ox is usually an excellent gardener and whenever possible he will always make sure he has a large area of ground to maintain. He usually prefers to live in the country rather than the town.

Due to his dedicated and dependable nature, the Ox will usually do well in his chosen career, providing he is given enough freedom to act on his own initiative. He invariably does well in politics, agriculture and in careers which need specialized training. The Ox is also very gifted in the arts and many Oxen have enjoyed considerable success as musicians or composers.

The Ox is not as outgoing as some and it often takes

him a long time to establish friendships and feel relaxed in another person's company. His courtships are likely to be long, but once he is settled he will remain devoted and loyal to his partner. The Ox is particularly well suited to those born under the signs of the Rat, Rabbit, Snake and Rooster. He can also establish a good relationship with the Monkey, Dog, Pig and another Ox, but he will find that he has little in common with the whimsical and sensitive Goat. He will also find it difficult to get on with the Horse, Dragon and Tiger – the Ox prefers a quiet and peaceful existence and those born under these three signs tend to be a little too lively and impulsive for his liking.

The female Ox has a kind and caring nature, and her home and family are very much her pride and joy. She always tries to do her best for her partner and can be a most conscientious and loving parent. She is an excellent organizer and also a very determined person who will often succeed in getting what she wants in life. She usually has a deep interest in the arts and is often a talented artist or musician.

The Ox is a very down-to-earth character. He is sincere, loyal and unpretentious. He can, however, be rather reserved and to some he may appear distant and aloof. He has a quiet nature, but underneath he is very strong-willed and ambitious. He has the courage of his convictions and is often prepared to stand up for what he believes is right, regardless of the consequences. He inspires confidence and trust and throughout his life he will rarely be short of people who are ready to support him or who admire his strong and resolute manner.

THE FIVE DIFFERENT TYPES OF OX

In addition to the 12 signs of the Chinese zodiac, there are five elements and these have a strengthening or moderating influence on the sign. The effects of the five elements on the Ox are described below, together with the years in which the elements were exercising their influence. Therefore all Oxen born in 1901 and 1961 are Metal Oxen, those born in 1913 and 1973 are Water Oxen, and so on.

Metal Ox: 1901, 1961

This Ox is confident and very strong-willed. He can be blunt and forthright in his views and is not afraid of speaking his mind. He sets about his objectives with a dogged determination, but he can become so involved in his various activities that he is oblivious to the thoughts and feelings of those around him, and this can sometimes be to his detriment. He is honest and dependable and will never promise more than he can deliver. He has a good appreciation of the arts and usually has a small circle of very good and loyal friends.

Water Ox: 1913, 1973

This Ox has a sharp and penetrating mind. He is a good organizer and sets about his work in a methodical manner. He is not as narrow-minded as some of the other types of Oxen and is more willing to involve others in his plans and aspirations. He usually has very high moral standards and is often attracted to careers in public service. He is a good judge of character and has such a friendly and persuasive manner that he usually experiences little difficulty in securing his objectives. He is popular and has an excellent way with children.

Wood Ox: 1925, 1985

The Wood Ox conducts himself with an air of dignity and authority and will often take a leading role in any enterprise in which he gets involved. He is very self-confident and is direct in his dealings with others. He does, however, have a quick temper and has no hesitation in speaking his mind. He has tremendous drive and will-power and has an extremely good memory. The Wood Ox is particularly loyal and devoted to the members of his family and has a most caring nature.

Fire Ox: 1937, 1997

The Fire Ox has a powerful and assertive personality and is a hard and conscientious worker. He holds strong views and has very little patience when things do not go his own way. He can also get carried away in the excitement of the moment and does not always take into account the views of those around him. He nevertheless has many leadership qualities and will often reach positions of power, eminence and wealth. He usually has a small group of loyal and close friends and is very devoted to his family.

Earth Ox: 1949

This Ox sets about everything he does in a sensible and level-headed manner. He is ambitious, but also realistic in his aims and is often prepared to work long hours in order to secure his objectives. He is shrewd in financial and business matters and is a very good judge of character. He has a quiet nature and is greatly admired for his sincerity and integrity. He is also very loyal to his family and friends and his views and opinions are often sought by others.

PROSPECTS FOR THE OX IN THE YEAR 2000

The Chinese New Year starts on 5 February 2000. Until then, the old year, the Year of the Rabbit, is still making its presence felt.

The Year of the Rabbit (16 February 1999 to 4 February 2000) will have been a positive one for the Ox and in what remains it he can accomplish a great deal. He should continue to set about his activities with his customary resolve, promoting his ideas and following up any opportunities that arise as well as setting about any tasks and projects that he has given himself.

In particular, the Ox can look forward to making pleasing headway in his work at this time, and his determined and conscientious nature will impress those around him. For those Oxen eager to transfer to a new position, October and November 1999 could hold some interesting possibilities. There could be an ideal opening during these months, and even if only on a temporary basis, it will still provide the Ox with the chance of gaining useful experience and could develop into something more substantial in the future.

As far as financial matters are concerned, most Oxen will have enjoyed a reasonable improvement in their situation over the year and will generally have used their money well. Indeed, many will have taken the opportunity to change their present style, buying new clothes as well as other items for themselves and their home. What the Ox has acquired during the Rabbit year will bring him considerable pleasure. However, as the year draws to a close, if there any expensive purchases the Ox still has in mind, it could be in his interest to delay them until the year 2000. In the post-Christmas sales he could pick up some excellent bargains and make some shrewd purchases.

The closing stages of the year will also be a favourable time for the Ox's relations with others. Both his domestic and social life will bring him much pleasure and he will find himself very much caught up in the festivities and celebrations at the end of 1999. There will be parties and get-togethers to attend and, although the Ox tends to be one of the more reserved of the Chinese signs, he will find himself opening up and truly enjoying himself, while appreciating the significance and sense of occasion as the new millennium approaches.

In most respects the closing stages of the Rabbit year will be a happy and rewarding time for the Ox.

The Year of the Dragon starts on 5 February and will be a variable one for the Ox. Some parts of the year will go well, bringing the Ox personal satisfaction and allowing him to make reasonable progress, but there will also be times of disappointment, pressure and uncertainty. The Ox may also not feel entirely at ease with some of the sudden changes that the Dragon year so often produces and this too will temper his outlook. However, provided he proceeds with care and keeps his expectations modest, he can still make headway and place himself in a good position to benefit from the improved trends that will emerge towards the end of the year and continue in 2001.

As far as the Ox's work is concerned, this will be a challenging year. Although the Ox is one who likes to plan and work to a pattern, in the year 2000 new situations will arise which will have a bearing on some of his goals. These changes could involve him being given or taking on different duties, or having to adapt to new colleagues, procedures or working practices. At the time, this will cause the Ox some unease, but by making the most of the situations in which he finds himself, he will often be able to turn circumstances to his advantage. The Ox should show some willingness to adjust rather than appear too 'set in his ways'. He will find it better to move with the tide than swim against it, and once matters have settled down, he could find opportunities and possibilities emerging which he will be well placed to pursue. As he has so often found in the past, a period of progress and advance comes as a consequence of change, and so it will be this time, with the benefits becoming truly apparent in 2001.

For those Oxen seeking work or feeling that the time is now right to change their present position, the year will hold some interesting possibilities. However, in order to discover these the Ox will need to take action rather than just wait for opportunities to become available. Neither should he allow himself to be put off after any initial setback or reversal; instead he should only make this increase his resolve. As he will find, his tenaciousness will ultimately be rewarded. In his quest, the Ox could find it particularly helpful to approach companies he might like to work for, setting out his experience and qualifications and actively seeking out those who may be able to advise on possible openings, including professional bodies. Sometimes an innovative and direct approach will pay off, and throughout the year the Ox would do well to remember the old saying, 'Nothing ventured, nothing gained.' For employment matters, the months of May, July and September could see some important activity.

This is also a good year for all Oxen to consider extending their skills. If the Ox has the opportunity to undertake any training or follow up a subject that he considers might be useful, he should do so. He will not only find this a satisfying use of his time but can do much to advance his prospects. In so many respects, what the Ox accomplishes, learns and gains in experience in the Dragon year will prepare the way for the more substantial progress he is soon to make.

As far as financial matters are concerned, this will be a reasonable year for the Ox. Many Oxen will enjoy a modest but noticeable improvement in their situation, and as usual, the Ox will deal with his finances with care, but he would do well to consider setting some of his money aside for a holiday or break later in the year. The Ox does tend to drive himself hard and should make sure he enjoys the fruits of his labours rather than slogs away relentlessly.

A holiday could prove an enjoyable and well-deserved reward for his efforts.

Also, if the Ox's current lifestyle does not allow him the opportunity to get much exercise, he should try to remedy this, perhaps by taking up some suitable activity. Cycling, swimming and additional walking could prove ideal for maintaining and even improving fitness.

The Ox will also take much satisfaction in his domestic and social life over the year. Although he does tend to be reserved, only letting a privileged few share his innermost thoughts, he will be heartened by the support and encouragement he receives from others – not only from those close to him but also from unexpected quarters. Many do think highly of the Ox and over the year will do much to try to help him. Admittedly, the Ox may not always be aware of this, as others may put in a good word for him behind his back, but he is truly admired and appreciated.

The support the Ox receives will also turn out to be invaluable at times when he may face uncertainty or have important decisions to take. On these occasions, rather than keep his concerns to himself, he should speak to others and listen to the advice he is given. Sometimes the Ox feels he has to shoulder all his problems by himself, but this is not the case and in the year 2000 he should take advantage of the real willingness of others to help.

In addition to the support he receives, the Ox will obtain considerable pleasure and satisfaction from general family activities during the year. He will take a keen interest in the activities of those around him and will have good reason to be proud of the achievements of those close to him. He will also enjoy any projects and interests that he can share with others and should make a point of encouraging these. They will produce some meaningful occasions over the year and will help preserve (and even strengthen) the strong relations the Ox has with those around him.

The Ox's social life will generally go well and he will value the occasions when he can meet up with his friends, even if just for a chat. He will also enjoy the often interesting and varied social occasions he attends over the year. The spring and summer months in particular will contain some agreeable times and, for those Oxen who are unattached and seeking new friendships, this would be an excellent time to go out more and meet others. The Ox does take great care in choosing his friends and a friendship made around the middle of the year, perhaps arising from a chance encounter, could become significant in the future.

Although this may not be the easiest of years for the Ox, by adapting, making the most of existing and changing situations and giving of his best he will still be able to make useful headway. Significantly, what he accomplishes now will do much to contribute to the progress he will make in the near future. For the Ox, the Dragon year often brings about the changes that are necessary for greater advance and success. Also, despite the year's pressures and challenges, the Ox will be greatly encouraged by the supportive attitude of those around him and will appreciate the often happy and meaningful times spent with family and friends. Indeed, his personal life will do much to brighten the year for him.

As far as the different types of Ox are concerned, this will be an important year for the *Metal Ox* and one which will allow him to learn more about himself and his abilities as well as gain valuable experience. Admittedly, not all the events will go in his favour and there will be times when he will feel he should be making greater progress, but overall what he accomplishes now will prove helpful for his long-term future. One area which will see much activity is work and here all Metal Oxen should remain alert to changing situations. When new plans are being proposed or the Metal Ox takes on or is given different duties, he should aim to make the most of them and show a willingness to adapt and learn, despite any misgivings he might have. When new situations arise, the Metal Ox would do well to assess their potential and look at ways in which he might benefit from them. It is those Metal Oxen who are prepared to be forward-looking and show flexibility in their approach who will fare the best. Such Metal Oxen could open up some interesting possibilities for themselves. Those seeking work should continue to pursue any openings that interest them, but would also be helped by looking at their own talents and experience and thinking of how they could draw on them. Some enterprising thinking could widen the scope of positions they could try for and for some Metal Oxen an idea they have now could lead to considerable success in the future. As far as work activities are concerned, the Dragon year will not be a smooth or easy one for the Metal Ox, but its potential for setting in motion events and sparking ideas which will have a favourable bearing on the future should not be under-estimated. The Metal Ox will, however, fare well in financial matters, and by making allowance for specific obligations and forthcoming items of expenditure, he will be satisfied with his general situation. As with all Oxen, though, the Metal Ox should aim to take a holiday or break over the year and if he has any funds he does not immediately need, consider saving or investing some of these for his longer term future. The Metal Ox's domestic life will be quite active over the year, with many matters requiring his attention. These will include helping others, including a relation who has a complex matter to deal with. The Metal Ox's judgement and support will be greatly valued and throughout the year those around him will appreciate his many fine qualities, not least his considerate nature and level-headed approach. In addition to his often busy home life, the Metal Ox will decide to tackle some projects on his home over the year, improving both the comfort and decor. In undertaking practical work, though, he should make sure he allows himself plenty of time rather setting himself too tight a deadline. Also, should any of this work involve tasks which he feels uncomfortable about, he should seek advice or expert help. Better this than risk his personal safety. Although his home life and the practical projects he tackles will take up much of his time over the year, the Metal Ox should still make sure he leaves himself adequate time for his hobbies, interests and social life. These will all help to provide him with a valuable break from his usual preoccupations and allow him to unwind. For one who tends to drive himself hard, this is both important and necessary. The Metal Ox should also pay careful regard to his well-being over the year and if he does not get much daily exercise or is reliant on fast convenience food, more exercise and a balanced diet could leave him feeling fitter and with more energy. Again this is something the Metal

Ox should give thought to over the year, particularly if he wishes to remain on peak form. Although the year will contain its pressures and uncertainties, generally these will not prevent the Metal Ox's onward progress and the experience he gains now will serve him well in the years ahead. In addition, his relations with those close to him will bring him joy and contentment and will certainly help to make up for some of the more testing aspects of the year.

The *Water Ox* has a fine and ambitious nature. Always keen to give of his best, he is certainly not afraid of hard work and over the years his drive and talent will enable him to achieve much. However, although along the route there will be times when his progress is swift and smooth, there will also be occasions when the going is tough and the ride bumpy. In the Dragon year the Water Ox must expect a few bumps! Despite his best endeavours, he will find his progress more difficult than he would like and he could have to revise some of his plans and objectives, particularly those regarding his work. Water Oxen who have recently changed positions or taken on new duties should aim to build on what they have achieved, learn about the different aspects of their role and, if the opportunity arises, go on any training courses. As they will find, this is a good year to consolidate, learn and gain experience. However, the Water Ox could still find himself subject to further change and this could include adapting to new procedures or personnel or taking on additional or different duties. While he may have reservations about some of this, the Water Ox must be careful not to jeopardize what he has already achieved by acting or speaking too rashly. Also, he could find that once some of the changes are in place, new opportunities could become available and he may be well placed to benefit from them. Those Water Oxen looking for work should persist in following up any openings that interest them, but again also take advantage of any training opportunities that become available. It could also be worth the Water Ox's while to consider learning a new skill over the year, perhaps something different from what he has done before. He could, by chance, discover a new forte, one which he can build on and develop successfully in future years. Admittedly, the Water Ox may not always find his quest for a position easy this year, but with enterprise and determination, many Water Oxen will be able to secure a post which will add to their experience and give them a platform from which to develop. As far as financial matters are concerned, this will be a reasonable year and, as usual, the Water Ox will handle his finances with care. He may, however, have to meet some large expenses in the year 2000, especially connected with his accommodation and transport. At such times, he could find it helpful to conduct a review of his present financial situation. This way he might be able to modify and reduce some of his less essential items of expenditure. The Water Ox's personal life will, though, bring him considerable pleasure and he will take a keen and active part in following and encouraging the activities of those around him. He should also make an effort to involve others in his own undertakings and will find that interests and projects he can share will lead to some truly satisfying occasions. His social life, too, can provide some agreeable times over the year. The Water Ox will enjoy meeting friends as well as making some new ones and attending a variety of often interesting social functions. Although he will need to proceed carefully and adapt to the situations in which he finds himself, the year will provide him with the chance to gain valuable experience and will help to set him on course for more substantial progress in the future. To offset any difficulties he may face, the Water Ox will be able to take comfort in his personal life and the happiness and support his loved ones will bring.

This will be a reasonable year for the *Wood Ox* and while he may not always be able to accomplish as much as he would like, he will still obtain some worthwhile results. However, throughout the year, he should keep his objectives at a realistic level and will find that his progress, while not necessarily smooth or problem free, will come from steady and persistent effort. For those Wood Oxen in education this will be a useful and important year, with many taking up new subjects or starting projects which will interest and inspire them. However, while in some areas of school work the Wood Ox will greatly impress, there could also be some subjects which he finds difficult. Rather than struggle on unaided or worry himself too much over his situation, he should seek help and extra guidance. Those around do think highly of him and can do much to help, but the initiative must come from the Wood Ox. Young Wood Oxen, do take note and take advantage of the willingness of others to assist. All Wood Oxen, whether born in 1925 or 1985, can, however, look forward to obtaining much pleasure from their hobbies and interests over the year, especially those that allow them to extend their practical and creative abilities. Also, if the

Wood Ox's hobbies allow him to produce work he can show, he should do so, even perhaps entering an appropriate competition. He will be encouraged by the response and could be given some valuable advice by those who recognize his gifts and potential. Similarly, any Wood Oxen born in 1925 who feel able to write or talk about their interests, specialist knowledge or even family or personal history, should consider doing so. They will find the process both absorbing and illuminating. The Wood Ox should not experience any undue financial problems over the year, although when making sizeable purchases he could sometimes save himself considerable outlay by shopping around and waiting for favourable opportunities. Also, if he has any important paperwork to complete, he does need to deal with this carefully and check any points that he is unclear about. A mistake or delayed response could be to his detriment. When dealing with forms and official correspondence, the Wood Ox does need to be his vigilant and thorough self. As always, he places great value on his domestic and social life, and will be thankful for the support, friendship and affection both his family and friends offer. If he has any personal matter that may be concerning him, he should not hesitate to speak to those around him. They do have his best interests at heart and, once asked, will do all they can to assist. Also, if he has suffered any recent adversity or would like more company, the Wood Ox really would find it in his interests to contact others and perhaps consider joining a society or friendship group. He will find this will do much to help. Similarly, those Wood Oxen born in 1985 who are keen to further their interests and social life could do so by joining a club or youth group where they will be able to forge some good friendships as well as have some enjoyable times. However, as with so much of his life in 2000, the initiative to get positive results does rest with the Wood Ox himself. While the year may not be entirely problem or pressure free, there is still much that will bring him satisfaction, not least his personal interests and favourable relations with those around him.

This *can* be a pleasant and productive year for the *Fire Ox* provided he set about his activities with care and consideration. If, however, he succumbs to some of the more negative aspects of his character, it could prove a disappointment. The reason why the year is so finely balanced is that the Dragon year is rarely straightforward for the Ox and problems can and do arise. Many times these can be quickly dealt with but sometimes the Fire Ox takes hold of an issue and tackles it in such a manner that it assumes a far greater importance than necessary and takes up a lot of his time. If he is not careful, this could happen in the year 2000. When and if problems arise, no matter what area of his life they may concern, the Fire Ox should look at them in their true light, consider his options and try to work out a speedy and effective solution. Also, rather than tackle awkward matters single-handedly, he should consult those around him and, if the situation calls for it, seek professional advice. If not, matters could so easily escalate and, with the Fire Ox being the redoubtable person he is, he will immerse himself so much in their resolution that it will prevent him from carrying out other sometimes more productive pursuits. Hopefully these words of warning will only apply to a minority of Fire

Oxen, but is something that all do need to be aware of during the year. At difficult moments, keep things in perspective! More positively, the year will offer the Fire Ox the chance to carry out some of the plans he has been contemplating for some time. Some of these will concern his accommodation and many Fire Oxen will decide to go ahead with some improvements over the year, particularly relating to the decor, comfort and style of their home. While the work may take longer than envisaged, what the Fire Ox accomplishes will bring him and his loved ones much satisfaction. His own personal hobbies and interests too will provide him with many pleasurable moments, especially those in which the Fire Ox can use his practical or creative talents. If he is able to take one of his hobbies further, perhaps by learning about different aspects or, if appropriate, obtaining new equipment, he could find his pastime all the more interesting and rewarding. One area which could prove especially satisfying is photography and for those Fire Oxen interested in taking photographs or making films, it certainly would be worth while spending time on this over the year and perhaps experimenting with new techniques. Similarly, for those interested in computers, this would be a good year in which to find out more and extend their skills. The Fire Ox will also find much contentment in his domestic and social life, and will take considerable pleasure in encouraging the activities of those dear to him, with the progress and success enjoyed by a younger relation being especially meaningful. The Fire Ox will be heartened too by the support he receives for his own activities, but here again he should take care. The Fire Ox does like to have his own way and if at any time he

THE OX

encounters any form of dissension he must take this into account; otherwise, if he becomes intractable, friction could arise which might take some time to settle. Fire Oxen, do take careful note – enjoy the companionship and love of those around you, but do not jeopardize good relationships through a little awkwardness. An area which will bring the Fire Ox pleasure over the year is travel and all Fire Oxen should aim to go away at some time. They will not only benefit from the rest and change a holiday brings but will be impressed by some of the destinations they visit. Generally, this can be a productive year for the Fire Ox, but so much rests upon his own reaction to events. In the year 2000 he needs to proceed carefully, remain mindful of the views of others and take things in his stride. There is much in his favour, but a too negative or single-minded approach could prevent him from realizing and enjoying all he otherwise might. If he bears this in mind the year can work out well for him, however, and produce some pleasing and fulfilling times.

The *Earth Ox* is blessed with a methodical nature, recognizing the value of order, good planning and consistency. These qualities have, in the past, led him to some worthy achievements. However, the Dragon year could prove disruptive to him, throwing uncertainty on some of his plans and causing him to rethink some of his current objectives. Parts of the year will be unsettling and the Earth Ox will feel ill at ease with some of the situations in which he finds himself. However, while there will be some challenging aspects to the year, out of these will often come positive and far-reaching benefits. Sometimes the changes that occur will usher in opportunities that had not been available before or will cause the Earth Ox to look again at some of his plans and either strengthen these or come up with better ones. In addition, some of the events that occur, particularly related to work, will bring fresh and interesting challenges which will not only keep the Earth Ox on his mettle but also help keep alight his incentive to get on. Indeed, change, although not always welcome, is often a necessary prerequisite for development and success. The work changes could involve the introduction of new schemes, restructuring or changes in personnel, or the Earth Ox could find himself taking on different duties, some of which he had not quite anticipated. In view of these possibilities it is important he remains alert to all that is going on and aware of any imminent proposals. This way he can better prepare and position himself for any changes that may occur. Also, although he may hold reservations about some of what is being proposed or taking place, the Earth Ox should proceed carefully and tactfully. In time, when events have become more settled, he could find some new and excellent opportunities emerging, but in the meantime he should not do anything that could undermine his position. For those Earth Oxen who are currently seeking work or who want to move from their present position, the Dragon year will bring some interesting openings. These may not always be in the area in which the Earth Ox was intending to work, but could nevertheless usefully extend his experience, provide him with some interesting challenges and give him better scope for progress in the future. As far as financial matters are concerned, this will be a reasonable year, with some Earth Oxen receiving an additional sum of money, either as a gift, the fruition of an investment or payment for earlier work. As usual, the Earth Ox will deal with his finances with care, often deciding to save or invest some of the money he does not immediately need and putting the rest towards items of household equipment, travel, holidays and personal interests. However, when he is involved in any large purchase, he would do well to take his time comparing the prices and ranges on offer; by looking around he could make some noticeable and, in some cases, quite startling savings. This will also be an active year personally, with family matters and household projects keeping the Earth Ox busy. As usual he will play a full and active role in family life, encouraging and helping others and dispensing advice, as well as taking much personal delight in the successes of those close to him. Just as the Earth Ox will give much useful advice over the year, like-wise, whenever he has matters concerning him or feels in need of a helping hand, he should not hesitate to ask those around him. By doing so he will not only be given assis-tance but will also gain much from the reassurance and views given. He will be heartened, too, by the esteem and affection shown towards him throughout the year. The Earth Ox will also obtain much value from his own hobbies and interests over the year; those that allow him to meet others or provide some additional exercise could prove particularly beneficial. The Earth Ox should try to ensure that he goes away for a holiday or has a proper break over the year, as this too will do him a great deal of good. Although the Dragon year will contain some testing and challenging moments, much of it will nevertheless bring the Earth Ox contentment. His relations with those around him and his personal interests will be particularly pleasurable. Added to which, the events in his professional life will often have an important bearing on the next few years and will allow him to develop skills as well as bring him some interesting challenges and opportunities. For many Earth Oxen, the Dragon year will mark the start of a new and more fulfilling period, with considerable rewards coming in 2001 and beyond.

FAMOUS OXEN

Madeleine Albright, Martin Amis, Hans Christian Andersen, Johann Sebastian Bach, Warren Beatty, Tony Benn, William Blake, Napoleon Bonaparte, Rory Bremner, Benjamin Britten, Frank Bruno, Albert Camus, Jim Carrey, Johnny Carson, Barbara Cartland, Charlie Chaplin, Melanie Chisholm (Sporty Spice), George Clooney, Martin Clunes, Jean Cocteau, Natalie Cole, Bill Cosby, Tom Courtenay, Tony Curtis, Donald Dewar, Diana, Princess of Wales, Marlene Dietrich, Walt Disney, Patrick Duffy, Harry Enfield, Jane Fonda, Gerald Ford, Edward Fox, Michael J. Fox, Peter Gabriel, Richard Gere, William Hague, Handel, King Harald V of Norway, Robert Hardy, Nigel Havers, Adolf Hitler, Dustin Hoffman, Anthony Hopkins, Saddam Hussein, Billy Joel, Don Johnson, Lionel Jospin, King Juan Carlos of Spain, B. B. King, Mark Knopfler, Burt Lancaster, k. d. Lang, Jessica Lange, Angela Lansbury, Jack Lemmon, Nicholas Lyndhurst, Mary Tyler Moore, Kate Moss, Mo Mowlam, Alison Moyet, Eddie Murphy, Benjamin Netanyahu, Paul Newman, Jack

Nicholson, Leslie Nielsen, Billy Ocean, Gwyneth Paltrow, Oscar Peterson, Colin Powell, Robert Redford, Lionel Richie, Rubens, Greg Rusedski, Meg Ryan, Monica Seles, Jean Sibelius, Sissy Spacek, Bruce Springsteen, Rod Steiger, Meryl Streep, Lady Thatcher, Scott F. Turow, Dick van Dyke, Vincent van Gogh, Zoë Wanamaker, the Duke of Wellington, Barbara Windsor, Ernie Wise, W. B. Yeats.

8 FEBRUARY 1902 ∼ 28 JANUARY 1903   *Water Tiger*

26 JANUARY 1914 ∼ 13 FEBRUARY 1915   *Wood Tiger*

13 FEBRUARY 1926 ∼ 1 FEBRUARY 1927   *Fire Tiger*

31 JANUARY 1938 ∼ 18 FEBRUARY 1939   *Earth Tiger*

17 FEBRUARY 1950 ∼ 5 FEBRUARY 1951   *Metal Tiger*

5 FEBRUARY 1962 ∼ 24 JANUARY 1963   *Water Tiger*

23 JANUARY 1974 ∼ 10 FEBRUARY 1975   *Wood Tiger*

9 FEBRUARY 1986 ∼ 28 JANUARY 1987   *Fire Tiger*

28 JANUARY 1998 ∼ 15 FEBRUARY 1999   *Earth Tiger*

THE
TIGER

THE PERSONALITY OF THE TIGER

You cannot dream yourself into a character; you must
hammer and forge one for yourself.

James A. Froude: a Tiger

The Tiger is born under the sign of courage. He is a charis-
matic figure and usually holds very firm views. He is
strong-willed and determined, and sets about most of the
things he does with tremendous energy and enthusiasm.
He is very alert and quick-witted and his mind is forever
active. He is a highly original thinker and is nearly always
brimming with new ideas or full of enthusiasm for some
new project or scheme.

The Tiger adores challenges and loves to get involved in
anything which he thinks has an exciting future or which
catches his imagination. He is prepared to take risks and does
not like to be bound either by convention or the dictates of
others. The Tiger likes to be free to act as he chooses and at
least once during his life he will throw caution to the wind
and go off and do the things he wants to do.

The Tiger does, however, have a somewhat restless
nature. Even though he is often prepared to throw himself
wholeheartedly into a project, his initial enthusiasm can
soon wane if he sees something more appealing. He can
also be rather impulsive and there will be occasions in his
life when he acts in a manner which he later regrets. If the
Tiger were to think things out or to persevere in his
various activities, he would almost certainly enjoy a greater
degree of success than he would otherwise obtain.

Fortunately, the Tiger is lucky in most of his enterprises, but should things not work out as he had hoped, he is liable to suffer from severe bouts of depression and it will often take him a long time to recover. His life often consists of a series of ups and downs.

The Tiger is, however, very adaptable. He has an adventurous spirit and rarely stays in the same place for long. In the early stages of his life he is likely to try his hand at several different jobs and he will also change his residence fairly frequently.

The Tiger is very honest and open in his dealings with others. He hates any sort of hypocrisy or falsehood. He is also well known for being blunt and forthright and has no hesitation in speaking his mind. He can be most rebellious at times, particularly against any form of petty authority, and while this can lead the Tiger into conflict with others, he is never one to shrink from an argument or avoid standing up for what he believes is right.

The Tiger is a natural leader and can invariably rise to the top of his chosen profession. He does not, however, care for anything too bureaucratic or detailed and he also does not like to obey orders. He can be stubborn and obstinate, and throughout his life he likes to retain a certain amount of independence in his actions and be responsible to no one but himself. He likes to consider that all his achievements are due to his own efforts and unless he cannot avoid it, he will rarely ask for support from others.

Ironically, despite his self-confidence and leadership qualities, the Tiger can be indecisive and will often delay making a major decision until the very last moment. He can also be sensitive to criticism.

Although the Tiger is capable of earning large sums of money, he is rather a spendthrift and does not always put his money to its best use. He can also be most generous and will often shower lavish gifts on friends and relations.

The Tiger cares very much for his reputation and the image that he tries to project. He carries himself with an air of dignity and authority and enjoys being the centre of attention. He is very adept at attracting publicity, both for himself and for the causes he supports.

The Tiger often marries young and he will find himself best suited to those born under the signs of the Pig, Dog, Horse and Goat. He can also get on well with the Rat, Rabbit and Rooster, but will find the Ox and Snake a bit too quiet and too serious for his liking, and he will also be highly irritated by the Monkey's rather mischievous and inquisitive ways. The Tiger will also find it difficult to get on with another Tiger or a Dragon – both partners will want to dominate the relationship and could find it difficult to compromise on even the smallest of matters.

The Tigress is lively, witty and a marvellous hostess at parties. She is usually most attractive and takes great care over her appearance. She can also be a very doting mother and while she believes in letting her children have their freedom, she makes an excellent teacher and will ensure that her children are brought up well and want for nothing. Like her male counterpart, she has numerous interests and likes to have sufficient independence and freedom to go off and do the things that she wants to do. She also has a most caring and generous nature.

The Tiger has many commendable qualities. He is honest, courageous and often a source of inspiration for others. Providing he can curb the wilder excesses of his restless nature, he is almost certain to lead a most fulfilling and satisfying life.

THE FIVE DIFFERENT TYPES OF TIGER

In addition to the 12 signs of the Chinese zodiac, there are five elements and these have a strengthening or moderating influence on the sign. The effects of the five elements on the Tiger are described below, together with the years in which the elements were exercising their influence. Therefore all Tigers born in 1950 are Metal Tigers, those born in 1902 and 1962 are Water Tigers, and so on.

Metal Tiger: 1950
The Metal Tiger has an assertive and outgoing personality. He is very ambitious and, while his aims may change from time to time, he will work relentlessly until he has obtained what he wants. He can, however, be impatient for results and also become highly strung if things do not work out as he would like. He is distinctive in his appearance and is admired and respected by many.

Water Tiger: 1902, 1962
This Tiger has a wide variety of interests and is always eager to experiment with new ideas or go off and explore

distant lands. He is versatile, shrewd and has a kindly nature. The Water Tiger tends to remain calm in a crisis, although he can be annoyingly indecisive at times. He communicates well with others and through his many capabilities and persuasive nature he usually achieves what he wants in life. He is also highly imaginative and is often a gifted orator or writer.

Wood Tiger: 1914, 1974

The Wood Tiger has a very friendly and pleasant personality. He is less independent than some of the other types of Tiger and is more prepared to work with others to secure a desired objective. However, he does have a tendency to jump from one thing to another and can get easily distracted. He is usually very popular, has a large circle of friends and invariably leads a busy and enjoyable social life. He also has a good sense of humour.

Fire Tiger: 1926, 1986

The Fire Tiger sets about everything he does with great verve and enthusiasm. He loves action and is always ready to throw himself wholeheartedly into anything which catches his imagination. He has many leadership qualities and is capable of communicating his ideas and enthusiasm to others. He is very much an optimist and can be most generous. He has a likeable nature and can be a witty and persuasive speaker.

Earth Tiger: 1938, 1998

This Tiger is responsible and level-headed. He studies everything objectively and tries to be scrupulously fair in all his dealings. Unlike other Tigers, he is prepared to specialize in certain areas rather than get distracted by other matters, but he can become so involved in what he is doing that he does not always take into account the opinions of those around him. He has good business sense and is usually very successful in later life. He has a large circle of friends and pays great attention to both his appearance and his reputation.

PROSPECTS FOR THE TIGER IN THE YEAR 2000

The Chinese New Year starts on 5 February 2000. Until then, the old year, the Year of the Rabbit, is still making its presence felt.

The Year of the Rabbit (16 February 1999 to 4 February 2000) will have been a positive one for the Tiger, with the closing months being a particularly fulfilling and rewarding time.

During the Rabbit year the Tiger will have impressed others with his personable approach, keen ideas and enterprising nature, and this will place him in a good position to make further headway as the year draws to an end. Many Tigers will find themselves being offered the chance to take on other, more interesting duties at work or will be given some recognition for what they have achieved. If the Tiger sees any opportunities for further advancement, he should follow them up, drawing on his experience and skills to do so. With a positive attitude, he can make headway and also prepare for the continuing progress he will make in 2000. Those Tigers seeking work should remain particularly active in their quest, as a chance remark or advert that they follow up now could have some interesting consequences.

With its cultural overtones, the Rabbit year is an excellent time for self-development and the Tiger should take full advantage of any training opportunities that become available to him. Similarly, if there are any skills or subjects that he would like to learn, this would be a good time to follow them up. With the Tiger's prospects so favourable in the forthcoming Dragon year, what he can set in motion now will often work to his longer term advantage.

On a domestic and social level, the Tiger will find himself in fine form in the closing stages of the Rabbit year. He will be invited to a wide range of functions and social events and he will enjoy them very much. For Tigers who are unattached, who would like new friends or who are seeking additional company, opportunities to meet others will abound. Personally this will be a busy, rewarding and happy time.

However, while so much will go in the Tiger's favour, there are two points that he should bear in mind. The first is to watch his outgoings. Without a certain care, the Tiger could find he has spent considerably more in the closing months of 1999 than he anticipated and more control over his spending would not come amiss. The second point is that he should keep his commitments to a manageable level. Sometimes the Tiger's enthusiasm and willingness do get the better of him. Without a certain restraint, he could find his life becoming a whirl, with him having to rush from one activity to another with little free time. The Tiger should watch this and certainly in December 1999 he would do well to organize his time and commitments, particularly in view of all that he wants to fit in.

The Year of the Dragon starts on 5 February and heralds an interesting and exciting time for the Tiger. As the new millennium starts, the Tiger will feel more determined than ever to build on his achievements and make more of his potential. The Dragon year will certainly give him his chance.

In recent times, particularly during the Rabbit year, the Tiger will have accomplished and learnt a great deal. However, despite these achievements, many Tigers will feel there is still much more they can offer and will make an even greater effort to improve their position and realize some of their aspirations. In order to do this, though, the Tiger should give serious thought to just what it is he does want to do and how best he might to achieve it. It is one thing to have a dream, another to turn it into reality.

One particularly positive area, however, is the Tiger's work and during the year many Tigers will take up some interesting and, perhaps more importantly from their point of view, fulfilling challenges. Many will be offered new responsibilities, the chance to transfer to different duties or promotion. While some of what is on offer may initially be daunting, it will provide the Tiger with an added incentive to make better use of his skills. The Tiger will also be helped by his enterprising nature and fertile mind, and again he should use these abilities to his advantage. If he has any ideas which he would like to take further, he should talk them over with others and gauge the initial response. If his work is of an imaginative or artistic nature, or if he has creative aspirations, he should draw on his talents and promote himself. The Dragon year is all for enterprise, innovation and creativity, and here the Tiger can score well and make an impact.

For those Tigers who are seeking work or who decide that now is the right time to move from their present position, the year will contain some excellent possibilities. However, identifying openings will sometimes require ingenuity and boldness on the Tiger's part and he does need to seek out opportunities rather than just wait for them. In his quest he could be helped by considering different ways in which he could draw on his experience as well as by investigating areas of interest to him, even though these may be different from anything he has done before. The Tiger will find that his keen, enterprising approach will often help him to secure a position and that an opening he is offered now could easily become a stepping-stone to greater progress. The early months of the year and then again from September to late November could see some particularly interesting and positive developments as far as his work prospects are concerned. The Dragon year does hold considerable potential for the Tiger, but the onus is on him to take the initiative and to seize the opportunities the year holds.

In matters of finance the Tiger will, though, need to exercise care. This is not a year in which he can be too complacent and if he becomes involved in any large transaction he should make sure that he has studied the small print and is aware of any obligations he may be placed under. Sometimes the Tiger can be just a little lax or trusting in his financial dealings and without extra vigilance this year he could find his outlay and obligations greater than he thought. Similarly, he should keep a watch over his level of spending, as again this could sometimes creep up and as a result lead to him having to make cutbacks later. The Tiger can certainly end the year in an improved financial position, but this does require care and some restraint.

The Tiger will, however, lead an active personal life over the year and, for the unattached, romance, engagement and marriage are all splendidly aspected. There will also be many opportunities and occasions for the Tiger to add to his circle of friends and acquaintances, with the spring and summer months being particularly busy. However, in his relations with others, the Tiger does need to be his honourable self and if he lets his attentions wander, problems, difficulties and heartache could ensue. This word of warning only applies to a minority of Tigers, but it is one to heed. Enjoy the year and enjoy yourself – but do not tempt fate.

On a domestic level this will be an active year, with many family activities and commitments keeping the Tiger occupied. In some cases these could involve changes within the home, such as family members moving out for the purposes of education or work or for other reasons. Alternatively, some Tigers will themselves decide to move and will spend time choosing where they want to live and setting the process in motion. Whatever happens in the

Tiger household in the year 2000, others will admire the Tiger's ability to take command, and during times of pressure and change he will often be a source of strength and inspiration.

Although there will be considerable activity in the Tiger's domestic life over the year, there will be much for him to enjoy. In particular, those interests that he can share or household projects he can carry out with others will lead to some satisfying occasions. The Tiger will also do much to assist and encourage those around him, and his kindnesses will be greatly appreciated.

Travel too is favourably aspected and the Tiger will enjoy any holiday and breaks that he takes. During the year he will have the chance to visit some often remarkable and unusual destinations. For any Tiger who has been thinking of furthering his experience by living and working in another country, this would be a good year in which to do it. The Dragon year does hold a spirit of adventure and for those Tigers keen to do something different and challenging, the year 2000 will offer some interesting opportunities!

Similarly, this is an excellent year for the Tiger to consider extending his personal interests. He will find that those which provide some sort of challenge or are different from anything he has done before will provide him with some absorbing and stimulating occasions.

Generally, this will be a fulfilling year for the Tiger. However, to get the most from it he does need to give some thought to what he wants to accomplish and then go after his objectives in an organized manner. By planning and using his time wisely he can make significant strides and achieve some well-deserved successes. He can also look forward to an active domestic and social life, and will find himself much in demand. In the year 2000 the Tiger has much in his favour and really should take advantage of the opportunities. For the bold, enterprising and creative Tiger, this is a year which holds great potential.

As far as the different Tigers are concerned, this will be an interesting year for the *Metal Tiger* and one which will see some important and far-reaching changes. Indeed, many Metal Tigers will view this, the first year of the new millennium, as a time for action, and will make a concerted effort to realize some of their plans and ideas. One area which will see much activity will be the Metal Tiger's work. Although over the years the Metal Tiger has already accomplished a great deal, there are many Metal Tigers who feel they have not yet realized their full potential or who are unfulfilled in their present role. To help correct this, some will actively seek promotion and greater responsibilities while others will look for new and different duties, perhaps even switching careers. However, whatever the Metal Tiger decides upon, once he has set himself upon a course he will pursue it in his usual steadfast way. Admittedly, his path will not always be straightforward, but the Metal Tiger is always one who enjoys challenges and his determination over the year will pay off. He should, though, not expect instant results nor become disheartened if his initial attempts to improve his position come to nothing; success will ultimately come, and sometimes on the heels of a setback or disappointment. Similarly, those Metal Tigers seeking work can attain a position over the year, but again this will require determination and resourcefulness on their part. These Metal Tigers should not only follow up any openings that interest them but also look at their own skills and experience and consider different ways in which they can draw on them. Some enterprising thinking could open up new possibilities and once they have secured a position, it will serve as a valuable base from which to make further headway. As far as finances are concerned, however, the year will call for a certain care. If the Metal Tiger has any doubts over a financial matter in which he becomes involved he should seek further clarification and, if need be, professional advice. This is not a year in which he can take undue risks or become complacent in his financial dealings. Also, if he does not keep financial records and accounts, he could find it useful to start doing so. By putting his finances on a more organized footing, he will find he is able to make more effective use of his money as well as make some additional savings. For personal matters this will be an active year. The Metal Tiger's home life will be busy and he will do much to assist family members, including helping someone with an awkward problem. Although sometimes there may be moments of anxiety and pressure over family matters, the Metal Tiger's considerate nature, combined with his fine judgement, will do much to help and he will earn the gratitude of many. However, while there may be some demanding periods in his home life, there will still be much that will bring the Metal Tiger satisfaction, including not only any household projects and mutual interests that he can share but also the many pleasurable activities in which he is involved, such as

outings, visits to places of interest and any breaks and holidays. The Metal Tiger will also derive much pleasure from
his own personal interests and should aim to further these
over the year, perhaps by learning about new aspects, tackling more ambitious projects or meeting fellow enthusiasts.
By doing something positive, he can make his interests all
the more fulfilling and enjoy some particularly satisfying
occasions. The Metal Tiger's social life will also go well and
he will not only enjoy times spent with existing friends
but, by joining local or special interest groups, will be able
to strike up new, and in some cases important, friendships.
The prospects are certainly favourable for the Metal Tiger,
but to get the most from the year, he should decide upon
his objectives and set about them in earnest. He will find
that positive action towards specific goals will lead to some
important, fulfilling and often far-reaching results.

This will be a demanding but satisfying year for the
Water Tiger, with some of what happens having considerable bearing on his future. One area which will see much
activity will be work, particularly as many Water Tigers
will take positive steps to improve on their present position
over the year. Some will try for promotion or greater
responsibilities elsewhere or even consider changing
careers. While not all their initial attempts may work out,
by going determinedly after what they want they will
eventually make progress. As has been shown in the past,
once the Water Tiger is given his chance, he will quickly
impress and make his mark. The Dragon year will also
bring some positive developments for those Water Tigers
seeking work. In addition to following up any openings
that they see, they might well find it useful to make direct

contact with companies they might like to work for or people currently in the type of position they would like. By taking the initiative these Water Tigers could be given some useful advice which could ultimately lead to the opening they want. However, it does rest with the Water Tiger himself to take action. As all Water Tigers will find over the year, progress and success will often result from applied effort towards specific goals. The progress the Water Tiger will make in his work will also often lead to an improvement in his income. However, in spite of this, he does still need to take care when dealing with money matters. This is not a year for taking unnecessary risks, entering into speculative ventures or spending too freely. The Water Tiger will make money over the year, but without care he could all too easily lose or squander it. Water Tigers, take note! The Water Tiger's domestic life will, however, bring him considerable pleasure. He will enjoy following the progress of those dear to him and will also get much satisfaction from carrying out various projects on his home and garden. Many Water Tigers will decide to move over the year and those that do will spend some time selecting their new accommodation. At times they will despair of getting what they want or wonder whether the effort will be worthwhile, but once they have moved, they will quickly settle down and be pleased with their new home – as well as relieved! Throughout the year, the Water Tiger will be well supported by others and should not hesitate to seek additional assistance or advice if he has any matters concerning him or if jobs (particularly household) seem to be mounting up. In view of the active nature of the year there may be a temptation for the Water

Tiger to neglect his own interests or perhaps not socialize as much as he would like. However it is important he finds time for these activities; both his interests and social life will help him to unwind and relax as well as provide a valuable break from his usual preoccupations. In addition, the Water Tiger should try to make sure he takes a break or holiday over the year as this will not only prove beneficial but will also lead to some enjoyable occasions and often give him the chance to visit some interesting locations. Generally, the year 2000 will be a busy one for the Water Tiger, partly because of the objectives he has set himself. However, as he realizes, to make progress does require effort on his part. In the Dragon year, he will make a supreme effort to realize some of his goals and will achieve much as a result. This is very much an active year for the Water Tiger and one which will lay the groundwork for the success he can look forward to in the coming years.

Although not everything may work out as the *Wood Tiger* intended in the year 2000, this will still be a significant and important time for him. During the Dragon year he could find some of his plans being affected by new and changing situations and may sometimes find it difficult to progress in the way he desires. However, while the Dragon year will throw some challenges at him and disrupt some of his plans, this is not necessarily to the Wood Tiger's disadvantage. The changing circumstances will help keep him on his mettle and by confronting and overcoming problems, he will learn a great deal about himself. In this way his character will be strengthened and he will devise new and sometimes superior plans. The Wood Tiger can therefore derive much value from the year, even though some of it will work out differently from how he envisaged. As far as his work is concerned, several important changes are indicated. For many Wood Tigers this will mean a change of duties or job, and while again these new duties may not always be what the Wood Tiger would have wanted, they will allow him to extend his skills and experience, and will thereby work to his future advantage. Also, while the Wood Tiger may possess clear ideas about what he would ultimately like to do, this year he would find it in his interest to adopt a flexible approach and take advantage of the opportunities that arise rather than hold rigidly to his existing plans. Those Wood Tigers seeking work would also do well to broaden the scope of the positions they are trying for. By doing this, they will find they have more openings to pursue and one position they are offered could provide a useful foothold for future progression. For work matters, the Dragon year holds considerable potential, but it does require the Wood Tiger to show some flexibility and to accept and take advantage of the situations as they are rather than what he hopes might exist. The Wood Tiger will also need to deal carefully with financial matters over the year and in view of his many outgoings he could find it helpful to maintain a set of accounts and so keep better track of his situation. With fine financial management he should be able to avoid problems, but this is not a year for taking risks or neglecting money matters. The Wood Tiger's personal life will, though, be particularly busy, with some important and memorable developments. Some Wood Tigers will marry, see an addition to their family or take especial delight in following the progress of family members. However, while personal and family matters will bring the Wood Tiger much happiness, mixed in with this there could also be a few niggling problems. At such times the Wood Tiger should not hesitate to seek the advice of those around him, as he will find reassurance in the assistance others are able to offer. At awkward times it is important for him to remember that he is not on his own. Indeed, there are many who love and respect him and are prepared to help him out. The problems will not, however, detract from the many rich and happy times that the year will bring the Wood Tiger, especially over the summer months. In addition to enjoying the company of those around him, he will also take pleasure in carrying out his hobbies and interests, especially those he can share with his loved ones or which bring him into contact with others. On a social level the year is finely aspected and the Wood Tiger will find himself much in demand with his friends, as well as having the opportunity to make some new ones, and can look forward to attending a variety of social occasions, parties and events. Again, the summer will be an active time. In most respects, the Wood Tiger will enjoy and benefit from the Dragon year and even if he has to modify some of his existing plans and ideas, he will have an excellent chance to add to his experience and learn from life's rich learning process, challenging though this sometimes may be. The year will also provide him with some memorable occasions, particularly in his personal life.

The *Fire Tiger* is very much one who likes to keep himself active and invariably has a range of different ideas and projects to try out. In the year 2000 he can look forward to obtaining some pleasing results, but early in the year he should decide upon his more immediate priorities and then set about achieving these in a planned and organized manner. This way he will not only make better use of his time but will also obtain more satisfying results. His plans may concern practical projects or personal interests, but whatever he decides, purposeful action on his part will be well rewarded. During the year many Fire Tigers will involve themselves with home improvement projects or decide to move. While they will have every reason to be pleased with what they accomplish, they should allow plenty of time for practical tasks and major undertakings. Although the end results will certainly be delightful, the execution will not necessarily be quick or problem free! Also, if these Fire Tigers have to tackle complex tasks with which they are not fully conversant, or move heavy items, they should seek help rather than risk an accident or mishap. In addition to what he undertakes in his home, the Fire Tiger will also get much satisfaction from his own interests. If he is able to extend them in any way, such as learning about new aspects, contacting fellow enthusiasts, starting new projects or even writing about his experiences, he will find this will help make them all the more rewarding. The Fire Tiger will also get considerable pleasure from his domestic and often active social life over the year. He can look forward to playing a full and appreciated role in family activities, with some pleasing family news and occasions bringing him much satisfaction. He will also find himself in demand socially and will enjoy time spent with friends and attending various social functions. Another area which is well aspected is travel and the Fire Tiger should take advantage of any opportunity he gets to go away, perhaps visiting destinations he has been keen to see for some time or relations and friends living some distance away. Travel will lead to some fine and memorable occasions over the year. Those Fire Tigers born in 1986 will make good progress in their schoolwork. However, with often many activities to fit in, both pleasurable and educational, it would be worth such Fire Tigers setting about their activities in an organized manner rather than trying to cram too much in at any one time. Also, if tests and exams are approaching, the Fire Tiger would do well to leave sufficient time for revision. Although he still has several years of education in front of him, his results now could have an important bearing on his future and it would be worth him making that extra effort. Also, if he does have any worries, he should not hesitate to speak to others about them. As he will find, those around can do much to help him and allay his concerns. Generally, this will be a pleasant year for the Fire Tiger, but to make the most of the encouraging trends that prevail, he does need to give some thought to what he wants to do over the year and to use his time wisely. With care and good organization, however, this can be a fulfilling and rewarding year.

This will be a positive year for the *Earth Tiger* with constructive developments in most areas of his life. His own personal hobbies and interests will be particularly satisfying and he should not only spend time on these but also aim to develop them, perhaps by learning about another aspect or tackling a more ambitious project. By extending his interests and setting himself some challenges the Earth Tiger will enjoy some stimulating and fulfilling times over the year. It is even possible that he might be able to put an interest or skill of his to profitable use. With enterprising thinking, some Earth Tigers could develop an additional source of income over the year. For those Earth Tigers who do not have a particular hobby at the moment or have just retired and have more time at their disposal, it really would be worthwhile considering a new hobby or learning a new skill, perhaps one that has long intrigued them but they have never had the chance to take up. As the Earth Tiger will discover, his personal interests really will be a source of considerable pleasure over the year. His domestic life too will go well and he will greatly enjoy the family activities and projects he is involved in. These may well include some highly agreeable trips out. The Earth Tiger will also take particular delight in the successes and progress of those considerably younger than himself and if there is advice he would like to pass on, he should not hesitate to do so. Although there may be an age gap of many years, those younger than the Earth Tiger do hold him in special regard and will listen to his words carefully. Also, many Earth Tigers will decide to mount an efficiency drive over the year, sorting and clearing out unwanted papers and belongings, and so making their home tidier and more efficient. This in itself will bring the Earth Tiger much satisfaction. His social life too will go well and he can look forward to many enjoyable times meeting and conversing with friends as well as attending a variety of often interesting social functions, particularly during the summer. Any Earth Tiger who may be feeling lonely or wanting a more active social life really should make an effort to help bring this about over the year. By becoming more involved with group activities, perhaps by joining a local society or special interest group, the lonely Earth Tiger will soon meet others, some of whom may become firm friends and add a new interest to his life. As far as financial matters are concerned, however, the year does call for care. If the Earth Tiger becomes involved in any important transaction or has doubts over any financial matter, he should seek clarification. This is not a year for taking risks or jumping to conclusions. Similarly, if the Earth Tiger has any important forms to complete, especially concerning finance or tax, he should proceed with care. Otherwise he could find himself involved in some protracted correspondence and possibly paying more than he need or even losing out on some benefit or entitlement. Earth Tigers, do take note and remain vigilant! More positively, the Earth Tiger will greatly enjoy the travelling that he undertakes over the year and should aim to go away at least once, perhaps visiting a destination he has had in mind for some time or visiting relations or friends he has not seen for a while. His travels can lead to some particularly pleasing and memorable occasions. Generally, the Dragon year will go well for the Earth Tiger and by using his time effectively he will be satisfied with what he is able to accomplish. Added to which, his relations with those around him will go well and this, to one who is so caring and has so much to give, will make the year all the more meaningful and gratifying for him.

FAMOUS TIGERS

Victoria Adams (Posh Spice), Kofi Annan, Sir David Attenborough, Queen Beatrix of the Netherlands,

Beethoven, Tony Bennett, Tom Berenger, Chuck Berry, Jon Bon Jovi, Richard Branson, Garth Brooks, Mel Brooks, Isambard Kingdom Brunel, Agatha Christie, Phil Collins, Robbie Coltrane, Alan Coren, Sheryl Crow, Tom Cruise, Paul Daniels, Charles de Gaulle, Leonardo DiCaprio, Emily Dickinson, David Dimbleby, Isadora Duncan, Dwight Eisenhower, Queen Elizabeth II, Enya, Roberta Flack, E. M. Forster, Frederick Forsyth, Jodie Foster, Connie Francis, Crystal Gayle, Elliott Gould, Buddy Greco, Sir Alec Guinness, Ruud Gullit, Prince Naseem Hamed, Tim Henman, William Hurt, Derek Jacobi, Bianca Jagger, Jewel, Stan Laurel, Louise, Karl Marx, Marilyn Monroe, Demi Moore, Eric Morecambe, Alanis Morissette, Neil Morrissey, Jeremy Paxman, Marco Polo, Beatrix Potter, John Prescott, Renoir, Kenny Rogers, the Princess Royal, Dame Joan Sutherland, Dylan Thomas, Liv Ullman, Jon Voight, Julie Walters, Oscar Wilde, Robbie Williams, Tennessee Williams, Terry Wogan, Stevie Wonder.

29 JANUARY 1903 ～ 15 FEBRUARY 1904   *Water Rabbit*

14 FEBRUARY 1915 ～ 2 FEBRUARY 1916   *Wood Rabbit*

2 FEBRUARY 1927 ～ 22 JANUARY 1928   *Fire Rabbit*

19 FEBRUARY 1939 ～ 7 FEBRUARY 1940   *Earth Rabbit*

6 FEBRUARY 1951 ～ 26 JANUARY 1952   *Metal Rabbit*

25 JANUARY 1963 ～ 12 FEBRUARY 1964   *Water Rabbit*

11 FEBRUARY 1975 ～ 30 JANUARY 1976   *Wood Rabbit*

29 JANUARY 1987 ～ 16 FEBRUARY 1988   *Fire Rabbit*

16 FEBRUARY 1999 ～ 4 FEBRUARY 2000   *Earth Rabbit*

THE
RABBIT

THE PERSONALITY OF THE RABBIT

The talent of success is nothing more than doing what
you can well, and doing well whatever you do, without a
thought of fame.

Henry Wadsworth Longfellow: a Rabbit

The Rabbit is born under the signs of virtue and prudence.
He is intelligent, well-mannered and prefers a quiet and
peaceful existence. He dislikes any sort of unpleasantness
and will try to steer clear of arguments and disputes. He is
very much a pacifist and tends to have a calming influence
on those around him.

He has wide interests and usually has a good appreciation of the arts and the finer things in life. He also knows
how to enjoy himself and will often gravitate to the best
restaurants and night spots in town.

The Rabbit is a witty and intelligent speaker and loves
being involved in a good discussion. His views and advice
are often sought by others and he can be relied upon to be
discreet and diplomatic. He will rarely raise his voice in
anger and will even turn a blind eye to matters which
displease him just to preserve the peace. The Rabbit likes to
remain on good terms with everyone, but he can be rather
sensitive and takes any form of criticism very badly. He
will also be the first to get out of the way if he sees any
form of trouble brewing.

The Rabbit is a quiet and efficient worker and has an
extremely good memory. He is very astute in business and
financial matters, but his degree of success often depends

on the conditions that prevail. He hates being in a situation which is fraught with tension or where he has to make sudden decisions. Wherever possible he will plan his various activities with the utmost care and a good deal of caution. He does not like to take risks and does not take kindly to changes. Basically, he seeks a secure, calm and stable environment, and when conditions are right he is more than happy to leave things as they are.

The Rabbit is conscientious in most of the things he does and, because of his methodical and ever-watchful nature, can often do well in his chosen profession. He makes a good diplomat, lawyer, shopkeeper, administrator or priest and he excels in any job where he can use his superb skills as a communicator. He tends to be loyal to his employers and is respected for his integrity and honesty, but if he ever finds himself in a position of great power he can become rather intransigent and authoritarian.

The Rabbit attaches great importance to his home and will often spend much time and money maintaining and furnishing it and fitting it with all the latest comforts – the Rabbit is very much a creature of comfort! He is also something of a collector and there are many Rabbits who derive much pleasure from collecting antiques, stamps, coins, *objets d'art* or anything else which catches their eye or particularly interests them.

The female Rabbit has a friendly, caring and considerate nature, and will do all in her power to give her home a happy and loving atmosphere. She is also very sociable and enjoys holding parties and entertaining. She has a great ability to make the maximum use of her time and, although she involves herself in numerous activities, she always manages to find time to sit back and enjoy a good read or a chat. She has a great sense of humour, is very artistic and is often a talented gardener.

The Rabbit takes considerable care over his appearance and is usually smart and very well turned out. He also attaches great importance to his relations with others and matters of the heart are particularly important to him. He will rarely be short of admirers and will often have several serious romances before he settles down. The Rabbit is not the most faithful of signs, but he will find that he is especially well suited to those born under the signs of the Goat, Snake, Pig and Ox. Due to his sociable and easy-going manner he can also get on well with the Tiger, Dragon, Horse, Monkey, Dog and another Rabbit, but will feel ill at ease with the Rat and Rooster as both these signs tend to speak their mind and be critical in their comments, and the Rabbit just loathes any form of criticism or unpleasantness.

The Rabbit is usually lucky in life and often has the happy knack of being in the right place at the right time. He is talented and quick-witted, but he does sometimes put pleasure before work and wherever possible will tend to opt for the easy life. He can at times be a little reserved and suspicious of the motives of others, but generally will lead a long and contented life and one which – as far as possible – will be free of strife and discord.

THE FIVE DIFFERENT TYPES
OF RABBIT

In addition to the 12 signs of the Chinese zodiac, there are five elements and these have a strengthening or moderating influence on the sign. The effects of the five elements on the Rabbit are described below, together with the years in which the elements were exercising their influence. Therefore all Rabbits born in 1951 are Metal Rabbits, those born in 1903 and 1963 are Water Rabbits, and so on.

Metal Rabbit: 1951
This Rabbit is capable, ambitious and has very definite views on what he wants to achieve in life. He can occasionally appear reserved and aloof, but this is mainly because he likes to keep his thoughts to himself. He has a quick and alert mind and is particularly shrewd in business matters. He can also be very cunning in his actions. The Metal Rabbit has a good appreciation of the arts and likes to mix in the best circles. He usually has a small but very loyal group of friends.

Water Rabbit: 1903, 1963
The Water Rabbit is popular, intuitive and keenly aware of the feelings of those around him. He can, however, be rather sensitive and tends to take things too much to heart. He is very precise and thorough in everything he does and has an exceedingly good memory. He tends to be quiet and

at times rather withdrawn, but he expresses his ideas well and is highly regarded by his family, friends and colleagues.

Wood Rabbit: 1915, 1975

The Wood Rabbit is likeable, easy-going and very adaptable. He prefers to work in groups rather than on his own and likes to have the support and encouragement of others. He can, however, be rather reticent in expressing his views and it would be in his own interests to become a little more open and let others know how he feels on certain matters. He usually has many friends and enjoys an active social life, and is noted for his generosity.

Fire Rabbit: 1927, 1987

The Fire Rabbit has a friendly, outgoing personality. He likes socializing and being on good terms with everyone. He is discreet and diplomatic and has a very good understanding of human nature. He is also strong-willed and provided he has the necessary backing and support he can go far in life. He does not, however, suffer adversity well and can become moody and depressed when things are not working out as he would like. The Fire Rabbit is very intuitive and there are some who are even noted for their psychic ability. The Fire Rabbit has a particularly good manner with children.

Earth Rabbit: 1939, 1999

The Earth Rabbit is a quiet individual, but he is nevertheless very shrewd and astute. He is realistic in his aims and is prepared to work long and hard in order to achieve his objectives. He has good business sense and is invariably lucky in financial matters. He also has a most persuasive manner and usually experiences little difficulty in getting others to fall in with his plans. He is held in high esteem by his friends and colleagues and his views are often sought and highly valued.

PROSPECTS FOR THE RABBIT IN THE YEAR 2000

The Chinese New Year starts on 5 February 2000. Until then, the old year, the Year of the Rabbit, is still making its presence felt.

The Year of the Rabbit (16 February 1999 to 4 February 2000) will have been a favourable one for the Rabbit and in what remains of his own year he can still achieve a great deal, as most areas of his life are positively aspected. Accordingly, if there are any projects the Rabbit would like to complete before the year's end, now is the time to make a concerted effort. Purposeful action will lead to some excellent and gratifying results, but the initiative does rest with the Rabbit himself.

Particularly well aspected are the Rabbit's work prospects. During the year he will have impressed others with his diligent and conscientious manner and if he now wishes to make further advances, he should actively explore ways to move on. Those Rabbits seeking work should keep especially alert. From September 1999 onwards some particularly interesting possibilities could emerge.

The Rabbit will also fare well in financial matters in the last quarter of the year and could make some pleasing acquisitions for his home at this time. These will do much to add to its decor and comfort and will bring the Rabbit considerable pleasure. Also, with the coming of the new millennium, many Rabbits will decide to buy themselves some treats and will enjoy adding to and improving their wardrobe.

The Rabbit's personal life will also bring him much happiness, with both his family and friends being supportive of his various activities. As the Rabbit year closes, the Rabbit can look forward to many agreeable occasions with those around him and to attending parties, social events and some memorable and high-spirited occasions. For those seeking new friends and romance, there will be some splendid chances to meet others. When it comes to enjoying himself, the Rabbit certainly knows how, and he will have a splendid and memorable time in the closing weeks of the year.

The Year of the Dragon starts on 5 February and will be a variable one for the Rabbit. Some parts of the year will be pleasant, but it will not be free from anxieties or problems. However, provided the Rabbit remains his usual alert and tactful self and sets about his activities with care, he can do much to negate some of the more awkward aspects that prevail.

In his work the Rabbit would do well to stick with the familiar and concentrate on his areas of expertise. This is not a year for embarking on overly ambitious ventures or for trying to progress in areas in which he has little or no experience. Progress will come from steady and persistent effort as well as from adapting and making the most of changing situations.

Although many Rabbits will content themselves with remaining in their present position in the year 2000, there will still be changes that could have a bearing on their plans and prospects. Sometimes these could arise because of new personnel or changes in company strategy and procedures or workload. The Rabbit will understandably feel on edge and concerned, particularly as he is one who prefers a stable existence. In times of change he should aim to adapt and make the best of the situations in which he finds himself. As he appreciates (although does not always welcome), change is a necessary part of progression and new possibilities and openings will often emerge as a result. In the Dragon year the Rabbit should go with the flow of events rather than remain resistant or distance himself too much from the changes that do take place. Although some of the year will be unsettling, the Rabbit will still be able to make headway and obtain impressive results, again in the areas he knows best.

This also applies to those Rabbits seeking work or wanting to change their present position. In the Dragon year they should draw on what they know and have an affinity for rather than trying for positions for which they have little training. By promoting their experience and skills, most will eventually be successful in getting the sort of position they seek. Admittedly this may not be easy, and many Rabbits will face disappointment and rejection along the way, but they should persevere, keep faith with themselves and their abilities and remain resolute in their search. Quite often the position they do attain will come unexpectedly but will ideally suit them and will provide them with an excellent opportunity to add to their experience.

The months of April, May and the last quarter of the year could see some important activity concerning the Rabbit's work. From early October onwards work matters will become easier, problems will resolve themselves, life will become more settled and the Rabbit will receive credit – some of it overdue – for what he has done. The main thing is for the Rabbit not to lose heart in the face of obstacles or difficulties – these are only temporary and once out of the way, the Rabbit will again be able to resume his progress, having benefited from some of the opportunities that have arisen and the experience gained.

The Rabbit will fare reasonably well in financial matters over the year and by handling his finances with his usual skill he will enjoy a modest improvement in his situation. The one cautionary note that should be sounded is that the Rabbit should be wary of any particularly risky venture or investment. In the year 2000 it is best for him to concentrate on areas he knows best or in which he has done some research rather than to take risks. If he has any doubts over any financial matter it really would be in his interests to check it out and, if need be, obtain additional advice. Over the year the Rabbit should not let his usually shrewd nature slip.

As with last year, the Rabbit will be able to make some useful acquisitions for his home and those who have a fondness for art or craftwork, antiques or more aesthetic items will make some pleasing purchases during the year. The Rabbit would also do well to set some money aside for a break or holiday. With the pressures and demanding nature of some of the year, he will benefit from a change of scene and the chance to get away from his usual routine and preoccupations.

On a domestic level this will be a pleasant year and the Rabbit can look forward to many meaningful times with his loved ones. As always, he will take a caring interest in their activities and will do much to encourage and advise. The Rabbit may not always realize just what an important part he plays in the lives of those around him, but the esteem and affection shown him over the year will considerably hearten him. In addition to usual family activities, he can look forward to some notable family events, with good cause for celebration, particularly regarding successes enjoyed by family members.

However, while much of his domestic life will go well, there are certain points which the Rabbit should bear in mind. With some of the pressures and uncertainties he will face, particularly concerning his work, he should try not take out feelings of frustration, tension or even tiredness on others. He would do well to talk over any anxieties with those around him and make sure he gives himself the chance to relax rather than become too stressed. In this, the Rabbit's own personal interests will be a great asset. He could also find it beneficial to take regular exercise, particularly if he is sedentary for much of the day. A suitable fitness course or walking, swimming or cycling could all be worth considering.

The Rabbit sets great store by his social life and this will be of value to him over the year. In addition to enjoying the company of his friends, there will be quite a range of different social events for him to attend and for those Rabbits seeking new friends and romance, there will be some excellent opportunities to meet others. The Rabbit is one who relates well to others and his ability to make friends and strike up a rapport will certainly be to his advantage over the year. For social and personal matters the months of March, May, August and September could bring him particular joy.

Although this may not be the easiest of years for the Rabbit, it will still contain many pleasant moments and his relations with others, which mean so much to him, will provide him with some rich and meaningful times. Work-wise the year may present its obstacles and challenges, but these will often prove to be opportunities in the making, allowing the Rabbit to gain experience and opening the way for new possibilities, both for now and more significantly for the future. Testing though some parts of the year may be, the Rabbit should remember that there are many willing to offer him advice and support. So often those he does consult will be pleased to help, delighted that they can reciprocate the many kindnesses that the Rabbit himself has so frequently given.

As far as the different types of Rabbit are concerned, the Dragon year will be a satisfying one for the *Metal Rabbit*. The Metal Rabbit possesses a shrewd and perceptive nature and has an excellent sense of timing. He is able to read situations well and plans his moves and activities accordingly. When situations are favourable and opportunities are there he acts swiftly and with fortitude, while at other times he is prepared to be patient, assessing the situation and preparing his next move. His approach and abilities will, over the years, have brought him many successes and will continue to do so in the year 2000. For much of the year the Metal Rabbit will content himself with following all that happens around him, setting about his activities in his usual conscientious way and, for the most part, biding his time. But when a new opening presents itself, particularly in his work, he will seize it and as a result substantially improve his position and future prospects. Admittedly, opportunities may not be plentiful, but when they occur, the Metal Rabbit will certainly make the most of them, particularly in areas where he has specialist knowledge. The Metal Rabbit should note that some of the events of the Dragon year will be unexpected and it is those who remain alert and act swiftly who will benefit most. The months of April and May and the last quarter of the year could prove active for work matters. Many of those Metal Rabbits seeking work will also enjoy some success over the year. Not only should they remain alert for openings to pursue and useful pieces of information, but they should also listen carefully to any advice given by those with authority. Again, the Metal Rabbit's ability to sense interesting and developing situations will serve him well. The Metal Rabbit can also look forward to some success in financial matters and by managing his money with his usual consummate skill will enjoy a noticeable improvement in his situation. If he feels able to make any savings or investments with a view to his longer term future he could find these will develop into a useful asset in years to come. The Metal Rabbit's domestic life will, though, keep him busy. He will not only have to contend with the usual household chores, of which there will seem to be so many, but will also spend time attending to the interests of those around him and making some home improvements. In view of the many demands on his time, he would find it helpful to prioritize his activities rather than spread his energies too widely. If that means putting a project on hold, so be it. Better that than put himself under too much strain or rush tasks and have unsatisfactory results as a consequence. Also, at busy times, the Metal Rabbit should not hesitate to call upon others. He will find their help both welcome and forthcoming. However, despite all the activity in his home life, the Metal Rabbit's family will be a source of great comfort to him and over the year he will value the love and encouragement they provide. Mixed in with all the activity will be several memorable events which will give rise to a celebration, including the possible engagement or marriage of someone dear or the birth of a grandchild. The Metal Rabbit's social life too will be rewarding and he can look forward to some enjoyable times meeting friends and attending a wide range of social gatherings. For those Metal Rabbits who are seeking additional company, the Dragon year will contain some truly marvellous opportunities. The early weeks of the Dragon year and the summer months will be particularly good times for social matters. Generally, the Metal Rabbit will be content with how much of the year works out and by making the most of the opportunities that arise, he can do much to improve on his present situation, while his personal life will bring him much satisfaction. Overall a pleasant, busy and constructive year.

This will be a variable year for the *Water Rabbit* with some aspects of his life bringing joy while others will give him cause for concern. However, in all that he does the Water Rabbit will be well supported and if at any time he has uncertainties or problems he should not hesitate to seek the advice of those around him. By doing so he will gain both reassurance and encouragement, and as the Water Rabbit tends to feel things keenly, this is something he will value. His domestic life is one of the more favourably aspected areas of the Dragon year and will provide him with many gratifying moments. In addition to the support he will receive, he will delight in following the activities of those around him, with the successes of a younger relation being a particular source of pride. Although the Water Rabbit may not wish to appear interfering, any advice and additional instruction he feels able to give to someone in education will prove helpful and effective. The Water Rabbit's caring and attentive ways are appreciated by those around him and the important role he plays in the life of those dear to him will often be made clear; this is why when the Water Rabbit himself needs advice, he should be forthcoming and ask. He will also obtain pleasure from his own interests over the year and again those he can share with others will lead to some especially meaningful occasions. Any Water Rabbit who has interests of a creative nature, such as photography, writing, art or music, would do well to take his interest further and, if appropriate, obtain some feedback. This way he will not only learn a great deal but will also be given some useful advice and encouragement which will inspire him to do more. In addition, the Water Rabbit will enjoy tackling projects on his home and garden, particularly those which add new features, change the decor or improve his home comforts in some way. In undertaking practical projects, though, the Water Rabbit should make sure he follows all the recommended procedures, and if lifting heavy weights, he should seek assistance. To avoid problems and mishaps, Water Rabbits, do take sensible precautions! Although the Water Rabbit will have much to fill his time in the year 2000 he should not let his other activities encroach too much on his social life. He does, after all, enjoy this and in the Dragon year he can look forward to many agreeable times attending social gatherings, with the summer months being particularly active. Also, someone he meets on a social level will be greatly impressed with his personable nature and will turn out to be a useful contact and friend. As far as the Water Rabbit's work is concerned, however, care is required. Although he will have accomplished much in recent times, he should be wary of taking undue risks or of setting ambitious targets for the year. Rather, he should view this as a time to consolidate any recent gains he has made and continue to set about his activities in his usual diligent way. This is a time for steady rather than rapid progress, with results coming from persistent effort in those areas in which the Water Rabbit already has specialist knowledge. Those Water Rabbits who are seeking work or are keen to move from their current position will again fare best by going after openings which have a bearing on their previous experience. To try for anything too different could result in disappointment. Also, if the Water Rabbit can undertake any training, especially refresher courses, and/or extend his computer skills, he will find that not only will this enhance his prospects but also that an opportunity follows on as a result. Although this may not be the easiest of years for the Water Rabbit, there will be much that will bring him satisfaction. This includes the pleasure he derives from his hobbies, home projects and domestic and social life. By setting about his activities in his usual diligent way, he will continue to impress and win the admiration of others, and, as he will find, this will certainly be to his longer term advantage.

This will be an active year for the *Wood Rabbit*, with his personal life bringing particular pleasure. In the year 2000 he can look forward to many happy and meaningful times with those close to him and will have good reason for a personal celebration. As usual, he will play a full part in family activities and will do much to assist and encourage those dear to him. However, while the Wood Rabbit's home life will bring him much happiness, there are certain points that he should bear in mind. As with any year, problems and pressures will occur which will give rise to tension and anxiety. At such times the Wood Rabbit should recognize that either he or others are on edge and make allowances for this. If not, arguments and bickering could result and sour an otherwise meaningful time. Also, if the Wood Rabbit feels tired or below par he would find it helpful to tell others and, if need be, ask for additional assistance, including with household duties. Similarly, if he has any concerns, rather than keep them to himself, he should talk them over with others. In the year 2000 an open and forthcoming approach will lead to a far more conducive and co-operative atmosphere as well as help maintain the good relations the Wood Rabbit so values. In addition to the pleasure his domestic life will bring, his social life will contain some enjoyable occasions and he can look forward to attending some interesting functions and gatherings over the year. With his warm and friendly manner, the Wood Rabbit makes popular company and he will not only find himself much in demand but will also have the chance to add to his circle of friends. Any Wood Rabbit who may have had some personal problems of late would do well to look to the Dragon year as the start of a new phase and concentrate on the present rather than dwell too much on what has gone before. By making the effort and adopting a more positive attitude – together with the support of others – these Wood Rabbits can bring about a substantial upturn in their fortunes. The Wood Rabbit's hobbies will bring him much satisfaction over the year, with outdoor activities being particularly favoured. For those Wood Rabbits who enjoy travel or are sportingly inclined, the year will contain some fine moments. The area which could be most problematical, however, is the Wood Rabbit's work. In the year 2000 he will need to set about his duties with care, remaining ever watchful for new and developing situations. Although the Wood Rabbit very much enjoys stability and security, to ignore any new proposals could undermine his position. At times of change he will need to show himself adaptable both in outlook and approach. In addition, he should remain realistic in what he attempts. Although he may be keen to launch some of his ideas or attain certain ambitions, these will often require experience which he does not yet fully possess. In the Dragon year, to avoid disappointment, he should set his work expectations at attainable rather than over-ambitious levels. Those Wood Rabbits who are keen to move on from their present position or who are seeking work would do well to give serious thought to the direction they would like their future career to take and then aim for positions which would give them the necessary experience. Again, they should be realistic in what they try for, but their enthusiasm as well as their commitment to their longer term goals will impress and will often lead to them being given the chance they require. Also, if the Wood Rabbit is able to add to his skills over the year or take appropriate courses he will find that this too will help his prospects. Overall, this will be a pleasant and constructive year for the Wood Rabbit, with his personal life bringing many happy and memorable moments. However, he does need to proceed with care in his work and would find it helpful to be forthcoming with any problems or uncertainties. He can, though, take comfort in the knowledge that what he accomplishes in the year 2000 will do much to prepare for the progress and success he will deservedly enjoy in future years.

The Year of the Dragon holds considerable promise for the *Fire Rabbit*, but in order to make the most of the year, he should give some thought to what he would like to accomplish over the next 12 months and discuss his ideas with others. By planning his activities and setting himself some objectives he will find he is able to direct his energies in a more purposeful way than by going through the year with no particular aims in mind. His plans could relate to almost any part of his life, but one area which he should give particular thought to is his leisure time. If there has been an interest or subject that he would like to pursue, he really should take positive steps to do this. This applies to all Fire Rabbits, whether born in 1927 or 1987. By taking up something they are interested in, they can make this an especially rewarding year. Similarly, if there are practical tasks the Fire Rabbit would like to carry out on his home or garden, again he should aim to set his plans in motion. To use the old phrase, 'There is no time like the present' and the Dragon year will be supportive of the Fire Rabbit's efforts to realize his goals, but the initiative does rest with him. He will, though, find those around him highly supportive of his endeavours and by discussing his ideas and aspirations, he will obtain some useful advice and assistance. For those Fire Rabbits born in 1987 this will also be an important year for their education. Not only will they cover much material but many will be also inspired by some project work they are given or by a subject which captures their imagination. By setting about their work in their usual diligent manner they will make pleasing progress. However, while the Fire Rabbit will be strong in certain subjects, there could also be others that prove more troublesome and cause him anxiety. With these, it really would be in his interests to be forthcoming and obtain guidance rather than struggle on unaided. Those around can do much to help, advise and ease his concerns. The Fire Rabbit will, however, enjoy his family life and play a full and important role in the activities of those around him.

He will particularly treasure times spent on joint activities, including home improvements that he and his loved ones carry out, mutual interests and the holidays and visits to places of interest that he and his family go on. His social life too will go well and he can look forward to many pleasing occasions with his friends and to attending a variety of parties, functions and other events. Over the year there will be several opportunities for him to add to his circle of friends and any Fire Rabbit who may have been feeling lonely or have experienced some recent sadness will find that both his existing friends and some new ones will prove important as the year progresses. Overall, this will be a pleasant year for the Fire Rabbit. However, he does need to give some thought to just what he wants to accomplish and then set about achieving it. Positive effort on his part will lead to some satisfying and rewarding results and, in almost all he does, he will greatly benefit from the support and encouragement of those around him.

This will be an agreeable year for the *Earth Rabbit* and by planning his activities and making good use of his time, he will be well satisfied with what he is able to accomplish. One area which will prove particularly fulfilling is practical activities and the Earth Rabbit will find this an excellent year in which to carry out alterations on his home, redecorate certain rooms or add new features. He may have had some of these ideas in mind for some time, but the Dragon year is the ideal time to turn his thoughts into reality. In carrying out major projects, though, the Earth Rabbit should allow plenty of time and if he intends to do the work himself rather than engaging someone, he should involve those around him rather than aim to do all the work single-handed. This way the projects will be easier to complete as well as mean that much more to those involved. However, if any practical project the Earth Rabbit undertakes involves complex tasks which he is unsure about, he should seek professional help rather than risk his personal safety. Care is also required when moving heavy items. While many Earth Rabbits will content themselves with carrying out improvements on their existing accommodation, some will decide to move altogether. For these Earth Rabbits, much time will be spent viewing various possibilities before making a final decision but once the moving process is underway, they will be pleased with what they have acquired. In addition to the time and effort spent on accommodation matters during the year, the Earth Rabbit will also derive much satisfaction from his own interests. Again, those of a practical and creative nature will prove especially fulfilling, and if the Earth Rabbit is able to meet fellow enthusiasts, he will find this will not only usefully extend his knowledge but also lead to some enjoyable social occasions. For those Earth Rabbits who are keen gardeners or who enjoy outdoor pursuits, the year will contain some truly satisfying moments. The Earth Rabbit can also look forward to doing well in financial matters over the year, with many Earth Rabbits receiving a sum of money, either for work previously carried out, as the fruition of a policy or as a gift. This financial upturn will be another factor which will persuade many Earth Rabbits to carry out some of the plans they have had in mind, particularly those relating to their accommodation. The Earth Rabbit should also aim to set some money aside for travel and a holiday. The journeys he makes and places he visits, especially those new to him, could really impress as well as provide a much-needed break. In most of his activities and plans the Earth Rabbit will be well supported, but throughout the Dragon year he does need to remain mindful of the views of those around him. He may be sure about what he wants to do, but he should not let this close his mind to suggestions made and advice given. If he does, he could find certain tensions arising, which, with consideration, could have been avoided. The Earth Rabbit could also find it helpful, especially during busy or demanding times, to suggest activities all could enjoy – perhaps an outing, a meal out or some other treat. He will find that this will help ease some of the pressure that might have built up and these treats will be appreciated and enjoyed by all. For the most part, the Earth Rabbit's relations with his family and friends will go well and bring him much happiness, but to preserve the conviviality the Earth Rabbit so values, care and consideration are needed. Those Earth Rabbits in work should continue to set about their activities in their usual conscientious way, taking careful note of imminent changes and any proposals being considered. Some of the year will require the Earth Rabbit to proceed carefully and tactfully, but given his shrewd and alert nature, he should be able to do this and emerge from the year with much to his credit. In many respects this will be a satisfying year for him, with home projects and personal interests bringing particular pleasure. Travel and financial matters will also go well and the Earth Rabbit can look forward to many pleasant times with both family and friends. However, it would be in the interests of all if he were to avail himself more of the support, advice and assistance others are so ready and willing to give.

FAMOUS RABBITS

Paula Abdul, Bertie Ahern, Drew Barrymore, David Beckham, Harry Belafonte, Ingrid Bergman, Melvyn Bragg, Gordon Brown, Melanie Brown (Scary Spice), Emma Bunton (Baby Spice), James Caan, Nicolas Cage, Lewis Carroll, Fidel Castro, John Cleese, Confucius, Christopher Cross, Jack Cunningham, Marie Curie, Kenny Dalglish, Peter Davison, Johnny Depp, Albert Einstein, George Eliot, Peter Falk, Fatboy Slim, W. C. Fields, Bridget Fonda, Peter Fonda, James Fox, Sir David Frost, James Galway, Cary Grant, Edvard Grieg, Oliver Hardy, Seamus Heaney, Paul Hogan, Bob Hope, Whitney Houston, John Howard, John Hurt, Anjelica Huston, Chrissie Hynde, Clive James, Henry James, David Jason, Michael Jordan, Garry Kasparov, Michael Keaton, John Keats, Kevin Keegan, Danny La Rue, Cheryl Ladd, Julian Lennon, Patrick Lichfield, Gina Lollobrigida, Robert Ludlum, Ali MacGraw, Trevor McDonald, George Michael, Arthur Miller, Colin Montgomerie, Roger Moore, James Naughtie, Nanette Newman, Brigitte Nielsen, Christina Onassis, George Orwell, John Peel, Edith Piaf, Sidney Poitier, John Redwood, Ken Russell, Mort Sahl, Elisabeth Schwarzkopf, Neil Sedaka, Jane Seymour, Neil Simon, Frank Sinatra, Sting, Jimmy Tarbuck, Sir Denis Thatcher, J. R. R. Tolkien, Arturo Toscanini, Tina Turner, Luther Vandross, Queen Victoria, Orson Welles, Walt Whitman, Robin Williams, Tiger Woods.

16 FEBRUARY 1904 ～ 3 FEBRUARY 1905   *Wood Dragon*

3 FEBRUARY 1916 ～ 22 JANUARY 1917   *Fire Dragon*

23 JANUARY 1928 ～ 9 FEBRUARY 1929   *Earth Dragon*

8 FEBRUARY 1940 ～ 26 JANUARY 1941   *Metal Dragon*

27 JANUARY 1952 ～ 13 FEBRUARY 1953   *Water Dragon*

13 FEBRUARY 1964 ～ 1 FEBRUARY 1965   *Wood Dragon*

31 JANUARY 1976 ～ 17 FEBRUARY 1977   *Fire Dragon*

17 FEBRUARY 1988 ～ 5 FEBRUARY 1989   *Earth Dragon*

5 FEBRUARY 2000 ～ 23 JANUARY 2001   *Metal Dragon*

THE
DRAGON

THE PERSONALITY OF THE DRAGON

Activity is the only road to knowledge.
George Bernard Shaw: a Dragon

The Dragon is born under the sign of luck. He is a proud and lively character and has a tremendous amount of self-confidence. He is also highly intelligent and very quick to take advantage of any opportunities that occur. He is ambitious and determined and will do well in practically anything he attempts. He is also something of a perfectionist and will always try and maintain the high standards he sets himself.

The Dragon does not suffer fools gladly and will be quick to criticize anyone or anything that displeases him. He can be blunt and forthright in his views and is certainly not renowned for being either tactful or diplomatic. He does, however, often take people at their word and can occasionally be rather gullible. If he ever feels that his trust has been abused or his dignity wounded he can sometimes become very bitter and it will take him a long time to forgive and forget.

The Dragon is usually very outgoing and is particularly adept at attracting attention and publicity. He enjoys being in the limelight and is often at his best when he is confronted by a difficult problem or tense situation. In some respects he is a showman and he rarely lacks an audience. His views and opinions are very highly valued and he invariably has something interesting – and sometimes controversial – to say.

He has considerable energy and is often prepared to work long and unsocial hours in order to achieve what he wants. He can, however, be rather impulsive and does not always consider the consequences of his actions. He also has a tendency to live for the moment and there is nothing that riles him more than to be kept waiting. The Dragon hates delay and can get extremely impatient and irritable over even the smallest of hold-ups.

The Dragon has an enormous faith in his abilities, but he does run the risk of becoming over-confident and unless he is careful he can sometimes make grave errors of judgement. While this may prove disastrous at the time, the Dragon does have the tenacity and ability to bounce back and pick up the pieces again.

The Dragon has such an assertive personality, so much will-power and such a desire to succeed that he will often reach the top of his chosen profession. He has considerable leadership qualities and will do well in positions where he can put his own ideas and policies into practice. He is usually successful in politics, show business, as the manager of his own department or business, and in any job which brings him into contact with the media.

The Dragon relies a tremendous amount on his own judgement and can be scornful of other people's advice. He likes to feel self-sufficient and there are many Dragons who cherish their independence to such a degree that they prefer to remain single throughout their lives. However, the Dragon will often have numerous admirers and many will be attracted by his flamboyant personality and striking looks. If he does marry, the Dragon will usually marry young and will find himself particularly well suited to those born under the signs of the Snake, Rat, Monkey and Rooster. He will also find that the Rabbit, Pig, Horse and Goat make ideal companions and will readily join in with many of his escapades. Two Dragons will also get on well together, as they understand each other, but the Dragon may not find things so easy with the Ox and Dog, as both will be critical of his impulsive and somewhat extrovert manner. He will also find it difficult to form an alliance with the Tiger, for the Tiger, like the Dragon, tends to speak his mind, is very strong-willed and likes to take the lead.

The female Dragon knows what she wants in life and sets about everything she does in a determined and positive manner. No job is too small for her and she is often prepared to work extremely hard until she has secured her objective. She is immensely practical and somewhat liberated. She hates being bound by routine and petty restrictions and likes to have sufficient freedom to be able to go off and do whatever she wants. She will keep her house tidy but is not one for spending hours on housework – there are far too many other things that she feels are more important and that she prefers to do. Like her male counterpart, she has a tendency to speak her mind.

The Dragon usually has many interests and enjoys sport and other outdoor activities. He also likes to travel and often prefers to visit places that are off the beaten track rather than head for popular tourist attractions. He has a very adventurous streak in him and providing his financial circumstances permit – and the Dragon is usually sensible with his money – he will travel considerable distances during his lifetime.

The Dragon is a very flamboyant character and while he can be demanding of others and in his early years rather precocious, he will have many friends and will nearly always be the centre of attention. He has charisma and so much confidence in himself that he can often become a source of inspiration for others. In China he is the leader of the carnival and he is also blessed with an inordinate share of luck.

THE FIVE DIFFERENT TYPES OF DRAGON

In addition to the 12 signs of the Chinese zodiac, there are five elements and these have a strengthening or moderating influence on the sign. The effects of the five elements on the Dragon are described below, together with the years in which the elements were exercising their influence. Therefore all Dragons born in 1940 and 2000 are Metal Dragons, those born in 1952 are Water Dragons, and so on.

Metal Dragon: 1940, 2000
This Dragon is very strong-willed and has a particularly forceful personality. He is energetic, ambitious and tries to be scrupulous in his dealings with others. He can also be blunt and to the point and usually has no hesitation in speaking his mind. If people disagree with him, or are not prepared to co-operate, he is more than happy to go his own way. The Metal Dragon usually has very high moral values and is held in great esteem by his friends and colleagues.

Water Dragon: 1952

This Dragon is friendly, easy-going and intelligent. He is quick-witted and rarely lets an opportunity slip by. However, he is not as impatient as some of the other types of Dragon and is more prepared to wait for results than to expect everything to happen at once. He has an understanding nature and is prepared to share his ideas and co-operate with others. His main failing, though, is a tendency to jump from one thing to another rather than concentrate on the job in hand. He has a good sense of humour and is an effective speaker.

Wood Dragon: 1904, 1964

The Wood Dragon is practical, imaginative and inquisitive. He loves delving into all manner of subjects and can quite often come up with some highly original ideas. He is a thinker and a doer and has sufficient drive and commitment to put many of his ideas into practice. He is more diplomatic than some of the other types of Dragon and has a good sense of humour. He is very astute in business matters and can also be most generous.

Fire Dragon: 1916, 1976

This Dragon is ambitious, articulate and has a tremendous desire to succeed. He is a hard and conscientious worker and is often admired for his integrity and forthright nature. He is very strong-willed and has considerable leadership qualities. He can, however, rely a bit too much on his own judgement and fail to take into account the views and feelings of others. He can also be rather aloof and it would certainly be in his own interests to let others join in more with his various activities. The Fire Dragon usually gets much enjoyment from music, literature and the arts.

Earth Dragon: 1928, 1988

The Earth Dragon tends to be quieter and more reflective than some of the other types of Dragon. He has a wide variety of interests and is keenly aware of what is going on around him. He also has clear objectives and usually has no problems in obtaining support and backing for any of his ventures. He is very astute in financial matters and is often able to accumulate considerable wealth. He is a good organizer, although he can at times be rather bureaucratic and fussy. He mixes well with others and has a large circle of friends.

PROSPECTS FOR THE DRAGON IN THE YEAR 2000

The Chinese New Year starts on 5 February 2000. Until then, the old year, the Year of the Rabbit, is still making its presence felt.

The Year of the Rabbit (16 February 1999 to 4 February 2000) will have been a pleasant one for the Dragon and while it may have lacked the activity and pace of some years, the closing months will prove an important and interesting time. The next Chinese year is the Dragon's own year and as such offers the Dragon magnificent opportunities for success in many areas of his life. However, to take advantage of the excellent aspects that are about to prevail, the Dragon should use the remaining months of the Rabbit year as a time of preparation.

At this time the Dragon should give some thought to what he would like to accomplish over the next 12 months and discuss his ideas with those around him. Plans made now could develop in a significant way as well as give the Dragon added incentive to set about his activities in a more purposeful manner. If, in order to achieve what he has in mind, he feels he needs some additional experience or training, he should take steps to obtain this. By preparing for the auspicious and exciting times that lie ahead, the Dragon can do much to help his prospects.

This would also be a good time for the Dragon to deal with any outstanding matters, including unanswered correspondence, projects he might not have finished or even those he might have been putting off! By making a concerted effort, he will be able to accomplish a great deal and once these matters are out of the way, he will find himself better able to turn his attention to the more pleasurable activities at the end of the year.

Indeed, the Dragon will find himself much in demand at this time, particularly with Christmas and the celebrations surrounding the new millennium. There will be parties, social and family gatherings to look forward to and the Dragon will greatly enjoy himself. He will also have the opportunity to meet friends and relations he has not seen for some time, with such a reunion being a truly pleasurable occasion. At one of these gatherings he will find himself being given some advice by someone he has not seen for some time. He should heed their words well, as there will be much wisdom in them and they could prove highly relevant in view of the upturn in fortunes the Dragon is about to enjoy.

The Year of the Dragon starts on 5 February and almost at once interesting developments will take place. Indeed, the Dragon, with his determined and enthusiastic nature, is never one to do things by halves and when he has set himself a target to aim for, he can expect things to start moving quickly. So it will be in the year 2000. Within weeks, the Dragon will find, discover or create some interesting opportunities to pursue.

Often these will relate to his work and over the year the Dragon will see some important changes in his career. He may take on a different position, obtain promotion or even switch career altogether, but by setting out to improve his situation, the Dragon will be able to make significant headway. Sometimes changes will begin in a relatively low key manner but turn into major developments. The year really does hold considerable potential for the Dragon, with his enterprise, drive and sheer enthusiasm enabling him to secure some excellent results.

Those Dragons seeking work will also benefit from the favourable aspects. Again, the Dragon's persistent and positive attitude will be recognized and rewarded, and he should actively pursue any opportunities that he sees. He could also find it helpful to make a direct approach to companies and organizations he would like to work for, emphasizing his experience and how he could make a contribution. It may be bold, but such positive action could produce valuable leads or information which the Dragon will be able to benefit from. Indeed, throughout the year he would do well to remember the proverb 'Nothing ventured, nothing gained' and by venturing, he will most certainly gain.

The whole year is well aspected for work matters and any month could bring opportunities. However, particularly significant developments could take place in February and March and again in September and November.

With the spirit of enterprise that prevails over the year, the Dragon should also promote any business ideas he has and test the initial response. Some of what he proposes and develops now has the potential to grow in a major way and it rests with him to take action. Better this than looking back in future years and wondering 'What if?' Also, in most of what he does, the Dragon will be well supported by others and if he discusses his ideas and seeks the advice of experts, he will be given some helpful information. One point that the Dragon should bear in mind, though, is that he does need to proceed in an organized manner rather than be tempted to act too hastily. It is often the time and care taken in the initial stages of any enterprise that can make the difference between success and failure. Dragons, take note of this: plan, prepare and take the time to consult others.

This will also be a positive year for financial matters, with many Dragons seeing an increase in their income and improvement in their overall financial situation. While the Dragon will naturally enjoy this, he would find it to his advantage to deal with his finances on a more regulated basis, including keeping a set of accounts. This way he will be better able to budget for major purchases as well as make more effective use of his money. This could prove particularly helpful as many Dragons will decide to spend money on their accommodation over the year, replacing furnishings, altering the look and style of some rooms and buying items to improve their general comfort. Home entertainment equipment could also figure prominently, although with this, especially if computers are concerned, the Dragon would do well to take his time and check that what he is buying meets his present and likely future requirements. He would also do well to consider making some savings over the year and could find that a regular savings scheme started now could build into a handy sum in the future. While luck and good fortune may accompany the Dragon in the year 2000, he would be wise not to push this too far by committing himself to risky or highly speculative schemes.

The Dragon's personal life is splendidly aspected over the year and he can look forward to many meaningful and fulfilling times with those around him. In addition to the support he receives with his own activities, he will do much to encourage those around him and will have good reason to feel proud of the achievements of certain family members. If any Dragon has been experiencing problems recently in any of his relationships, he should make every attempt to heal them rather than let the difficulties linger and possibly sour the year. A positive and conciliatory approach will really make a big difference and it is worth these Dragons making the extra effort. For those who are unattached and are looking for company and romance, the year is superbly aspected and a chance encounter could literally sweep the Dragon off his feet. For many unat-tached Dragons love will beckon, with many getting engaged or married during the year, such are the splendid aspects that prevail.

The year also favours travel and if the Dragon has been longing to visit a certain destination, it would be worth him investigating whether this is now possible. Again, by working purposefully towards what he wants, the Dragon will often be able to achieve his objectives over the year. Similarly, any Dragon who has been thinking of working in another country, perhaps to extend his experience or improve language skills, would find this an excellent year in which to try and follow this through.

In so many respects the year holds considerable poten-tial for the Dragon, but in order to benefit from the favourable aspects, he really does need to give some thought to his activities and either seize the opportunities available or create them. This is the Dragon's own year and is really an important one for him, allowing him to progress and make good use his talents. In most of his activities, he will enjoy pleasing and fulfilling results as well as savouring the personal happiness that the year will bring.

As far as the different types of Dragon are concerned, this will be an auspicious year for the *Metal Dragon*. This is his own year and, as such, it will usher in some significant developments and mark the start of a new and important phase in his life. Indeed, over the last few years the Metal Dragon will have given much thought to his future activi-ties and with the dawning of the new millennium, he will decide that now is the time to take action. As is so often the way with the Metal Dragon, by setting his mind to his tasks he will obtain some worthy results. From a work point of view the year will see some major developments. Some Metal Dragons will mark their sixtieth year by retiring and turning their attention to pursuits they have long wanted to take up. However for others, there will be the chance to take on new career responsibilities and make significant headway. This is also a favourable year for the Metal Dragon to advance any idea or enterprise he may have been nurturing. Again, by promoting himself and acting in a positive manner he could see some interesting and rewarding results, and throughout the year if there is something he wants to try out or achieve, he should set his ideas in motion. Another favoured area concerns the Metal Dragon's leisure pursuits and by devoting time to these, he can look forward to some fulfilling and absorbing occasions. He could also find that one of his interests will develop in an unexpected manner, bringing him credit for his knowledge and possibly even some remuneration. If he wishes to be enterprising, by using his skills or perhaps instructing others or writing up some of his specialist knowledge, he could find he has yet another outlet for his talents. The Metal Dragon will also decide to make some changes to his accommodation over the year. Some Metal Dragons will move while others will carry out projects on their existing accommodation, redecorating and altering certain rooms as well as adding new features. Those who are keen gardeners will also be tempted to try out some adventurous ideas, possibly altering certain areas or experimenting with new plants or crops as well as making some interesting additions. The practical work that the Metal Dragon undertakes, whether indoors or out, will bring him much satisfaction, but he should always allow himself plenty of time to complete his tasks. If not, he could find himself under increased pressure and that what was originally meant to be a pleasurable activity turns into something less than enjoyable. This will be a positive year for financial matters, however, and as a result the Metal Dragon will decide to go ahead with some important purchases he has been considering, particularly related to his accommodation, transport and travel. However, where large purchases are concerned, the Metal Dragon could find himself saving a considerable amount by taking the time and effort to compare what is on offer and waiting for sales or other favourable opportunities. With travel well aspected, he would also do well to try and go away over the year and perhaps visit a destination he has wanted to see for some time. His travels and any holidays he takes are likely to go well and will give him the chance to enjoy a well-deserved rest. On a domestic and social level this will also be a favourable year and the Metal Dragon can look forward to many agreeable times with both family and friends. He will delight in carrying out interests he can share with others as well as tackling projects that will bring pleasure both to himself and those around him. The progress of loved ones will also be a source of much joy. One point that should be mentioned, however, is that if a difference of opinion occurs, the Metal Dragon should not let it escalate or make it worse by being unnecessarily stubborn or intransigent. He may hold strong views, but he must not let his redoubtable character and opinions take the edge off what will otherwise be an excellent year. Also, any Metal Dragon who may have had some recent adversity would do well to concentrate on the present rather than dwell too much on what has gone before, difficult though this sometimes may be. Positive action will be rewarded and for those Metal Dragons who may be lonely, a new friendship made at the end of 1999 or early in 2000 could become important and bring much happiness. In so many respects, the Metal Dragon has much going for him in the year 2000 and by making good use of his time and pursuing his aims and aspirations, he can make this a fulfilling, enjoyable and successful year.

This will be a rewarding year for the *Water Dragon*, particularly as he will now be able to build on his past achievements and put his experience, training and skills to more effective use. This could be by switching to the type of position he has sought for some time, gaining promotion or taking on responsibilities more in line with what he wants. He will also receive much credit for what he has done, including the completion of projects that he has been responsible for or ideas he has advanced. The Water Dragon is highly thought of and his positive input will impress others and be much appreciated during the year. This, too, will help him advance. Those Water Dragons who are currently looking for a new position or fresh challenges, perhaps because they feel they have achieved all they want to in their present post, will also enjoy some pleasing developments. Over the year these Water Dragons should carefully consider the type of position they would now like and take positive steps to attain it. They should not only go after any opportunities that become available, but also contact companies they would like to work for and those already engaged in the type of work they want. An enterprising approach will produce some interesting results and in many cases provide the opening that the Water Dragon has been seeking for so long. He knows he has the skills and talents, and by using his initiative will be able to do himself justice. This will also be a successful year for financial matters. Many Water Dragons will enjoy an appreciable increase in their income or receive a sum of money from the fruition of a policy or some other source. As usual, the Water Dragon will handle his money with skill and would do well to consider adding to his savings and setting some money towards travel, recreational pursuits and some well-deserved treats for himself and his loved ones. Also, with travel well aspected, a holiday that the Water Dragon takes over the year could prove particularly pleasurable, especially if it is to a destination new to him and off the usual tourist map. Although there will be much to keep the Water Dragon occupied in the year 2000, he should also ensure that he devotes sufficient time to his personal hobbies and interests. As well as helping him to unwind and relax, he will find they will prove especially fulfilling, particularly those that are in complete contrast to his usual occupation and allow him to draw on his creative abilities. As far as his personal life is concerned he will find himself much in demand. As usual, he will do much to assist others over the year and several times those dear to him will look to him for advice and support, which he will be glad to give. He will also take pleasure in the progress of those around him as well as in some good family news, but if there are any matters concerning him or he feels he has too much to do, he should not hesitate to seek assistance. This also applies to the times when much needs to be done around the home. However, despite the often active nature of the Water Dragon's domestic life, these will still be happy and meaningful times. His social life too will bring him much pleasure and he will enjoy meeting friends and attending social occasions. There will also be opportunities to add to his friends and contacts over the year and some of these will become important over the next few years. Overall, this will be a satisfying year for the Water Dragon. By making good use of his skills and the opportunities that arise, he can do much to improve on his current position. In addition, his relations with others and his personal interests will bring him pleasure, and this too will help make the first year of the new millennium all the more rewarding. Furthermore, the positive upturn the Water Dragon will enjoy in the year 2000 will continue for some time yet.

This will be an ideal year for the *Wood Dragon* and one he will greatly enjoy. The Wood Dragon possesses a most inventive mind and is capable of coming up with many original ideas. In the year 2000, he will be given every chance to develop some of his plans and will obtain some very satisfying results. In addition, he will be well supported by others and this too will give him the reassurance he so values. Almost all aspects of his life will see favourable developments, but his work in particular. During the last year many Wood Dragons will have seen changes in their duties, undertaken training or started new projects. Now they will be able to reap the rewards of their efforts and make further progress. The Wood Dragon makes an inspiring team member, and his diligent and co-operative nature will be appreciated. This too will help him advance. Several times over the year he will find himself with the right experience and right contacts, ideally placed to benefit from openings that become available. These include the chance of promotion, transferring to a more responsible position and being able to pursue some of his ideas. With such auspicious aspects prevailing, the Wood Dragon should look on this as a year in which to make the progress he has often dreamt about and he should actively seek to advance his position. Those Wood Dragons who have been thinking of starting out on their own and putting a business idea to the test should seek professional advice about the best way to proceed. The Dragon year is certainly good for enterprise, but for the Wood Dragon to maximize its potential, he does need to proceed in a planned and methodical manner, particularly where major commitments are concerned. Many of those Wood Dragons seeking work will be successful in their quest over the year, often in an unexpected way. Once in a new position, the Wood Dragon will find it will provide him with a valuable foothold for further development. This is a favourable year too for financial matters and the Wood Dragon can look forward to a noticeable improvement in his situation. If he feels able, he would do well to add to his savings over the year and so help build up a useful nest egg for the future. The Wood Dragon will also enjoy several strokes of good fortune in the year 2000 and if he sees a competition that particularly intrigues him he would do well to enter it. With luck, he could find himself among the winners! The Wood Dragon's personal life will also go well, with both his family and friends providing many happy and pleasurable occasions. During some parts of the year he will find his home life particularly busy, with various commitments as well as his own activities and the usual household chores. At such times the Wood Dragon should prioritize his tasks rather than attempt too many things all at once and should not hesitate to ask for assistance. He should also remain mindful of any advice given him, particularly by those older than himself, who speak with experience. There will be much of value in what he is told. The Wood Dragon will also enjoy the time he spends on his hobbies and interests, particularly those which contain some personal challenge or offer a finished product as a result. His social life will also be rewarding and he will enjoy meeting up with his friends and attending various social occasions. For the unattached Wood Dragon, or those who would like to make new friends, this will be an excellent year for meeting others and for some a new friendship could literally transform their lives. The Wood Dragon will indeed be in fine form throughout the Dragon year and will be determined to make something of the first year of the new millennium. With his experience, skills and ability to get on so well with others he has a tremendous amount in his favour and will do well. This is a productive and rewarding time and the Wood Dragon will not only make satisfying progress but will also enjoy himself.

The start of the millennium will have inspired the *Fire Dragon* and he will feel that a new phase of his life is about to begin. Accordingly he will set about his objectives with a renewed sense of determination and this will, over the year, lead to some interesting results. However, while all Fire

Dragons have the potential to do well in the year 2000, a note of caution does need to be sounded. In the Dragon year the Fire Dragon does need to remain realistic in his expectations; sometimes he can let his exuberant nature get the better of him and to go after almost unattainable targets will only lead to disappointment. Also, some of the things the Fire Dragon wants to achieve are more for the longer term and will only be possible once he has the necessary experience behind him. Substantial headway can be made in the year 2000, but the goals the Fire Dragon aims for must be within reach and preferably in line with his present experience. If he bears this in mind and gives of his best then he will obtain some truly worthwhile results and will build an excellent base from which to make even greater progress. Suitably motivated, all Fire Dragons should make real efforts to improve on their present position and go after the opportunities that arise or that they are able to create. At work, promotion, increased responsibilities or switching to another type of employment are all possible, but it does rest with the Fire Dragon to decide just what he wants to achieve and then set about attaining it. The Fire Dragon would also find it instructive to discuss his ideas with those around him and particularly seek out those with relevant experience, who may be in a position to give him advice. If he takes the initiative, his keen and enterprising nature will be noted and this too will help his progress. Many of those Fire Dragons currently seeking work will also find their patience and persistence rewarded, and even though their new position may not be the type of work they really wanted, they could find it more interesting than they thought and discover skills they did not know they had. Indeed, over the year, the

Fire Dragon will be given every opportunity to show his worth and by rising to the challenges he is given he will certainly enhance his reputation and add to his experience. What he is able to achieve now will often lead to greater progress over the next few years. In addition to the favourable aspects that prevail in his work, the Fire Dragon will also see some wonderful developments in his personal life which will bring him much happiness. This is a year for personal growth and many Fire Dragons will celebrate it with romance, an engagement, marriage or an addition to their family. On a personal level the year will be busy and sometimes demanding, but the Fire Dragon will be in fine form and will appreciate the love, company and support of those dear to him. Over the year he will also do much to assist more senior family members and the attention he is able to give will be truly valued. Those close to the Fire Dragon hold him in very high esteem and their faith in him will be amply justified during the year. In addition to the activity and pleasure of his home life, the Fire Dragon will find this a particularly good time for social matters, with a variety of events to attend. Over the year there is a tremendous amount in the Fire Dragon's favour, but there are two points he does need to bear in mind. With so much to occupy him he could sometimes be dilatory over paperwork and dealing with official correspondence, and he should watch this. Without care he could find a delayed response or neglected matter could rebound on him and be to his detriment. Similarly, with any large transaction or agreement he enters into, the Fire Dragon does need to check the terms and ensure that he can meet any obligations he is placed under. Again, care is required. Although this a good year for the Fire Dragon, he cannot push his luck too far or become complacent over important matters. These warnings apart, the year 2000 will be a splendid one for the Fire Dragon. It is a time when he should make every attempt to improve on his present position while, personally, this will be a time of much happiness and joy.

This will be a pleasant and constructive year for the *Earth Dragon*. However, to make the most of the favourable aspects that prevail, he would do well to give some thought to what he would like to accomplish over the year. This can include home projects, hobbies, learning new skills, travel plans or some other matter, but by deciding upon his objectives, the Earth Dragon will find the year that much more rewarding. One area which will give him particular satisfaction is carrying out projects on his home and garden. Some of these will be ideas he has been considering for some time; by setting them in motion he will be delighted with what he is able to achieve. In carrying out practical tasks, though, the Earth Dragon should allow plenty of time as well as be prepared for some disruption. Occasionally, ambitious undertakings will take him longer and cause more upheaval than he anticipated, but to compensate for this, he will consider the end result well worth the often considerable effort. There will also be some Earth Dragons who decide to move over the year. Again, while the moving process may take longer than originally envisaged, they will take much delight in settling into their new accommodation and arranging it as they want. For home matters, this will be an active but immensely satisfying year. Another well aspected area concerns travel and the Earth Dragon would do well to ensure he takes a break or holiday over the year, possibly

visiting an area he has had in mind for some time or friends
or relations he has not seen for a while. The Earth Dragon's
personal hobbies and interests will also bring him much
pleasure and he should make sure he devotes ample time to
them, possibly adding to his knowledge in some way. As in
so many areas of his life, the Earth Dragon can get much of
value from the year but he does need to use his time well
and follow through his ideas. However, while so much will
go in his favour, one area which could prove troublesome
involves important items of paperwork. If the Earth Dragon
has any doubts or concerns over any forms he has to
complete or transactions he is entering into, he does need to
check. If not, problems could ensue. Earth Dragons, take
note! Those Earth Dragons in education will, though, make
good progress and be particularly inspired by some new
subjects they take up. If they have any problems or concerns
over any aspect of their school or schoolwork, they should
not hesitate to seek advice. As they will find, those around
them are willing to provide additional help and can do much
to allay their concerns. These Earth Dragons will also lead an
active social life over the year and can look forward to
making new friends and generally having a good time. As
always, the Earth Dragon will greatly value his home life
and will be grateful for the love, support and consideration
he is shown. However, as well as being open about any
concerns he might have, he should also be forthcoming over
some of the ideas he is keen to try out. By discussing these,
he may discover that others can help. There will also be
several family events that will bring the Earth Dragon
considerable pleasure over the year. For those born in 1928
these could involve the progress of children or grandchil-

dren, while those born in 1988 will find some of their own personal achievements will bring them attention and well-deserved credit. Overall, this will be a positive and fulfilling year for the Earth Dragon, and by deciding upon and then setting about his activities in his usual keen and diligent way he will obtain some worthwhile results. Added to which, his personal life and relations with others will be a source of much happiness.

FAMOUS DRAGONS

Clive Anderson, Maya Angelou, Jeffrey Archer, Joan Baez, Michael Barrymore, Count Basie, Pat Benatar, Maeve Binchy, James Brown, Sandra Bullock, Neneh Cherry, James Coburn, Bing Crosby, Courteney Cox, Roald Dahl, Salvador Dali, Charles Darwin, Neil Diamond, Bo Diddley, Matt Dillon, Christian Dior, Frank Dobson, Placido Domingo, Fats Domino, Kirk Douglas, Faye Dunaway, Prince Edward, Bruce Forsyth, Sigmund Freud, James Garner, Sir John Gielgud, Graham Greene, Che Guevara, David Hasselhoff, Sir Edward Heath, Joan of Arc, Tom Jones, Imran Khan, Martin Luther King, John Lennon, Abraham Lincoln, Queen Margrethe II of Denmark, Yehudi Menuhin, Bob Monkhouse, Hosni Mubarak, Florence Nightingale, Nick Nolte, Al Pacino, Elaine Paige, Gregory Peck, Pele, Christopher Reeve, Keanu Reeves, Sir Cliff Richard, Harold Robbins, George Bernard Shaw, Ringo Starr, Dave Stewart, Karlheinz Stockhausen, Mr T, Shirley Temple, Andy Warhol, Johnny Weissmuller, Raquel Welch, Mae West, Frank Zappa.

4 FEBRUARY 1905 ~ 24 JANUARY 1906	*Wood Snake*
23 JANUARY 1917 ~ 10 FEBRUARY 1918	*Fire Snake*
10 FEBRUARY 1929 ~ 29 JANUARY 1930	*Earth Snake*
27 JANUARY 1941 ~ 14 FEBRUARY 1942	*Metal Snake*
14 FEBRUARY 1953 ~ 2 FEBRUARY 1954	*Water Snake*
2 FEBRUARY 1965 ~ 20 JANUARY 1966	*Wood Snake*
18 FEBRUARY 1977 ~ 6 FEBRUARY 1978	*Fire Snake*
6 FEBRUARY 1989 ~ 26 JANUARY 1990	*Earth Snake*

THE
SNAKE

THE PERSONALITY OF THE SNAKE

Learn to limit yourself, to content yourself with some definite thing and some definite work; dare to be what you are, and learn to resign with a good grace all that you are not, and to believe in your own individuality.

Henri-Frédéric Amiel: a Snake

The Snake is born under the sign of wisdom. He is highly intelligent and his mind is forever active. He is always planning and always looking for ways in which he can use his considerable skills. He is a deep thinker and likes to meditate and reflect.

Many times during his life he will shed one of his famous Snake skins and take up new interests or start a completely different job. The Snake enjoys a challenge and he rarely makes mistakes. He is a skilful organizer, has considerable business acumen and is usually lucky in money matters. Most Snakes are financially secure in their later years provided they do not gamble – the Snake has the distinction of being the worst gambler in the whole of the Chinese zodiac!

The Snake generally has a calm and placid nature and prefers the quieter things in life. He does not like to be in a frenzied atmosphere and hates being hurried into making a quick decision. He also does not like interference in his affairs and tends to rely on his own judgement rather than listen to advice.

The Snake can at times appear solitary. He is quiet, reserved and sometimes has difficulty in communicating with others. He has little time for idle gossip and will certainly not suffer fools gladly. He does, however, have a good sense of humour and this is particularly appreciated in times of crisis.

The Snake is certainly not afraid of hard work and is thorough in all that he does. He is very determined and can occasionally be ruthless in order to achieve his aims. His confidence, will-power and quick thinking usually ensure his success, but should he fail it will often take a long time for him to recover. He cannot bear failure and is a very bad loser.

The Snake can also be evasive and does not willingly let people into his confidence. This secrecy and distrust can sometimes work against him and it is a trait which all Snakes should try to overcome.

Another characteristic of the Snake is his tendency to rest after any sudden or prolonged bout of activity. He burns up so much nervous energy that without proper care he can, if he is not careful, be susceptible to high blood pressure and nervous disorders.

It has sometimes been said that the Snake is a late starter in life and this is mainly because it often takes him a while to find a job in which he is genuinely happy. However, the Snake will usually do well in any position which involves research and writing and where he is given sufficient freedom to develop his own ideas and plans. He makes a good teacher, politician, personnel manager and social adviser.

The Snake chooses his friends carefully and while he keeps a tight control over his finances, he can be particularly generous to those he likes. He will think nothing of buying expensive gifts or treating his friends or loved ones to the best theatre seats in town. In return he demands loyalty. The Snake is very possessive and he can become extremely jealous and hurt if he finds his trust has been abused.

The Snake is also renowned for his good looks and is never short of admirers. The female Snake in particular is most alluring. She has style, grace and excellent (and usually expensive) taste in clothes. A keen socializer, she is likely to have a wide range of friends and has the happy knack of impressing those who matter. She has numerous interests and her advice and opinions are often highly valued. She is generally a calm-natured person and while she involves herself in many activities, she likes to retain a certain amount of privacy in her undertakings.

Affairs of the heart are very important to the Snake and he will often have many romances before he finally settles down. He will find that he is particularly well suited to those born under the signs of the Ox, Dragon, Rabbit and Rooster. Provided he is allowed sufficient freedom to pursue his own interests, he can also build up a very satisfactory relationship with the Rat, Horse, Goat, Monkey and Dog, but he should try to steer clear of another Snake as they could very easily become jealous of each other. The Snake will also have difficulty in getting on with the honest and down-to-earth Pig, and will find the Tiger far too much of a disruptive influence on his quiet and peace-loving ways.

The Snake certainly appreciates the finer things in life. He enjoys good food and often takes a keen interest in the arts. He also enjoys reading and is invariably drawn to subjects such as philosophy, political thought, religion or the occult. He is fascinated by the unknown and his enquiring mind is always looking for answers. Some of the world's most original thinkers have been Snakes, and – although he may not readily admit it – the Snake is often psychic and relies a lot on intuition.

The Snake is certainly not the most energetic member of the Chinese zodiac. He prefers to proceed at his own pace and to do what he wants. He is very much his own master and throughout his life he will try his hand at many things. He is something of a dabbler, but at some time – usually when he least expects it – his hard work and efforts will be recognized and he will invariably meet with the success and financial security he so much desires.

THE FIVE DIFFERENT TYPES OF SNAKE

In addition to the 12 signs of the Chinese zodiac, there are five elements and these have a strengthening or moderating influence on the sign. The effects of the five elements on the Snake are described below, together with the years in which the elements were exercising their influence. Therefore all Snakes born in 1941 are Metal Snakes, those born in 1953 are Water Snakes, and so on.

Metal Snake: 1941
This Snake is quiet, confident and fiercely independent. He often prefers to work on his own and will only let a

privileged few into his confidence. He is quick to spot opportunities and will set about achieving his objectives with an awesome determination. He is astute in financial matters and will often invest his money well. He also has a liking for the finer things in life and has a good appreciation of the arts, literature, music and good food. He usually has a small group of extremely good friends and can be generous to his loved ones.

Water Snake: 1953

This Snake has a wide variety of interests. He enjoys studying all manner of subjects and is capable of undertaking quite detailed research and becoming a specialist in his chosen area. He is highly intelligent, has a good memory, and is particularly astute when dealing with business and financial matters. He tends to be quietly spoken and a little reserved, but he does have sufficient strength of character to make his views known and attain his ambitions. He is very loyal to his family and friends.

Wood Snake: 1905, 1965

The Wood Snake has a friendly temperament and a good understanding of human nature. He is able to communicate well with others and often has many friends and admirers. He is witty, intelligent and ambitious. He has numerous interests and prefers to live in a quiet, stable environment where he can work without too much interference. He enjoys the arts and usually derives much pleasure from collecting paintings and antiques. His advice is often very highly valued, particularly on social and domestic matters.

Fire Snake: 1917, 1977

The Fire Snake tends to be more forceful, outgoing and energetic than some of the other types of Snake. He is ambitious, confident and never slow in voicing his opinions – and he can be very abrasive to those he does not like. He does, however, have many leadership qualities and can win the respect and support of many with his firm and resolute manner. He usually has a good sense of humour, a wide circle of friends and a very active social life. The Fire Snake is also a keen traveller.

Earth Snake: 1929, 1989

The Earth Snake is charming, amusing and has a very amiable manner. He is conscientious and reliable in his work and approaches everything he does in a level-headed and sensible way. He can, however, tend to err on the cautious side and never likes to be hassled into making a decision. He is extremely adept at dealing with financial matters and is a shrewd investor. He has many friends and is very supportive towards the members of his family.

PROSPECTS FOR THE SNAKE
IN THE YEAR 2000

The Chinese New Year starts on 5 February 2000. Until then, the old year, the Year of the Rabbit, is still making its presence felt.

The Year of the Rabbit (16 February 1999 to 4 February 2000) is the type of year that suits the Snake. To a large extent he will have been able to pursue his activities and ideas in the way he wants, and as a result will have made satisfying progress.

With the year's cultural leanings, many Snakes will also have taken the opportunity to add to their skills, take up a new interest or improve themselves in some way, and this again will have brought the Snake much personal satisfaction. If in the remaining months of the Rabbit year the Snake has any opportunity to add to his training or skills he will find this a valuable and productive use of his time. Also, he has a canny knack for sensing developing opportunities or conceiving ideas that are right for the moment and if, in the closing stages of the Rabbit year, he sees a suitable opening or has an idea he wishes to advance, he should do so. For the astute and quick-witted Snake, excellent progress can be made.

The Snake can also look forward to some enjoyable and meaningful times with his family and friends as the Rabbit year ends. Although he may be one of the more reserved of the Chinese signs, he will really get caught up in the sense of occasion and festivities at the end of 1999 and will celebrate the coming of the new millennium in fine style. He will also be grateful for the support he receives at this time and should be forthcoming about his plans as well as any concerns he might have. In this way he will gain much from the help and input of others.

There are, though, two points that the Snake should bear in mind. While usually adept in financial matters, he should be wary of becoming involved in any risky ventures or of tempting his luck just a little too far. If he has doubts about any financial undertaking, he should check, otherwise he could find himself regretting his actions. The second point is that he should avoid acting in a way that could leave him open to embarrassment or censure. Without care, he could find himself embroiled in an awkward and potentially damaging situation, and he should avoid this if at all possible. In all his dealings, the Snake should aim to be his honourable self.

Provided he bears these warnings in mind, this will, however, be a positive and personally fulfilling time for the Snake. Also, with the memorable celebrations towards the end of the Rabbit year, it will be one that he thoroughly enjoys.

The Year of the Dragon starts on 5 February and will be a variable year for the Snake. The Dragon year is often characterized by bustle and activity, and the Snake may feel uneasy with some of the events that occur. However, while he may have misgivings and concerns, if he remains his watchful self, observing, assimilating and making the most of the situations in which he finds himself, then he can still emerge from the year with some far-reaching gains to his credit.

As far as the Snake's work is concerned, this will be a constructive year, with opportunities for the Snake to further his experience as well as develop some ideas. Admittedly, his actual progress may not always be as great or as swift as he may like, but what he does learn and accomplish will bring him much personal satisfaction and will do much to help the more substantial advances he will make in his own year, 2001.

For those Snakes who have recently taken on new duties, this would be an excellent year to familiarize themselves with the different aspects of their work, while those who are seeking to change their work should give serious thought to just what they want to do and how they would like their future to develop. In some cases, the Snake may decide to switch to a completely different type of work, feeling that he would benefit from the challenge this would bring. If, in order to do this, he needs to learn new skills, he should look to obtain these in the Dragon year.

In so many respects, this is an ideal year for the Snake to prepare for the next major upturn in his life, which will start late in 2000 and continue throughout 2001. By giving some thought to his future, the Snake will also find he is directing his energies in a more purposeful way and if he does see any suitable opportunities to pursue, he should follow them up. Admittedly, not all his initial attempts to change or improve his position may go his way, but all the time he will be learning and strengthening his ideas and approach, and his persistence will ultimately pay off.

The Snake is also an original thinker and during the Dragon year he could form some interesting and unusual ideas which he would do well to nurture. In time one or two could really take shape and develop in a meaningful way. Again, what the Snake starts in the Dragon year could become truly important later on.

As far as financial matters are concerned, the year will see a modest improvement for the Snake. However, while he is usually careful when dealing with money matters, he should be wary of taking undue risks or committing his money to anything too speculative or to schemes or investments he knows little about. Similarly, he should be alert to any dubious undertakings or supposedly 'get-rich-quick' schemes. All is not as it seems and where his money is concerned the Snake cannot afford to relax his guard.

He will, however, derive much satisfaction from his personal interests, especially those that allow him to draw on his creative abilities. For those Snakes who are keen on craftwork or who enjoy activities such as writing, art, music and photography, the year will certainly contain some absorbing and stimulating times. If the Snake is able to display or promote any work he produces he could find it highly appreciated and this could inspire him to begin more ambitious projects.

On a domestic level this will be a demanding year for the Snake, with many matters requiring his attention. In addition to his own commitments, the activities of those around will keep him occupied and throughout the year he will do much to advise, help and support his loved ones. As always, those around him will set great store by his usually sound judgement as well as value his caring and considerate nature. An older relation will, in particular, appreciate the support and attention the Snake is able to give, while those younger than himself will regularly seek his guidance. However, in view of the often considerable activity in his domestic life and the many calls upon his time, the Snake should keep his level of commitments to a manageable level and at busy times would find it helpful to set himself priorities. If this involves postponing some household projects until quieter and more suitable times, it will still be better than being under too much pressure. Also, should the Snake feel over-stretched, he should not hesitate to call on others for assistance. Help will certainly be forthcoming, but the Snake should ask rather than, as some Snakes are apt to do, soldier on in silence.

However, while his home life will see much activity, the Snake will take great satisfaction from it and will be pleased with the progress of others and the constructive and appreciated role he plays, as well as the many meaningful occasions that take place. These include activities that all can enjoy such as sharing joint interests, meeting mutual friends and taking trips out.

As far as the Snake's social life is concerned in the year 2000, it really will be what he makes of it. Some Snakes will be content to keep their social activities at a low level, preferring to devote time to their family and concentrate on their personal interests, while others will restrict themselves to their present circle of friends, enjoying their company and meetings, however regular or occasional they might be. Any Snakes who would like to make new friends and lead a more active social life will find that the aspects will support them well. However, they will need to take the initiative and go out more and give themselves the chance to meet others. Sometimes this will take a great deal of effort on their part, particularly for those Snakes who are more reserved, but they will be well rewarded for it. They could strike up some particularly good friendships by joining clubs and societies that specialize in their own interests, especially as they will meet people who are like-minded and of a similar age.

Travel is also favourably aspected and all Snakes should try to make sure that they take a holiday or break over the year. This will not only do them good but they could also find it especially interesting to visit places which are off the usual tourist map and which appeal to their liking for the unusual.

Although the Dragon year will bring moments of pressure and challenge, it is still an important year for the Snake. It is a time when he will consider the direction he would like his life, and particularly his work, to take in the future. What he decides upon, achieves and sets in motion now will serve him extremely well in the next, more favourable Chinese year. It is almost as if this year the Snake is preparing to lose one of his famous Snake skins and choosing which skin or guise he should now take on. From late September, the aspects will start to move in his favour and that is when his efforts, plans and ideas will start to gather momentum and bear fruit. Even more exciting prospects await in 2001!

As far as the different types of Snake are concerned, this will be a variable year for the *Metal Snake*. He possesses a determined nature and has clear ideas about what he wants to achieve, but while such clear-sightedness will have allowed him to accomplish much over the years, some of the problems he will face in the year 2000 could prevent him from achieving all he would like. However, while the

Dragon year will contain its disappointments, it need not be entirely negative. Some of its events will cause the Snake to reflect on his current situation and think about his longer term plans and aims, and this will often lead him to coming up with new and sometimes more suitable ideas. As he recognizes, it is better to adapt to circumstances as they are than stick with something that may not now be so appropriate. Some of the more awkwardly aspected areas of the year are work matters and the Metal Snake could have some tricky decisions to make. These could concern taking on different and in some cases daunting responsibilities, moving from his present position and either seeking a new one or deciding to retire. However, by considering his options and knowing that he can rise to the challenges (and opportunities) given him, the Metal Snake will find that new and interesting possibilities will emerge. As a result of what happens and some of the decisions he makes, he will also find he is tackling his plans and activities with a greater enthusiasm and commitment, more than ever determined to triumph – as indeed many Metal Snakes will. The latter part of the year will see more positive developments, with 2001 holding much promise. With any awkward situations that arise in the Dragon year, the Metal Snake would do well to discuss his concerns with others rather than keeping them to himself. He will find this will help ease any feelings of irritation or anxiety he might have as well as produce some useful information and advice. Just as work matters will need care over the year, so too will the Snake's financial dealings. Although he is usually shrewd in money matters, he will need to proceed cautiously. This is especially important as some Metal

Snakes will receive an additional sum of money over the year. They should consider their options particularly carefully. This is not a year for the Metal Snake to rush important financial decisions, take undue risks or tempt his luck too far. If he proceeds with care then he can prosper, but he does need to remain his thorough and vigilant self. The Metal Snake will, though, obtain much pleasure from his personal interests and should make sure he sets a regular time aside for these. For those who enjoy being out of doors, whether gardening, following sport, travelling or visiting places of interest, the year will contain some memorable and gratifying moments. If the Metal Snake receives any invitations to meet up with relations or friends living some distance away or has any other interesting travel opportunities, he should take advantage of them. His domestic and social life will also bring him satisfaction and he will be encouraged by the support he is given and the interest shown in his activities. He will also feel proud of the successes of a younger relation and any assistance or encouragement he feels able to give will be greatly appreciated. Indeed, throughout the year, the Metal Snake's sincere and caring ways will be truly valued by all those around him. He will also take particular satisfaction from some home improvements he carries out, although if these involve hazardous activities or moving heavy weights it is essential he seeks help and follows the recommended safety procedures. This is not a year in which he can take risks or compromise his personal safety. Although this may not be the easiest of years for the Metal Snake, by adjusting to the events and situations in which he finds himself, he will often form new ideas and plans, some of which hold considerable potential. In many respects the first year of the new millennium represents the culmination of one stage in his life, with a new and positive phase about to begin. The action and decisions the Metal Snake takes in the year 2000 will prepare him admirably for that future.

In recent times a great deal will have happened to the *Water Snake* and he will have many accomplishments of which he can be truly proud. Despite this, many Water Snakes will consider that they are still not fulfilling their potential and will have ambitions they are keen to realize. However, the Water Snake possesses a patient nature and is prepared to work steadily and persistently towards his goals. In the Dragon year, many Water Snakes will decide that the time has come to take stock and enjoy recent achievements but also to focus firmly on the direction they really want their lives to take. In this period of reflection and planning, the Water Snake would do well to discuss his ideas with others as well as seek out those who have already achieved whatever he is considering. By taking such positive steps, he will gain much from the advice and information given as well as be alerted to possible pitfalls to avoid. Those around the Water Snake can prove truly useful to him, but he must take the initiative and be forthcoming, particularly if he is to do himself justice. As he will later find, what he sets in motion in the year 2000 will prove instrumental to some of the future success he will enjoy. However, while he will give much thought to his future, as far as more immediate matters are concerned, the Water Snake will need to proceed with a certain caution. In his work he will need to watch new and developing situations carefully and adapt to any changes as they take place. These may include the introduction of new procedures or different responsibilities. In the year 2000 it is better for the Water Snake to show himself willing and flexible in his approach than remain too set in his ways. However, while he will need to tread carefully, throughout the year he should keep his eyes firmly set on the future and if he sees any opportunities which he feels could help him towards his objectives, he should follow them up. This applies to all Water Snakes, whether in work or seeking work. By keeping alert and acting whenever suitable opportunities arise, they can make headway. Admittedly, opportunities may not be plentiful, but, as the Water Snake himself realizes, patience and persistence have brought some impressive results in the past and will continue to do so. Also, if the Water Snake feels he needs any training that would enhance his prospects he should take steps to obtain it. Whether he goes on courses, takes up further education or studies by himself, what he learns now could certainly prove helpful in the future and his own personal development would be a stimulating use of his time. The Water Snake usually handles his finances with care and in the year 2000 he should not let his vigilance slip. He should be particularly wary of risky or speculative ventures or of entering into commitments without checking all the implications. If not, there is a danger that he could come to regret his actions. More positively, however, the Water Snake's personal life will bring him much pleasure and he can look forward to many satisfying times with both family and friends. Over the year he will be grateful for the support he is given as well as be heartened by the affection shown him. However, in return, he should strive to overcome his sometimes secretive nature and be more open about his ideas and concerns. Those around do genuinely want to assist him and see him realize his potential, but for them to do this it does require the Water Snake himself to be more forthcoming. The Water Snake will take much satisfaction from general family activities and in the second year half of the year will delight in some interesting developments and family achievements. His social life, too, will bring him pleasure and he will enjoy meeting friends and attending social functions. For the unattached Water Snake or those seeking new friends, there will be many opportunities to meet others, with the prospect of a new friendship developing in an important way in the future. Although the Water Snake's actual level of progress may not always be as great as he would like over the year, the long-term implications of what he sets in motion now will be significant, often even marking a turning-point in his life. This is very much a year in which the Water Snake will be preparing the way for the exciting times ahead!

This will be a reasonable year for the *Wood Snake* and while he may not always be able to achieve as much as he would like, he will still enjoy some rewarding and significant times. In his work the Wood Snake will be able to consolidate the gains he has made over the last few years and will continue to impress with his diligent and level-headed approach. Many Wood Snakes will decide to concentrate on their present position, particularly if they have recently taken on new duties, and over the year will do much to enhance their reputation. They should also take advantage of any training opportunities that arise and of any other ways in which they could extend their skills and experience. In the next, more auspicious year, many Wood Snakes will find that what they have accomplished during the Dragon year will prove an excellent base from which to make further progress. Those Wood Snakes who are anxious to move from their present position or are looking for work should remain active in following up any openings which interest them. Admittedly, these openings may not be plentiful and it may take several attempts to make the desired progress, but persistence will pay off. Also, many Wood Snakes will find that once they have obtained a foothold in an organization, further progress will be possible. Indeed, a lot of the success the Wood Snake will enjoy in the next few years will have its origins in the Dragon year. Similarly, if the Wood Snake has any ideas he is keen to try out, this is a good year in which to take those all-important initial steps, gauge the response of others and seek information and support. Again, projects started now could lead to pleasing developments later in the year and particularly in 2001. The Wood Snake will enjoy a modest improvement in his financial situation during the year, and by watching his spending and making allowance for his outgoings, he will be satisfied with money matters. However, as with all Snakes, he does need to be wary of committing himself to risky ventures and should not relax his usually cautious nature. The Wood Snake's personal life will be active over the year, with many matters requiring his attention. As always, he will be attentive to those around him and will encourage his loved ones in their various activities. He will also do much to assist a more senior relation during the year and the advice and support he is able to give will prove of considerable benefit as well as be truly appreciated. However, while the Wood Snake will do much to help others, he himself should not hesitate to seek assistance should any matters give him concern. This particularly applies to those demanding times when he has many commitments as well as what seem to be an ever-mounting number of household chores! In the year 2000 the Wood Snake should make sure that assistance operates on a two-way basis and that he does not shoulder too much by himself. With all the activity of the year he should also make sure he does not neglect his own well-being. This includes setting time aside for recreational pursuits, especially those that help him relax and unwind, as well as making sure he takes sufficient exercise and so does not get too out of condition. The Wood Snake should also make room for his social life as over the year this could provide him with some pleasurable occasions. For those Wood Snakes who are unattached and seeking friends, there will certainly be opportunities to meet others and to form some significant friendships, especially over the summer months. Although this will be a busy year for the Wood Snake, there will still be much that will bring him satisfaction and what he starts during the Dragon year will help prepare for the progress he will make in 2001.

This will be an interesting year for the *Fire Snake* and while not entirely free from pressures and problems, will be one in which he can lead a rewarding personal life as well as make useful progress. In all his activities, though, he must keep his expectations at a realistic level and aim to build on his present skills and experience rather than be over-ambitious. Admittedly, the Fire Snake does possess a determined and ambitious nature, but some of what he is aiming for does first require him to get the necessary experience, and he must concentrate on this now. There is plenty of time in the future for him to realize all his goals and more. In his work, the Fire Snake's earnest and enthusiastic nature will impress others and if he has the chance of taking on additional responsibilities or undergoing some training, he should do so. Also, he should remain alert to developments in his workplace, particularly any changes or new proposals under consideration. By keeping himself informed, he will be better able to make positive contributions and will be well placed should new openings arise. Similarly, any Fire Snakes who are keen to move on from their present position or are looking for work should actively follow up any opportunities that they see, but they will find they will fare best by concentrating on positions which draw specifically on their existing experience. Again, if these Fire Snakes find themselves eligible for courses or training, it would certainly be worth them taking advantage of it. As all Fire Snakes will find, what they learn and accomplish now will do much to help their prospects later. As far as work matters are concerned, this is very much a year for preparing for the exciting times that lie ahead! The Fire Snake will, though, need to be especially careful when dealing with finance. During the year he could face some large expenses, particularly related to his accommodation, and he will need to watch his outgoings carefully. Also, when entering into a new transaction, he should check any obligations he may be placed under as well as make allowance for new commitments. With care, problems can be avoided, but this is not a year for complacency or pushing his luck too far. One of the more favourably aspected areas of the year, however, concerns the Fire Snake's relations with others. He will find himself in great demand with both family and friends, with plenty of meaningful occasions to enjoy. He will also be heartened by the affection shown him and this too will help to motivate him as well as lift his spirits at awkward moments. The Fire Snake will also enjoy projects and interests that he can share and will find they will lead to some particularly rewarding occasions. Personally, he will feel in fine form and for any Fire Snake who may feel alone, perhaps because he has just moved to a new area and is seeking friends and perhaps romance, the aspects will encourage a livelier social life. However, this does require the Fire Snake to make that extra effort and go out more. He could find that joining a special interest group where he is likely to meet like-minded people will lead to some good friendships. However, while his relations with others will bring the Fire Snake much happiness, there is one point he should bear in mind. The Fire Snake does hold very firm views and there could be occasions when others do not quite agree with him. He should allow for this and rather than remain stubborn and intransigent should aim to sort out any difference of opinion quickly and amicably before it escalates and takes the edge off what could be happier times. Fire Snakes, take note of this and do not let what are sometimes relatively minor matters get out of hand! Overall, however, the Dragon year will be a constructive time for the Fire Snake. Determined and capable of so much, he knows he has a grand future ahead of him and what he accomplishes in the year 2000 will do much to prepare for that future, while on a personal level this will be a fine and happy year.

This will be a reasonable year for the *Earth Snake* and one which will allow him to obtain positive results in many areas of his life. However, to get the best from the Dragon year, the Earth Snake would do well to decide upon his objectives and, at busy times, give himself priorities. If not, there is a danger that he could end up spreading his energies too widely and not achieve as much as he otherwise might. For the Earth Snake born in 1989 there will be some interesting developments in his schooling, with the prospects of starting new subjects or project work, some of which will greatly inspire him. Indeed, the inquisitive young Earth Snake will impress those around him with his progress and earnest approach. However, if there is any matter that is concerning him, whether problems in a certain subject or even a personal matter, he should not hesitate to speak to others. Often his concerns can be quickly allayed and he can be given useful and practical help, but for that to be possible he does need to be forthcoming. In addition to the progress he will make academically, his interests will also bring him much satisfaction. For those Earth Snakes who are keen on sport and outdoor activities, the year will contain some truly memorable moments and these Earth Snakes would do well to take advantage of any opportunity they can to further their skills. Similarly, if there is an interest or hobby the Earth Snake has been considering taking up, again this would be an excellent year in which to do so. The Dragon year very much favours enterprise and initiative, and for the keen Earth Snake it can prove a fulfilling time. This also applies to those Earth Snakes born in 1929. In recent years they will have undertaken a great deal and seen many changes, and for some this will have included moving. In the year 2000 the Earth Snake will find himself better able to appreciate and enjoy what he has achieved as well as indulge in activities more of his own choosing. All this will be a great source of satisfaction to him and is another reason why he should decide just how he wishes to spend his time over the year. In addition to outdoor activities, the Earth Snake is likely to find interests of a creative nature particularly pleasing and for those keen on photography, music or some aspects of the arts the year will contain some gratifying moments. Some Earth Snakes will also have been particularly intrigued by recent computer developments and will enjoy finding out more and increasing their skills and knowledge. In most of what he does over the year, the Earth Snake will be well supported by others, although he should listen carefully to any advice he is given, even though this may sometimes run counter to his own thoughts. Those around him do have his best interests at heart and can sometimes see points that he may have overlooked. One of the more awkwardly aspected areas of the year concerns paperwork, particularly any official forms that the Earth Snake may have to complete. He should deal with these promptly and with care, otherwise he could find himself caught up in a welter of bureaucracy which may be to his financial detriment. Earth Snakes, do take careful note of this and if you are unsure about anything, do seek advice rather than jump to conclusions. Similarly, with financial matters, the Earth Snake should not take undue risks. Although usually so skilful when dealing with finance, he should not allow his vigilance to slip over the year and should check if he has any uncertainties. These warnings apart, the year 2000 will be a satisfying one for the Earth Snake and by using his time well he can enjoy many rewarding occasions, with his relations with others bringing him considerable pleasure.

FAMOUS SNAKES

Muhammad Ali, Ann-Margret, Yasser Arafat, Paddy Ashdown, Ronnie Barker, Kim Basinger, Bjork, Tony Blair, Heinrich Böll, Michael Bolton, Betty Boothroyd, Brahms, Pierce Brosnan, Casanova, Chubby Checker, Tom Conti, Randy Crawford, Alistair Darling, Jim Davidson, Bob Dylan, Elgar, Sir Alexander Fleming, Henry Fonda, Mahatma Gandhi, Greta Garbo, Art Garfunkel, J. Paul Getty, Dizzy Gillespie, W. E. Gladstone, Goethe, Princess Grace of Monaco, Stephen Hawking, Nigel Hawthorne, Audrey Hepburn, Jack Higgins, Michael Howard, Howard Hughes, Tom Hulce, Liz Hurley, Rev. Jesse Jackson, James Joyce, Stacy Keach, Howard Keel, J. F. Kennedy, Carole King, James Last, Cindi Lauper, Lennox Lewis, Courtney Love, Dame Vera Lynn, Nigel Mansell, Mao Tse-tung, Henri Matisse, Francis Maude, Robert Mitchum, Nasser, Bob Newhart, Alfred Nobel, Ryan O'Neal, Mike Oldfield, Aristotle Onassis, Jacqueline Onassis, Pablo Picasso, Mary Pickford, Brad Pitt, André Previn, Franklin D. Roosevelt, Jean-Paul Sartre, Franz Schubert, Brooke Shields, Paul

Simon, Delia Smith, John Thaw, Dionne Warwick, Charlie Watts, Ruby Wax, Oprah Winfrey, Victoria Wood, Virginia Woolf, Susannah York.

25 JANUARY 1906 ～ 12 FEBRUARY 1907   *Fire Horse*

11 FEBRUARY 1918 ～ 31 JANUARY 1919   *Earth Horse*

30 JANUARY 1930 ～ 16 FEBRUARY 1931   *Metal Horse*

15 FEBRUARY 1942 ～ 4 FEBRUARY 1943   *Water Horse*

3 FEBRUARY 1954 ～ 23 JANUARY 1955   *Wood Horse*

21 JANUARY 1966 ～ 8 FEBRUARY 1967   *Fire Horse*

7 FEBRUARY 1978 ～ 27 JANUARY 1979   *Earth Horse*

27 JANUARY 1990 ～ 14 FEBRUARY 1991   *Metal Horse*

THE

HORSE

THE PERSONALITY OF THE HORSE

Let us not look back in anger or forward in fear, but around in awareness.

James Thurber: a Horse

The Horse is born under the signs of elegance and ardour. He has a most engaging and charming manner and is usually very popular. He loves meeting people and likes attending parties and other large social gatherings.

The Horse is a lively character and enjoys being the centre of attention. He has considerable leadership qualities and is much admired for his honest and straightforward manner. He is an eloquent and persuasive speaker and has a great love of discussion and debate. He also has a particularly agile mind and can assimilate facts remarkably quickly.

He does, however, have a fiery temper and although his outbursts are usually short-lived, he can often say things which he will later regret. He is also not particularly good at keeping secrets.

The Horse has many interests and involves himself in a wide variety of activities. He can, however, get involved in so much that he can often waste his energies on projects which he never has time to complete. He also has a tendency to change his interests rather frequently and will often get caught up with the latest craze or 'in thing' until something better or more exciting turns up.

The Horse also likes to have a certain amount of freedom and independence. He hates being bound by petty rules and regulations and as far as possible likes to feel that he is answerable to no one but himself. But despite this spirit of freedom, he still likes to have the support and encouragement of others in his various enterprises.

Due to his many talents and likeable nature, the Horse will often go far in life. He enjoys challenges and is a methodical and tireless worker. However, should things work against him and he fail in any of his enterprises, it will take a long time for him to recover and pick up the pieces again. Success to the Horse means everything. To fail is a disaster and a humiliation.

The Horse likes to have variety in his life and he will try his hand at many different things before he settles down to one particular job. Even then, he will probably remain alert to see whether there are any new and better opportunities for him to take up. The Horse has a restless nature and can easily get bored. He does, however, excel in any position which allows him sufficient freedom to act on his own initiative or which brings him into contact with a lot of people.

Although the Horse is not particularly bothered about accumulating great wealth, he handles his finances with care and will rarely experience any serious financial problems.

The Horse also enjoys travel and he loves visiting new and far-away places. At some stage during his life he will be tempted to live abroad for a short period of time and due to his adaptable nature he will find that he will fit in well wherever he goes.

The Horse pays a great deal of attention to his appearance and usually likes to wear smart, colourful and rather distinctive clothes. He is very attractive to the opposite sex and will often have many romances before he settles down. He is loyal and protective to his partner, but, despite his family commitments, still likes to retain a certain measure of independence and have the freedom to carry on with his own interests and hobbies. He will find that he is especially well suited to those born under the signs of the Tiger, Goat, Rooster and Dog. The Horse can also get on well with the Rabbit, Dragon, Snake, Pig and another Horse, but he will find the Ox too serious and intolerant for his liking. The Horse will also have difficulty in getting on with the Monkey and the Rat – the Monkey is very inquisitive and the Rat seeks security, and both will resent the Horse's rather independent ways.

The female Horse is usually most attractive and has a friendly, outgoing personality. She is highly intelligent, has many interests and is alert to everything that is going on around her. She particularly enjoys outdoor pursuits and often likes to take part in sport and keep-fit activities. She also enjoys travel, literature and the arts, and is a very good conversationalist.

Although the Horse can be stubborn and rather self-centred, he does have a considerate nature and is often willing to help others. He has a good sense of humour and will usually make a favourable impression wherever he goes. Provided he can curb his slightly restless nature and keep a tight control over his temper, he will go through life making friends, taking part in a multitude of different activities and generally achieving many of his objectives. His life will rarely be dull.

THE FIVE DIFFERENT TYPES OF HORSE

In addition to the 12 signs of the Chinese zodiac, there are five elements, and these have a strengthening or moderating influence on the sign. The effects of the five elements on the Horse are described below, together with the years in which the elements were exercising their influence. Therefore all Horses born in 1930 and 1990 are Metal Horses, those born in 1942 are Water Horses and so on.

Metal Horse: 1930, 1990
This Horse is bold, confident and forthright. He is ambitious and also a great innovator. He loves challenges and takes great delight in sorting out complicated problems. He likes to have a certain amount of independence and resents any outside interference in his affairs. The Metal Horse has charm and a certain charisma, but he can also be very stubborn and rather impulsive. He usually has many friends and enjoys an active social life.

Water Horse: 1942
The Water Horse has a friendly nature, a good sense of humour, and is able to talk intelligently on a wide range of topics. He is astute in business matters and quick to take advantage of any opportunities that arise. He does, however, have a tendency to get easily distracted and can change his interests – and indeed his mind – rather frequently, and this can sometimes work to his detriment.

He is nevertheless very talented and can often go far in life. He pays a great deal of attention to his appearance and is usually smart and well turned out. He loves to travel and also enjoys sport and other outdoor activities.

Wood Horse: 1954

The Wood Horse has a most agreeable and amiable nature. He communicates well with others and, like the Water Horse, is able to talk intelligently on many different subjects. He is a hard and conscientious worker and is held in high esteem by his friends and colleagues. His opinions and views are often sought and, given his imaginative nature, he can quite often come up with some very original and practical ideas. He is usually widely read and likes to lead a busy social life. He can also be most generous and often holds high moral viewpoints.

Fire Horse: 1906, 1966

The element of Fire combined with the temperament of the Horse creates one of the most powerful forces in the Chinese zodiac. The Fire Horse is destined to lead an exciting and eventful life and to make his mark in his chosen profession. He has a forceful personality and his intelligence and resolute manner bring him the support and admiration of many. He loves action and excitement and his life will rarely be quiet. He can, however, be rather blunt and forthright in his views and does not take kindly to interference in his own affairs or to obeying orders. He is a flamboyant character, has a good sense of humour and will lead a very active social life.

Earth Horse: 1918, 1978

This Horse is considerate and caring. He is more cautious than some of the other types of Horse, but he is wise, perceptive and extremely capable. Although he can be rather indecisive at times, he has considerable business acumen and is very astute in financial matters. He has a quiet, friendly nature and is well thought of by his family and friends.

PROSPECTS FOR THE HORSE IN THE YEAR 2000

The Chinese New Year starts on 5 February 2000. Until then, the old year, the Year of the Rabbit, is still making its presence felt.

The Year of the Rabbit (16 February 1999 to 4 February 2000) will have been a satisfying one for the Horse, with the closing months being the best and most successful part. Personally the Horse will feel in fine form and can look forward to some pleasing occasions with those around him. He will also thoroughly enjoy the social events that he attends at this time, particularly the celebrations surrounding the new millennium. Indeed, the significance of this event will do much to inspire the Horse and he may well take the opportunity to reflect on all he has achieved and how he would now like his life to develop. Some of these thoughts and ideas could prove significant in the next Chinese year.

However, while the Horse's relations with both family and friends will go well at the end of the Rabbit year, it should be noted that new friendships, especially those of a romantic nature, will need care if they are to endure. As the Horse will find, it is better for a couple to get to know each other well than rush into a hasty commitment.

As far as his work is concerned, the Horse will get the best results by concentrating on the areas in which he already has some knowledge rather than venturing into more unfamiliar territory. During some parts of the Rabbit year, this will require him to exercise a certain self-discipline to avoid getting distracted by other, lesser activities, but the effort and commitment he makes will lead to some pleasing results.

The Horse will fare well in financial matters, although in view of the considerable amount of socializing he will be involved in, the closing months of the year will be a particularly expensive time. It could be in the Horse's interests to make allowances for this several months ahead and consider spreading out his purchases and buying presents in advance.

Generally the Rabbit year will be a positive time for the Horse and he will certainly enjoy himself as the year ends as well as be able to look back on his achievements with satisfaction.

The Year of the Dragon starts on 5 February and will be an interesting year for the Horse. Many aspects of his life will go well and he will make useful progress in much of what he does. However, to temper the good times there will also be a few problems and obstacles. Although annoying at the time, these will act as a cautionary check. For the most part, though, the Horse will do well and will enjoy the Dragon year.

As far as his work is concerned, this will be an important year. Indeed, many Horses will consider that the time is now right to move on from their present position and make more of themselves. In the year 2000 these Horses should actively follow up any opportunities that interest them. Admittedly, not all may initially go their way, but the Horse's persistence and tenaciousness will be rewarded and many Horses will obtain a new position which holds great potential for further development. However, while positive change is very much in the air, once in a new position the Horse should take time to familiarize himself with his duties rather than let his sometimes over-enthusiastic nature run away with him. There will be plenty of time for him to show his worth, but he must not jeopardize those all-important early stages through rash actions or impetuous decisions. Horses, take note!

Many of those Horses seeking work will also be successful in finding a position, sometimes in a rather unusual way. They may perhaps hear about an opening by chance, receive a tip or be recommended by someone. However they obtain their new position, in many cases it will enable them to make effective use of their skills and thereby sow the seeds for subsequent advance.

The months of February to April and September and November will be particularly favourable for work opportunities.

Also, the Horse possesses a keen and inventive mind, and if he has an idea he wants to advance, he would do well to take it further during the year and investigate the feasibility of putting it into practice. With the year favouring enterprise the Horse can fare well, but when promoting any idea or scheme, he should give thought to its presentation and possible outcome rather than plunging straight in. Again, it is a case of moderating his sometimes over-zealous nature and taking time to attend to the finer details.

As far as financial matters are concerned, this will be a year for caution and restraint. Throughout the year the Horse would find it helpful to keep a close watch over his level of spending – if not, he could find it could all too easily creep up and exceed what he had intended or allowed for. Similarly, if he enters into any new transaction, he should make allowance for it in his budget. With careful financial management, the Horse's position can remain sound, but this is not a year for complacency or spending without regard to his situation. The Horse should also be wary of any dubious or highly speculative schemes that he might come across. All may not be as straightforward as it might seem and, if tempted, the Horse would be wise to seek further advice before committing himself. Horses, take note and do take care with money matters.

The Horse's relations with others are, however, favourably aspected over the year and he can look forward to many rewarding times with both family and friends. As far as his home life is concerned, this will be a busy year. In addition to following and encouraging those around them, the Horse will decide to carry out some ambitious projects on his home. This can include making alterations and adding new features as well as redecorating. Practical work will bring the Horse much satisfaction, but he could find that projects take him longer than he envisaged, especially with some of the interruptions and snags he may encounter. In view of this, he should be wary of embarking on too much at any one time and would find it preferable to have one or a few jobs completed rather than a lot started and left unfinished.

In addition to practical projects, the Horse will get a great deal of pleasure from the interests he can share with those around him. He will also delight in any family holidays or breaks that he can take and travel is favourably aspected.

Domestically, this will be an active year and one which will contain many pleasing occasions. On a social level there will also be much activity. The Horse can look forward to a range of interesting social occasions and, for the keen party-goer, this will be a busy and active year. There will also be plenty of opportunities for the Horse to make new friends and, for the unattached, romance is splendidly aspected, with many Horses getting engaged or married over the year. The summer will be a particularly happy time.

In many areas of the Horse's life there will be positive and pleasing developments, but there are certain points that he does need to bear in mind. As with any year, problems will emerge and when they do the Horse should aim to deal with them quickly and with good sense. If not, he could find they will linger on and become an unwelcome distraction. Also, if any differences with others should arise, again the Horse should seek a speedy and amicable solution rather than adopt an intransigent attitude. There are too many positive aspects to the year to risk jeopardizing them by what can sometimes be relatively minor matters. While on the subject of relations with others, with his social life being so active, there could be temptations for the Horse to act in a manner he may later regret. To prevent problems Horses should take careful note of this.

One other area which requires care is the Horse's own well-being. With all the activity of the year the Horse will often drive himself hard and it is therefore important that he takes good care of himself and allows himself time to rest, relax and exercise as well as ensuring he has a well-balanced diet. If not, he could find himself becoming drained and susceptible to minor ailments. With all he so wants to do in the year 2000, it is important that he takes good care of himself.

Overall, though, the Horse will accomplish much in the Dragon year. Work-wise there will be new opportunities which will bring fresh challenges and allow the Horse to show his skills and potential, while on a personal level, this will be an active and pleasing year. Earnest, keen and able to relate so well to others, the Horse knows he has much to offer and the Dragon year will give him the chance to shine and enjoy himself.

As far as the different types of Horse are concerned, this will be an interesting year for the *Metal Horse*. Greatly inspired by the start of the new millennium, many Metal Horses will decide that the time has come for them to seize the moment and start something new. This could involve carrying out plans they have been considering for some time, taking up an additional interest, learning a skill or bringing some new and positive element into their lives. Rather than just thinking about this, in typical Metal Horse style, they will take positive and decisive action to set about achieving what they want. In doing this they will be greatly encouraged by others as well as heartened by the support they receive. Many will decide to carry out plans they have regarding their accommodation, with some choosing to move altogether. The moving process will keep these Metal Horses occupied for much of the year, however once they are installed in their new home, they will delight in settling into a new area and discovering its amenities and attractions as well as getting to know others. Whether they move or decide to remain where they are, almost all Metal Horses will decide to have a major sort out in their home and make it tidier and more efficient – and again, they will take genuine pleasure in what they achieve. In addition to all that the Metal Horse does in his home, his domestic and social life will provide him with many rewarding times over the year and, as usual, he will find himself much in demand. He will take a caring interest in the activities of those close to him and much pride in a family event, which could be the birth of a grandchild or great-grandchild or the marriage of a close relation. The Metal Horse will also enjoy his social life, especially the many convivial hours spent in the company of friends. Those Metal Horses who may have had some recent adversity to contend with or who are looking for additional company will find that the kindly influence of the Dragon year will do much to support them, give them the opportunity to meet others and put some happiness back in their lives. With travel well aspected, the Metal Horse should also explore the possibility of visiting a destination he has wanted to see for some time or relations he has not seen for a while. Again, positive action will produce results. This will also be an important year for those Metal Horses born in 1990, particularly concerning their education. With tests, new subjects and for many an imminent change of school, many of these young Metal Horses will feel under pressure and daunted by what is expected of them. However, by giving of their best they will emerge from the year with much to their credit. Whenever they do have concerns, they should not hesitate to raise these with others and throughout the year should remember that support is available should they need it. The one area that the Metal Horse does need to watch over the year is finance, particularly with the likelihood of travel, accommodation expenses and, for some, moving costs, plus all the other usual financial demands. To avoid problems, the Horse does need to keep a close watch on his spending. Without care, he could later discover his outgoings were far more than he thought and this could result in him having to make modifications and cutbacks. Metal Horses, take note! In most respects, though, the Metal Horse will find this a fulfilling year and by setting his ideas in motion and using his time well, he will achieve pleasing results. The Metal Horse has always been a doer and in the Dragon year he will feel inspired to do a great deal! He will enjoy many gratifying results as a consequence.

This will be a variable year for the *Water Horse* and, while it will certainly contain many pleasing elements, it will also have its vexations. In particular, the Water Horse could find that not all his plans will go as smoothly as he would like and he may have to look again at some of what he is hoping to achieve. However, while the year may bring a few disappointments, the Water Horse is both resilient and resourceful and will often be able to turn a situation to his advantage. In his work he will need to remain alert to all that goes on around him, particularly imminent changes and developments. Sometimes he could find himself affected by these and, by keeping himself well informed, he will find himself better able to gauge what to do and what opportunities might become available. Work-wise there will be pressures and changes, but long-term benefits will often result. In addition to adapting and making the best of what occurs, some Water Horses will make a deliberate effort to switch to a different type of work, feeling that they would benefit from a new challenge, while others may take the opportunity to retire in order to concentrate on other interests. However, before taking any major action, the Water Horse would do well to discuss his plans with others as well as consider the consequences of his actions. By being forthcoming he will obtain much useful advice as well as gain a clearer idea in his own mind of the course he should take. Admittedly, any major decisions he takes will, at the time, put him under pressure, but often the Dragon year will represent the starting of a new phase in the Water Horse's life, with some interesting and fulfilling times ahead. Also, if any Water Horse has a hobby or interest which he can put to profitable use he should look into it. As he is a good communicator, this could be by writing or passing on some of his knowledge and skills. Again, with resourcefulness, the Water Horse could discover some interesting possibilities. As far as financial matters are concerned, this is, though, a year for care. Many Water Horses will receive an additional sum of money in the year 2000, either as a gift, as the fruition of a policy or for some work done. However, the Water Horse should think carefully what to do with this sum rather than allow it to 'burn a hole in his pocket'. He could, for instance, consider saving part and spending some on his accommodation and on travel. By dealing with his finances in a planned rather than *ad hoc* way, he will certainly benefit more. The Water Horse's personal life will be quite active over the year. Domestically there will be many demands upon his time and in addition to the usual household activities, he will do much to assist those around him. However, while there will be many pleasurable family occasions, there could also be a few problems and strains. To help ease these, the Water Horse should use his superb diplomatic skills to sort out any differences, particularly between family members, as well as seek an amicable solution. He will find that action on his part will do much to help. Similarly, strains could occur when tiredness and pressure set in and if the Water Horse can suggest activities all could enjoy, perhaps an outing or suitable treat, he will find it helpful. However, despite the activity and occasional fraught moment, the Water Horse's family life will generally be satisfying and he will take much pride in the progress enjoyed by family members. His social life too will bring its pleasurable moments and over the year the Water Horse will attend a wide range of social functions as well as have the opportunity to widen his circle of friends and acquaintances. Although the Dragon year will contain its challenging moments, there will still be much that the Water Horse will enjoy, with some of the events and decisions of the year being very much to his future advantage.

This will be an interesting year for the *Wood Horse* and while not everything may go as smoothly or work out in the manner he would have liked, the overall results will prove significant. In their work many Wood Horses will take some important decisions which will have an important bearing on their future. Some will decide that the time has now come when they would benefit from new challenges and should make more of their potential, and as a result will actively pursue any openings that interest them as well as see what opportunities they themselves can create. Admittedly, their progress may not always be as swift as they would like nor openings that plentiful, but their determination and initiative will be rewarded, and the progress that they do make will often provide a useful base from which to develop and expand. As so many Wood Horses will find, the positive results that come from the Dragon year tend to become apparent in the longer rather than shorter term. Those Wood Horses who decide to remain in their present position should, though, take advantage of any chances of training, taking on additional duties or learning about different aspects of their work. All this will do much to help their future prospects. Similarly, those seeking work should also investigate any training opportunities that might be available as well as follow up any openings that interest them. Again, by drawing on their skills and thinking of ways in which they could use or adapt them, they could come up with some interesting possibilities which have the potential for development. As far as finance is concerned, however, the Wood Horse will need to exercise care. This is not a year for taking undue risks and the Wood Horse should carefully check the small print of any large commitment he enters into, particularly if it has long-term implications. Similarly, any important forms or correspondence he receives need careful attention; again, if he has any doubts, he should seek clarification rather than take risks. Also, to help prevent problems, the Wood Horse should aim to deal with his paperwork and financial record-keeping in an organized manner. Not only will this save him time but also efficiency drives such as this – and anything else the Wood Horse can do to keep his home tidier and more organized – will bring him a great deal of personal satisfaction. The Wood Horse's domestic life will be busy but pleasant over the year. As always, he will play a full and active part in family life and will delight in following the progress of those around him. However, with many calls upon his time, he should be wary of becoming involved in too many household projects at once and would be helped by planning and prioritizing his tasks. Although there will often be a high level of activity in his domestic life, he can look forward to many splendid and meaningful times with his loved ones, especially enjoying hobbies and mutual interests. The Wood Horse's social life will go well, with many agreeable times spent with his friends and attending various functions. Travel is also favourably aspected and all Wood Horses should take advantage of any travel opportunities that arise as well as aim to go away at least once during the year. They will not only find a break or holiday beneficial but also their chosen destination could surpass expectations. Although the year will bring its pressures and moments of uncertainty, what the Wood Horse is able to accomplish will do much to enhance his future prospects. The year will also contain many satisfying elements, with his personal life, interests and travel pleasingly aspected.

The *Fire Horse* will begin the year with high hopes. Inspired by the start of the new millennium and determined to make more of himself, he will resolve to make this a time for growth and personal development. His enterprise and determination will indeed produce results, some of which will have an important bearing on his future. However, to get the best results from the year the Fire Horse should think carefully about what he actually wants to achieve. Without specific aims he could find himself striving to better himself without knowing exactly what he wants. Also, despite his earnestness, he must be realistic in what he attempts and the time-scale he sets himself. To achieve some of his objectives will require considerable time and effort on his part and he must allow for this and not let his exuberant nature get the better of him. However, while the Fire Horse's actual level of progress may not always meet his high expectations, by working persistently towards his goals he will make headway, with what he accomplishes being to his longer term benefit. In his work he should look at ways in which he can develop his skills as well as keep alert for openings that will take him in the direction he wants. Sometimes such opportunities will arise in a sudden and unexpected way. By being alert and seizing them, the Fire Horse will be able to make progress and improve his longer term prospects. Those Fire Horses seeking work should also persist in following up any opportunities and will find that once they are given a chance to show their worth they will quickly impress and will sow the seeds for future progress.

The Fire Horse will also enjoy the time he spends on his own interests over the year and should aim to further these. Not only will he find them fulfilling but also one of them could even provide him with an additional source of income. This especially applies to Fire Horses who enjoy activities such as writing, photography, painting, craftwork or who possess technical skills. The Fire Horse's domestic life will be active but highly satisfying over the year. He will play a full and appreciated part in family activities, encouraging those dear to him and involving himself in joint projects and interests as well as family trips and holidays. He will also carry out some improvements on his home, but in undertaking these, he should not set himself an unrealistic schedule and should, if possible, concentrate on one project at a time. His social life will go well, and there will be a variety of interesting social events and functions for him to attend as well as agreeable meetings with friends. Indeed, with his wide interests and outgoing nature, the Fire Horse likes to enjoy life to the full and during the year 2000 his personal life will bring him considerable pleasure. There are, though, two areas that will require care. With this being an active and often demanding year, the Fire Horse does need to look after his own well-being. He should make sure he keeps himself in trim, exercises and eats well and takes the time to properly relax and unwind. If not, he could find he is getting tired, not making as much of himself as he would like and also falling prey to minor ailments. The other area that requires care is finance. In the year 2000 the Fire Horse should avoid taking unnecessary risks or stretching his resources too far. If he has doubts over any financial matter, he should seek further clarification. Overall, though, this will be a positive year for the Fire Horse and by giving thought to his activities and using his skills well, he will do much to enhance his prospects. On a personal level, this will be a busy but rewarding year, with the Fire Horse's interests and relations with others bringing him considerable pleasure.

This will be an important year for the *Earth Horse*, although while he can look forward to pleasing results in many areas of his life, they will often require a great deal of effort on his part. One of the more favourably aspected areas of his life, however, is personal matters and his relations with others will bring him much happiness over the year. Indeed, many Earth Horses will have excellent cause for a personal celebration, with the prospects being good for new friendships, engagement, marriage or an addition to the family. The spring and summer months will be a particularly rewarding time. Any Earth Horse who may start the year in low spirits or who would like to make some new friends will find the Dragon year marking an important upturn in his personal life, so much so that he could find it helpful to draw a line over past misfortunes and regard the year 2000 as the start of a new chapter in his life. The Earth Horse will also be well supported by others and if he has any problems or uncertainties, he should not hesitate to discuss them. A more senior relation will prove especially helpful and the Earth Horse would do well to listen to any words of advice he is given. Those around him do, after all, speak with his interests very much at heart and often with the benefit of many years of experience behind them. Another favoured area concerns travel and outdoor pursuits and for those Earth Horses who enjoy visiting new areas or are outdoor enthusiasts, the year will bring many opportunities to follow their interests, with the summer promising to be an active and satisfying time. However, with so much happening on a personal level, this will prove an expensive year and the Earth Horse will need to watch his level of outgoings and make sure he leaves himself enough to meet his various commitments. To help improve their finances, some Earth Horses may be tempted by money-making schemes, such as 'get-rich-quick' or speculative ventures, and if so they should proceed with caution. This is not a year to take undue risks and the Earth Horse could, without care, find himself losing rather than making money. Indeed, if he is seeking additional income, rather than pursuing more risky ventures, he could consider putting an interest or skill of his to profitable use. Some imaginative thinking could produce some ideas which would be well worth developing. Another challenging area is the Earth Horse's work and he may find his progress patchy over the year. Some Earth Horses could find themselves being given additional and sometimes onerous duties as well as having to adapt to unwelcome changes. As a result, they will face new pressures and there will be times when they will feel despondent about what is going on and about their immediate prospects. However, there is every reason for the Earth Horse to take heart. By giving of his best and rising to all he is asked, he will certainly impress and learn much and this will certainly be to his future benefit. Also, some of his aspirations first require him to get experience and he should use the present year to acquire this. He is still at a young age and there will be plenty of time for him to achieve all he wants and more, but for the moment he does need to concentrate on building up his skills and experience and preparing a base from which to advance. By the end of the year 2000 the Earth Horse will begin to see the results of his efforts and his progress will then be much easier. Those Earth Horses who do decide to change their present position over the year or who are seeking work should remain persistent in their efforts. Admittedly, not all the openings they pursue will come to anything, but by looking at any feedback they receive, particularly on improving interview technique and presentation, as well as following up any suggestions they are given, they will make headway. Once in a new position, they will quickly show themselves capable of further progress and will be encouraged to develop their talents. In work matters, the Earth Horse's actual level of progress may not always meet his expectations during the year, but he will do much to prepare the way for future successes and with his capabilities he does have an exciting future ahead of him. While work and financial matters may sometimes prove challenging, his personal life is superbly aspected and he can look forward to some truly happy and memorable times.

FAMOUS HORSES

Neil Armstrong, Rowan Atkinson, Margaret Beckett, Samuel Beckett, Ingmar Bergman, Leonard Bernstein, Sir John Betjeman, Karen Black, Cherie Blair, Helena Bonham Carter, James Cameron, Eric Cantona, Ray Charles, Chopin, Sean Connery, Billy Connolly, Catherine Cookson, Ronnie

Corbett, Elvis Costello, Kevin Costner, Cindy Crawford, Michael Crichton, James Dean, Clint Eastwood, Thomas Alva Edison, Britt Ekland, Chris Evans, Harrison Ford, Aretha Franklin, Sir Bob Geldof, David Ginola, Samuel Goldwyn, Billy Graham, Gene Hackman, Rolf Harris, Rita Hayworth, Jimi Hendrix, Bob Hoskins, Ted Hughes, Janet Jackson, Neil Kinnock, Calvin Klein, Helmut Kohl, Lenin, Annie Lennox, Desmond Lynam, Sir Paul McCartney, Nelson Mandela, Princess Margaret, Curtis Mayfield, Spike Milligan, Ben Murphy, Jimmy Nail, Sir Isaac Newton, Louis Pasteur, Ross Perot, Harold Pinter, J. B. Priestley, Puccini, Lou Reed, Rembrandt, Ruth Rendell, Jean Renoir, Theodore Roosevelt, Helena Rubenstein, Peter Sissons, Lord Snowdon, Alexander Solzhenitsyn, Lisa Stansfield, Barbra Streisand, Kiefer Sutherland, Patrick Swayze, John Travolta, Kathleen Turner, Mike Tyson, Vivaldi, Robert Wagner, Denzel Washington, Billy Wilder, Andy Williams, the Duke of Windsor, Tammy Wynette, Boris Yeltsin, Michael York.

13 FEBRUARY 1907 ～ 1 FEBRUARY 1908   *Fire Goat*

1 FEBRUARY 1919 ～ 19 FEBRUARY 1920   *Earth Goat*

17 FEBRUARY 1931 ～ 5 FEBRUARY 1932   *Metal Goat*

5 FEBRUARY 1943 ～ 24 JANUARY 1944   *Water Goat*

24 JANUARY 1955 ～ 11 FEBRUARY 1956   *Wood Goat*

9 FEBRUARY 1967 ～ 29 JANUARY 1968   *Fire Goat*

28 JANUARY 1979 ～ 15 FEBRUARY 1980   *Earth Goat*

15 FEBRUARY 1991 ～ 3 FEBRUARY 1992   *Metal Goat*

THE
GOAT

THE PERSONALITY OF THE GOAT

The surest way not to fail is to determine to succeed.
Richard Brinsley Sheridan: a Goat

The Goat is born under the sign of art. He is imaginative, creative and has a good appreciation of the finer things in life. He has an easy-going nature and prefers to live in a relaxed and pressure-free environment. He hates any sort of discord or unpleasantness and does not like to be bound by a strict routine or rigid timetable. The Goat is not one to be hurried against his will, but despite his seemingly relaxed approach to life, he is something of a perfectionist and when he starts work on a project he is certain to give of his best.

The Goat usually prefers to work in a team rather than on his own. He likes to have the support and encouragement of others and if left to deal with matters on his own he can get very worried and tends to view things rather pessimistically. Wherever possible he will leave major decision-making to others while he concentrates on his own pursuits. If, however, he feels particularly strongly about a certain matter or has to defend his position in any way, he will act with great fortitude and precision.

The Goat has a very persuasive nature and often uses his considerable charm to get his own way. He can, however, be rather hesitant about letting his true feelings be known and if he were prepared to be more forthright he would do much better as a result.

The Goat tends to have a quiet, somewhat reserved nature but when he is in company he likes he can often become the centre of attention. He can be highly amusing, a marvellous host at parties and a superb entertainer. Whenever the spotlight falls on him, his adrenalin starts to flow and he can be assured of giving a sparkling performance, particularly if he is allowed to use his creative skills in any way.

Of all the signs in the Chinese zodiac, the Goat is probably the most gifted artistically. Whether in the theatre, literature, music or art, he is certain to make a lasting impression. He is a born creator and is rarely happier than when occupied in some artistic pursuit. But even in this the Goat does well to work with others rather than on his own. He needs inspiration and a guiding influence, but when he has found his true *métier*, he can often receive widespread acclaim and recognition.

In addition to his liking for the arts, the Goat is usually quite religious and often has a deep interest in nature, animals and the countryside. He is also fairly athletic and there are many Goats who have excelled in some form of sporting activity or who have a great interest in sport.

Although the Goat is not particularly materialistic or concerned about finance, he will find that he will usually be lucky in financial matters and will rarely be short of the necessary funds to tide himself over. He is, however, rather indulgent and tends to spend his money as soon as he receives it rather than make provision for the future.

The Goat usually leaves home when he is young but he will always maintain strong links with his parents and the other members of his family. He is also rather nostalgic and is well known for keeping mementoes of his childhood and souvenirs of places that he has visited. His home will not be particularly tidy but he knows where everything is and it will also be scrupulously clean.

Affairs of the heart are particularly important to the Goat and he will often have many romances before he finally settles down. Although he is fairly adaptable, he prefers to live in a secure and stable environment and will find that he is best suited to those born under the signs of the Tiger, Horse, Monkey, Pig and Rabbit. He can also establish a good relationship with the Dragon, Snake, Rooster and another Goat, but he may find the Ox and Dog a little too serious for his liking. Neither will he care particularly for the Rat's rather thrifty ways.

The female Goat devotes all her time and energy to the needs of her family. She has excellent taste in home furnishings and often uses her considerable artistic skills to make clothes for herself and her children. She takes great care over her appearance and can be most attractive to the opposite sex. Although she is not the best organized of people, her engaging manner and delightful sense of humour create a favourable impression wherever she goes. She is also a good cook and usually gets much pleasure from gardening and outdoor pursuits.

The Goat can win friends easily and people generally feel relaxed in his company. He has a kind and understanding nature and although he can occasionally be stubborn, with the right support and encouragement he can live a happy and very satisfying life. The more he can use his creative skills, the happier he will be.

THE FIVE DIFFERENT TYPES OF GOAT

In addition to the 12 signs of the Chinese zodiac, there are five elements, and these have a strengthening or moderating influence on the sign. The effects of the five elements on the Goat are described below, together with the years in which the elements were exercising their influence. Therefore all Goats born in 1931 and 1991 are Metal Goats, those born in 1943 are Water Goats, and so on.

Metal Goat: 1931, 1991

This Goat is thorough and conscientious in all that he does and is capable of doing very well in his chosen profession. Despite his confident manner, he can be a great worrier and he would find it helpful to discuss his concerns with others rather than keep them to himself. He is loyal to his family and employers and will have a small group of extremely good friends. He has good artistic taste and is usually highly skilled in some aspect of the arts. He is often a collector of antiques and his home will be very tastefully furnished.

Water Goat: 1943

The Water Goat is very popular and makes friends with remarkable ease. He is good at spotting opportunities but does not always have the necessary confidence to follow them through. He likes to have security both in his home life and at work and does not take kindly to change. He is articulate, has a good sense of humour and is usually very good with children.

Wood Goat: 1955
This Goat is generous, kind-hearted and always eager to please. He usually has a large circle of friends and involves himself in a wide variety of different activities. He has a very trusting nature but he can sometimes give in to the demands of others a little too easily and it would be in his own interests if he were to stand his ground a little more often. He is usually lucky in financial matters and, like the Water Goat, is very good with children.

Fire Goat: 1907, 1967
This Goat usually knows what he wants in life and he often uses his considerable charm and persuasive person-ality in order to achieve his aims. He can sometimes let his imagination run away with him and has a tendency to ignore matters which are not to his liking. He is rather extravagant in his spending and would do well to exercise a little more care when dealing with financial matters. He has a lively personality, many friends and loves attending parties and social occasions.

Earth Goat: 1919, 1979
This Goat has a very considerate and caring nature. He is particularly loyal to his family and friends and invariably creates a favourable impression wherever he goes. He is

reliable and conscientious in his work but he finds it difficult to save and never likes to deprive himself of any little luxury which he might fancy. He has numerous interests and is often very well read. He usually gets much pleasure from following the activities of various members of his family.

PROSPECTS FOR THE GOAT IN THE YEAR 2000

The Chinese New Year starts on 5 February 2000. Until then, the old year, the Year of the Rabbit, is still making its presence felt.

The Year of the Rabbit (16 February 1999 to 4 February 2000) will have been a favourable one for the Goat and in what remains of it he can look forward to some interesting and enjoyable times.

In the closing months of the Rabbit year the Goat will find himself much in demand, with both his domestic and social life being active. Also, with the festivities at the end of the year, he will become very much caught up in the prevailing mood and will attend quite a few parties, events and get-togethers. Indeed, he is always one who savours the finer things in life and the last months of the Rabbit year will see him in fine form and thoroughly enjoying himself.

For the unattached Goat, the Rabbit year is splendidly aspected, with the prospects excellent for romance. For those seeking new friends, there will be some marvellous opportunities for meeting others, especially in the last quarter of the year. Indeed, a friendship that the Goat forms during the Rabbit year could play an important part in his future.

However, with so much activity, there will be many expenses for the Goat to meet. As far as possible, he should aim to budget for some of these in advance and could find it helpful to spread his more seasonal purchases out. He should also keep watch on what he does spend at this time; it could quickly mount up and if he is not careful, in the new year he could face some bills that are larger than expected.

The Rabbit year will also see some positive developments in the Goat's work, with many Goats being given the chance to take on new responsibilities and develop some of their ideas. However, for the Goat to benefit from the favourable aspects that prevail, he does need to use his initiative and be prepared to take action. There are some Goats who tend to lose out through their reticence and in the Rabbit year it really would be in their interests to try and correct this. The bold and decisive Goat can really make significant headway at this time, with November being an especially positive month.

The Rabbit year is one of the best for the Goat, with the closing months going particularly well. By making the most of himself, he will make pleasing progress as well as greatly enjoy himself.

The Year of the Dragon starts on 5 February and will be a variable one for the Goat. Although parts of the year will be satisfying and bring much pleasure, the Goat could also face some niggling problems and difficulties.

In his work the Goat will need to proceed with care. Although so many will have enjoyed considerable success in the Rabbit year, in the year 2000 the Goat will need to remain alert and mindful of any changes that are being considered. This is not a year when he can afford to just concentrate on his own activities without regard to what is happening around him, much as he may like to. If he does, he could all too easily find himself out on a limb and sometimes vulnerable to change.

The Goat may also find that some of his plans and projects may take a little while to get going and many will have to wait for the following year before they show more substantial results. However, while some of the Dragon year may be frustrating, it is an excellent time for the Goat to take stock of his present position and look at what he is hoping to achieve and how he would like his career to develop. If he feels it would be beneficial to acquire new skills or he is eligible for any training, he should follow this up. As he will find, what he learns now, together with some of the ideas he forms, will have a positive bearing on his future.

This also applies to those Goats seeking work. If there are courses available or they have the opportunity to add to their experience they should take advantage of it; anything they can do to enhance their prospects will serve them well. These Goats should also persist in following up any opportunities that do become available. While there may be times when they feel despondent or discouraged, they should keep trying. Their efforts will eventually produce results and sometimes these could follow directly on from a setback or disappointment. The Dragon year is indeed capable of producing surprises for the Goat, particularly regarding the nature of some of the openings that become available. Once in a position, the Goat will find it a useful foothold from which to develop and again what he accomplishes now will have the potential to lead on to better things over the next year. For work matters the months of April, May, September and November could see some interesting developments.

Another area which requires care is finance. In view of the activities and expenses of the preceding year, some Goats will start the Dragon year with their resources depleted and quite a few bills to pay. To cope with these, the Goat would find it helpful to take greater control over his financial affairs and set them on a more regulated basis. This includes keeping records and accounts and regularly reviewing his spending, outgoings and commitments. By doing this, the Goat could find that he is able to make some useful modifications and so help his situation. He should also be wary of taking undue risks over the year or of committing himself to large undertakings without checking the obligations or small print. Any extra care that the Goat does take with money matters in the Dragon year will be very much to his advantage.

One of the more favourably aspected areas of the year, however, is the Goat's hobbies and if he has an interest he is keen to develop or one that has been intriguing him, he should find out more. He might find it useful to contact fellow enthusiasts or join an appropriate society, even, if he is able, a News Group on the Internet. He could also find that some projects that he starts this year will come to a successful conclusion in 2001.

The Goat always attaches great importance to maintaining good relations with those around him and while he will find happiness in these areas over the year, some care and consideration will be needed. In his domestic life the Goat could find that some of the events and activities of the year bring moments of pressure and stress, and as a result he may become edgy and preoccupied, as may those around him. To help with this, the Goat should be prepared to be open in his feelings as well as encourage others to be forthcoming. He will find a spirit of openness and understanding far better than letting worries brew and linger unspoken. Also, by speaking of his concerns, he will find others better able to assist, advise and reassure him.

However, while the Dragon year will bring its awkward moments, it will still contain many happy and agreeable times for the Goat. There will be family successes and achievements to enjoy and home projects, although sometimes disruptive, will bring him much satisfaction. The Goat would also find it helpful to encourage mutual interests and hobbies and will find that the occasional family treat or trip out will do much to help relieve some of the pressures that may have built up.

The Goat's social life will bring him pleasure over the year, with friendships made during the Rabbit year or at the start of the Dragon year developing well and bringing him considerable happiness. In view of the challenging nature of some of the year, if the Goat finds his friends can advise or help him in any way, he should not hesitate to ask. They will often be glad to assist as well as be honoured that he should consult them. It would also be in the Goat's interests to ensure that he takes a break or holiday over the year. He will find the rest and change of scene this brings both enjoyable and beneficial.

Although the Dragon year may not be the easiest of years for the Goat, by rising to its challenges he will do much to prepare himself for the significant upturn that awaits him. Despite its pressures, the year 2000 will still have its enjoyable and fulfilling times, with the Goat's personal interests going well and his family and friends being supportive and meaning a great deal to him.

As far as the different types of Goat are concerned, this will be a fair year for the *Metal Goat*. Admittedly, some parts of it may not go as well or as smoothly as he would like, but there will still be other areas which will bring him much satisfaction. The problems will tend to arise when the Metal Goat proceeds with some of his more ambitious plans, particularly with regard to his accommodation. For those Metal Goats who decide to move over the year, there could be problems in selling their existing home or finding somewhere else that is suitable and the whole process could take far longer and be more complex than they envisaged. There will indeed be occasions when the Metal Goat will wonder whether all the effort he is making is really worth it, but when everything is finally sorted out, he will be able to heave a sigh of relief and enjoy what he has accomplished. He can also take comfort in the knowledge that while the Dragon year will be a disruptive one, the Snake year that follows will be much more settled. Many of the Metal Goats who decide to remain where they are will carry out alterations and improvements to their home and again these could be more disruptive than anticipated but the end result will bring much pleasure. However, in view of some of the ambitious plans that the Metal Goat aims to carry out, it is important that he takes especial care when dealing with his finances, costing projects carefully and checking the terms and obligations of any new commitment. Paperwork concerning tax and benefits also needs to be given attention, otherwise the Metal Goat could find himself involved in some lengthy and protracted correspondence. Metal Goats, take note! However, while there will be awkward moments over the year, the Metal Goat will be well supported by others and rather than keep his concerns to himself, he should be forward in discussing them. He will often be reassured as well as relieved by the assistance others can give, whether family, friends or those in a professional capacity. One of the more positive areas of the year concerns the Metal Goat's own hobbies and interests, and whatever else might happen in the year 2000 he must not lose sight of these and should make sure he spends regular time on activities he enjoys. Also, if there has been a subject that has been intriguing him or there are skills he would like to learn, this would be a good year in which to find out more. The Metal Goat could find that learning something new will turn into a stimulating and absorbing challenge. This equally applies to those Metal Goats born in 1991. A new hobby or interest they take up could bring them considerable pleasure. These Metal Goats will also make good headway in their schoolwork over the year, although some new subjects could at first seem daunting. However, by giving of their best and asking at times of difficulty rather than struggling on unaided, they will learn a great deal and their achievements will please those around them. As always, the Metal Goat sets great store by his relations with others and in the year 2000 these will generally go well. In addition to the sterling support he is given, he can also look forward to many rewarding occasions with family and friends and to attending a variety of interesting social events. The late summer and the closing months of the Dragon year will be a particularly active time for social matters. Any Metal Goat who may have had some recent misfortune or be feeling lonely should make every effort to bring himself into greater contact with others rather than keeping his thoughts (and sometimes sadness) to himself. Positive effort on his part will certainly help bring back some happiness, and given his friendly nature and wide interests, he will soon be able to meet those with whom he has something in common and whose company he will appreciate. Generally, the Metal Goat will find the second half of the year better than the first, and that is when many of the problems and delays that have occurred will be more satisfactorily resolved. Despite the frustrations of the year, however, the Metal Goat will feel that what he has achieved has been worth all the pressure and aggravation he has been through, and he will come to appreciate this even more in the more settled Snake year that follows.

This will be a reasonable year for the *Water Goat*, although he will still need to proceed with a certain care in his activities. Many Water Goats will have made pleasing progress in their work in recent years and will have impressed others with what they have achieved. However, in the Dragon year some changes could occur which might give rise to some testing moments. These could arise through the introduction of new procedures and work practices, or changes in the Water Goat's responsibilities or personnel. The Water Goat is never entirely at ease during periods of change and will often view some of these developments with suspicion. However, over the year, it would be very much in his interests to watch developments carefully as well as show some readiness to adapt. If not, he could find himself in a vulnerable position as well as undermine some of the fine work he has done recently. The Water Goat could also find that some of his misgivings may turn out to be unfounded and that some opportunities and benefits do result from what occurs. The events of the year will, however, make him think much about his future and he would find it helpful if he were to give some thought to how he would like his life to develop over the next few years. In doing this, he will find himself coming up with some interesting possibilities and setting new goals and this, in turn, will help to motivate him, give him a greater sense of direction and lead him to setting about his activities in a more purposeful manner. Those Water Goats who are seeking work or who decide the time has now come to move from their present position would do well to consider the different ways in which they can draw on their skills and experience. Some enterprising thinking could widen the scope of positions they could try for and once they do gain a position, they could find it has the potential for future development. Admittedly, on a work level, the year will not be an easy one for the Water Goat, but what he accomplishes or sets in motion will often lead to satisfying results in the future, particularly in the more favourable Snake year that follows. As far as financial matters are concerned, many Water Goats can look forward to receiving an additional and often unexpected sum over the year. However, while the Water Goat will naturally welcome this, he should still handle his finances with care. If he does not already do so, he would find it helpful to establish some sort of record-keeping system. By managing his money he will find he is able to put it to more effective use as well as make better allowance for some of the more expensive items and projects he has in mind. However, while this can be a positive year for financial matters, the Water Goat should avoid taking unnecessary risks and be wary of any dubious or speculative schemes that he may come across. If in doubt, he should check. The Water Goat's personal life will, however, bring him pleasure and he will take considerable satisfaction from the activities of those around him. A younger relation will be the source of particular joy and any encouragement, help or advice the Water Goat feels able to give will be much appreciated. He himself will be well supported in his own activities and if troubled by any problems or uncertainties, he should not hesitate to raise his concerns with others. During the year he will often be reassured and heartened by the advice and assistance he is given as well as by the interest shown in what he does. The Water Goat will also enjoy the activities that he can share with family and friends, including any joint interests and projects, social events and outings. In addition, his own interests will bring him much satisfaction and he should make sure he sets a regular time aside for these. Not only will they provide a valuable break from his usual concerns, but the Water Goat will also take real pleasure in just immersing himself in what he wants to do. If his interests allow him to use his creative skills in any way, he will find them especially satisfying. Although this may not be the easiest of years for the Water Goat, provided he exercises care in his undertakings there will still be much that will bring him contentment, and at worrying or demanding times, it is important that he remembers that there are many around him he can turn to for advice and support.

The *Wood Goat* possesses many admirable qualities and among these is his desire to please and convey a favourable impression. But he is also sensitive and when things do not go well, or he faces criticism or challenging situations, he worries a great deal and can get despondent and disheartened. In the Dragon year, the Wood Goat will have to accept that not all areas of his life will go as well as he would like and he will have to face some difficulties. However, rather than despair or become too dejected, by taking action and rising to the challenges, he will learn a great deal and will find that new ideas and opportunities will come from some of the more challenging situations in which he finds himself. Indeed, the Dragon year will cause him to tap his reserves and resourcefulness and will enable him to create some interesting possibilities. Many Wood Goats will see significant changes in their work, particularly in the nature of their duties. Some of what they are given could prove a daunting challenge, but by rising to it the Wood Goat will be encouraged by what he achieves and in the process will add to his experience as well as enhance his reputation. Also, when changes are in the offing, the Wood Goat should avoid appearing too inflexible, otherwise he could find himself missing out on opportunities which have considerable potential. In his work he will need to proceed with care and to show a willingness to go with the current trends. Those Wood Goats who are seeking work will also see some important developments and many will be successful in obtaining a new position, although not necessarily in the type of work they may originally have had in mind. However different this sometimes might be, by giving of their best and showing willingness to learn new skills and procedures, these Wood Goats will impress and enhance their prospects. Also, all Wood Goats would benefit from any training or additional skills they can get, particularly in view of the more progressive aspects that prevail in the following year. In financial matters the Wood Goat will fare reasonably well, although he should keep a close watch over his level of spending. This is particularly important as some Wood Goats will decide to carry out considerable home improvements over the year. It would be in their interests to carefully cost this work as well as make allowances for any new obligations they take on. The Wood Goat could also find himself tempted by expensive indulgences or treats over the year. To succumb to too many of these could cause him to dip deeply into his savings and these may sometimes be more difficult to replenish than he would like. Financial matters do need careful management in the year 2000. In his domestic life the Wood Goat will have many calls upon his time. As usual, he will do much to support and encourage those around him as well as help sort out some problems or difficulties being experienced by a close relation. His considerate and kindly nature will be much appreciated. However, with helping others and the usual household chores, plus his own activities, there will be times during the year when the Wood Goat will feel weary and sometimes despondent, even though he may try to conceal this. At such times, it is important that he takes good care of himself, making sure he has adequate rest, is eating well and allowing himself time for relaxing and recreational pursuits. He should try not to let the busy nature of the year make too many incursions into his social life, as this too can provide him with some truly agreeable occasions, particularly in the second half of the year. The Wood Goat would also find it beneficial to make sure he has a proper holiday or break over the year, perhaps visiting somewhere he has had in mind for some time. Although this will be a demanding year for him, with some challenging elements, by rising to the tasks and situations before him he will find himself accomplishing a great deal and doing much to prepare the way for the more settled and productive times ahead.

This will be an important although challenging year for the *Fire Goat*. During the Dragon year he will find that not all his plans and activities will work out as he would like and he will face obstacles in some of what he wants to do. However, while this will lead to disappointment and frustration, the Fire Goat can still get an enormous amount of value from the year. By striving to overcome any problems that arise, as well as looking closely at what he wants to achieve, the Fire Goat will learn a great deal about himself as well as come up with some stronger plans. Indeed, the Dragon year is very much a time for taking stock, for evaluating his position and planning his future moves. So important is this that, for many Fire Goats, this year will come to be considered as one of the turning-points of their lives. One area which will see much activity will be the Fire Goat's work, with some significant changes to his role. Although at the time this may cause him some concern, the events that occur can sometimes be opportunities in the making and provided the Fire Goat shows some flexibility in his approach, he can emerge from the year with more experience and his reputation enhanced and in an excellent position to make further progress. Those Fire Goats seeking work or hoping to change their position could see the year developing in an interesting manner. Many could find themselves being offered a position unlike anything they have done before and while they may have doubts about what they are taking on, they will find that their new post will provide fresh and interesting challenges and will allow them to discover skills they did not know they had. For many Fire Goats the Dragon year will see, or start to see, a change in what they do, but a change which has exciting future possibilities. Although the Fire Goat's financial position will be reasonable over the year, he will still need to exercise care when dealing with money matters. Several times during the Dragon year, particularly in the first few months of the year 2000, he could find himself with some large bills to meet. To help with these, he could find it useful to examine his current financial position and see if there are any modifications he can make. He should also avoid taking unnecessary financial risks or succumbing to too many expensive whims or spending sprees. This year he does need to keep a close and watchful eye over the purse strings. He can, however, look forward to an active and rewarding domestic life. He will take particular pleasure in the progress of a younger relation and will also do much to assist someone much older than himself. His interest and considerate manner will be greatly appreciated. There will, though, be occasions when the Fire Goat's domestic life is busy and demanding, and at such times he should involve others in household activities rather than shouldering too much by himself, as well as prioritize what he has to do. Although he may be keen to get certain household projects completed – particularly when reorganizing and redecorating certain rooms – he should allow plenty of time for this and avoid starting too many jobs all at once. Although the Fire Goat will have much to keep him occupied over the year, he should not let this prevent him from pursuing his own personal interests or his social life. These will give him especial pleasure over the year and will provide a valuable and necessary break from his usual everyday activities. On a social level the Fire Goat can look forward to many agreeable meetings with friends and to attending various parties, events and get-togethers. He should also take advantage of any opportunities to travel and should take a holiday or break over the year as this again will not only prove pleasurable but also do him much good. Generally, this will be an active and demanding year for the Fire Goat, but he will emerge from it wiser, more experienced and often with a clearer idea of where his future lies. With this knowledge he will be able to build on his achievements and ideas and go forth and progress, with the next Chinese year holding much promise for him.

This will be an interesting year for the *Earth Goat* and while it will not be without problems or difficulties, for the most part it will be one that he will enjoy. Particularly well aspected is his personal life. For Earth Goats with a partner or those who have recently begun a new friendship there will be excellent cause for a personal celebration over the year. For Earth Goats who are unattached and would like to make new friends, the Dragon year will also mark a major improvement and will bring many opportunities to meet others. A new friendship – possibly one made after moving to a new location or in rather unusual circumstances – could develop in a significant manner. As always, the Earth Goat's family will prove important to him during the year and while he will be encouraged by the support he receives, he should listen carefully to any advice more senior relations give. They do hold the Earth Goat in high regard and speak with his best interests very much at heart. His work will also see some interesting developments. However, while the Earth Goat may hold firm ideas about what he wants to accomplish over the year, what he wants and what he actually achieves could turn out to be two different things! Some of his more ambitious aims require experience and skills which he does not yet possess and this year he would do better to concentrate on getting that expertise rather than set his sights too high. Sometimes this may mean he has to modify some of his existing ideas, particularly when he is looking for a position or to move on, but he will fare better by being flexible in his outlook and taking advantage of whatever opportunities do arise, even if they are slightly different from those he would like. The Earth Goat should also bear in mind that once he has a foothold in a company or organization there could be the possibility of later transferring to something more in line with his original intentions, or of using the position as a means of getting additional experience. The Earth Goat should also take advantage of any training or study opportunities that arise. He does have a grand future ahead of him and over the year he will do much to prepare for the more progressive times that lie ahead. He will, though, find this an expensive year, particularly with what promises to be an active social life and some of the obligations he may have taken on. In view of this, he should watch his level of spending carefully and avoid stretching his resources too far. He should also be wary of taking undue risks and while he may be keen to improve his situation, he should be suspicious about any dubious or risky money-making schemes he may hear about. All may not be as straightforward as it might appear and throughout the year the Earth Goat needs to remain prudent and cautious. More positively, however, it is possible that he may be able to turn a hobby or interest into an additional source of income. Any Earth Goat who has practical or creative skills would find it worthwhile considering freelance possibilities. Some enterprising thinking could be rewarded and in some cases develop in an encouraging manner over the next few years. In view of the activity of the year, particularly in his personal and social life, there could be the temptation for the Earth Goat to 'burn the candle at both ends' and not pay as much attention to his welfare as he should. In the year 2000 he does need to look after himself, particularly if he wishes to be at peak form, and this includes having a balanced and healthy diet, exercising well and giving his body the chance to catch up after a succession of late nights or bouts of considerable activity. He will feel much better for doing so! Overall though, this will be a satisfying year for the Earth Goat with his personal life bringing especial pleasure. While he will need to proceed carefully in financial matters and make the most of the opportunities available in his professional life, what he learns and achieves now will stand him in excellent stead for the future.

FAMOUS GOATS

Pamela Anderson, Isaac Asimov, W. H. Auden, Jane Austen, Anne Bancroft, George Benson, Cilla Black, Ian Botham, Elkie Brooks, George Burns, Lord Byron, Leslie Caron, John le Carré, Coco Chanel, Mary Higgins Clark, Nat 'King' Cole, Harry Connick Jr, Angus Deayton, Catherine Deneuve, John Denver, Charles Dickens, Angie Dickinson, Ken Dodd, Sir Arthur Conan Doyle, Daphne Du Maurier, Umberto Eco, Douglas Fairbanks, Dame Margot Fonteyn, Anna Ford, Noel Gallagher, Paul Gascoigne, Bill Gates, Mel Gibson, Paul Michael Glaser, Whoopi Goldberg, Mikhail Gorbachev, John Grisham, George Harrison, Sir Edmund Hillary, John Humphrys, Billy Idol, Julio Iglesias, Mick Jagger, Ben Kingsley, David Kossoff, Doris Lessing, Peter Lilley, Franz Liszt, John Major, Alun Michael, Michelangelo, Joni Mitchell, Rupert Murdoch, Mussolini, Randy Newman, Robert de Niro, Edna O'Brien, Des O'Connor, Sinead O'Connor, Lord Olivier, Michael Palin, Eva Peron, Marcel Proust, Keith Richards, William Shatner, Jerry Springer, Freddie Starr, Jacques Tati, Lord Tebbit, Lana Turner, Desmond Tutu, Mark Twain, Rudolph Valentino, Vangelis, Lech Walesa, Barbara Walters, John Wayne, Fay Weldon, Bruce Willis, Debra Winger, Tom Wolfe, Paul Young.

2 FEBRUARY 1908 ⁓ 21 JANUARY 1909   *Earth Monkey*

20 FEBRUARY 1920 ⁓ 7 FEBRUARY 1921   *Metal Monkey*

6 FEBRUARY 1932 ⁓ 25 JANUARY 1933   *Water Monkey*

25 JANUARY 1944 ⁓ 12 FEBRUARY 1945   *Wood Monkey*

12 FEBRUARY 1956 ⁓ 30 JANUARY 1957   *Fire Monkey*

30 JANUARY 1968 ⁓ 16 FEBRUARY 1969   *Earth Monkey*

16 FEBRUARY 1980 ⁓ 4 FEBRUARY 1981   *Metal Monkey*

4 FEBRUARY 1992 ⁓ 22 JANUARY 1993   *Water Monkey*

THE
MONKEY

THE PERSONALITY OF THE MONKEY

> The future belongs to those who believe in the beauty of their dreams.
>
> *Eleanor Roosevelt: a Monkey*

The Monkey is born under the sign of fantasy. He is imaginative, inquisitive and loves to keep an eye on everything that is going on around him. He is never backward in offering advice or trying to sort out the problems of others. He likes to be helpful and his advice is invariably sensible and reliable.

The Monkey is intelligent, well read and always eager to learn. He has an extremely good memory and there are many Monkeys who have made particularly good linguists. The Monkey is also a convincing talker and enjoys taking part in discussions and debates. His friendly, self-assured manner can be very persuasive and he usually has little trouble in winning people round to his way of thinking. It is for this reason that the Monkey often excels in politics and public speaking. He is also particularly adept at PR work, teaching and any job which involves selling.

The Monkey can, however, be crafty, cunning and occasionally dishonest, and he will seize on any opportunity to make a quick gain or outsmart his opponents. He has so much charm and guile that people often don't realize what he is up to until it is too late. But despite his resourceful nature, the Monkey does run the risk of outsmarting even himself. He has so much confidence in his abilities that he rarely listens to advice or is prepared to accept help from anyone. He likes to help others but prefers to rely on his own judgement when dealing with his own affairs.

Another characteristic of the Monkey is that he is extremely good at solving problems and has a happy knack of extricating himself (and others) from the most hopeless of positions. He is the master of self-preservation.

With so many diverse talents the Monkey is able to make considerable sums of money, but he does like to enjoy life and will think nothing of spending his money on some exotic holiday or luxury which he has had his eye on. He can, however, become very envious if someone else has got what he wants.

The Monkey is an original thinker and despite his love of company, he cherishes his independence. He has to have the freedom to act as he wants and any Monkey who feels hemmed in or bound by too many restrictions can soon become unhappy. Likewise, if anything becomes too boring or monotonous, the Monkey soon loses interest and turns his attention to something else. He lacks persistence and this can often hamper his progress. He is also easily distracted, a tendency which all Monkeys should try to overcome. The Monkey should concentrate on one thing at a time and by doing so will almost certainly achieve more in the long run.

The Monkey is a good organizer and, even though he may behave slightly erratically at times, he will invariably have some plan at the back of his mind. On the odd occasion when his plans do not quite work out, he is usually quite happy to shrug his shoulders and put it down to experience. He will rarely make the same mistake twice and throughout his life he will try his hand at many things.

The Monkey likes to impress and is rarely without followers or admirers. There are many who are attracted by his good looks, his sense of humour or simply because he instils so much confidence.

Monkeys usually marry young and for it to be a success their partner must allow them time to pursue their many interests and indulge in their love of travel. The Monkey has to have variety in his life and is especially well suited to those born under the sociable and outgoing signs of the Rat, Dragon, Pig and Goat. The Ox, Rabbit, Snake and Dog will also be enchanted by the Monkey's resourceful and outgoing nature, but he is likely to exasperate the Rooster and Horse, and the Tiger will have little patience for his tricks. A relationship between two Monkeys will work well – they will understand each other and be able to assist each other in their various enterprises.

The female Monkey is intelligent, extremely observant and a shrewd judge of character. Her opinions are often highly valued, and, having such a persuasive nature, she invariably gets her own way. She has many interests and involves herself in a wide variety of activities. She pays great attention to her appearance, is an elegant dresser and likes to take particular care over her hair. She can also be a caring and doting parent and will have many good and loyal friends.

Provided the Monkey can curb his desire to take part in all that is going on around him and can concentrate on one thing at a time, he can usually achieve what he wants in life. Should he suffer any disappointments, he is bound to bounce back. The Monkey is a survivor and his life is usually both colourful and very eventful.

THE FIVE DIFFERENT TYPES
OF MONKEY

In addition to the 12 signs of the Chinese zodiac, there are five elements and these have a strengthening or moderating influence on the sign. The effects of the five elements on the Monkey are described below, together with the years in which the elements were exercising their influence. Therefore all Monkeys born in 1920 and 1980 are Metal Monkeys, those born in 1932 and 1992 are Water Monkeys, and so on.

Metal Monkey: 1920, 1980
The Metal Monkey is very strong-willed. He sets about everything he does with a dogged determination and often prefers to work independently rather than with others. He is ambitious, wise and confident, and is certainly not afraid of hard work. He is very astute in financial matters and usually chooses his investments well. Despite his somewhat independent nature, the Metal Monkey enjoys attending parties and social occasions and is particularly warm and caring towards his loved ones.

Water Monkey: 1932, 1992
The Water Monkey is versatile, determined and perceptive. He has more discipline than some of the other Monkeys and is prepared to work towards a certain goal rather than be distracted by something else. He is not always open about his true intentions and when questioned can be

particularly evasive. He can be sensitive to criticism but also very persuasive and usually has little trouble in getting others to fall in with his plans. He has a very good understanding of human nature and relates well to others.

Wood Monkey: 1944

This Monkey is efficient, methodical and extremely conscientious. He is also highly imaginative and is always trying to capitalize on new ideas or learn new skills. Occasionally his enthusiasm can get the better of him and he can get very agitated when things do not quite work out as he had hoped. He does, however, have a very adventurous streak and is not afraid of taking risks. He also loves travel. He is usually held in great esteem by his friends and colleagues.

Fire Monkey: 1956

The Fire Monkey is intelligent, full of vitality and has no trouble in commanding the respect of others. He is imaginative and has wide interests, although sometimes these can distract him from more useful and profitable work. He is very competitive and always likes to be involved in everything that is going on. He can be stubborn if he does not get his own way and he sometimes tries to indoctrinate those who are less strong-willed than himself. The Fire Monkey is a lively character, popular with the opposite sex and extremely loyal to his partner.

Earth Monkey: 1908, 1968

The Earth Monkey tends to be studious and well read, and can become quite distinguished in his chosen line of work. He is less outgoing than some of the other types of Monkey and prefers quieter and more solid pursuits. He has high principles, a very caring nature and can be most generous to those less fortunate than himself. He is usually successful in handling financial matters and can become very wealthy in old age. He has a calming influence on those around him and is respected and well liked by those he meets. He is, however, especially careful about whom he lets into his confidence.

PROSPECTS FOR THE MONKEY IN THE YEAR 2000

The Chinese New Year starts on 5 February 2000. Until then, the old year, the Year of the Rabbit, is still making its presence felt.

The Year of the Rabbit (16 February 1999 to 4 February 2000) will have been a generally positive one for the Monkey with the closing months being a busy and enjoyable time. However, to make the most of what remains of it, the Monkey should try to plan his activities as well as prioritize them. Otherwise he could find the year ends in a rush, with him trying to fit in a lot all at once.

The Monkey's personal life will be particularly busy and in addition to the usual household activities, he will find himself arranging and attending a variety of events and get-togethers, especially with the approach of Christmas and the celebrations for the new millennium, both of which he will thoroughly enjoy. In addition to having some splendid times with family and friends, he will also get to meet others who he has not seen for a considerable time and such a reunion will prove a truly meaningful occasion. Indeed, from late November 1999 to early January the Monkey's domestic and social life will be a whirl of activity, which is why it would be helpful for him to give consideration to all he wants to do beforehand. He would also find it useful to make a concerted effort to deal with any outstanding matters he might have as well as start seasonal preparations and purchases early. This includes writing letters and cards. The more the Monkey can do before the festivities really begin, the less pressure he will be under and the freer he will be to enjoy all that takes place.

As far as his work is concerned, the Monkey will have greatly impressed during the Rabbit year and now, with his extra experience and enhanced reputation, he would do well to give some thought to how he would like his career to progress. Ideas formulated towards the end of the Rabbit year could develop significantly in the year 2000. There will be also opportunities for those Monkeys seeking work at this time and many could be successful in gaining a position, even though for some this might be on a temporary basis. However, what they are given could still offer an interesting personal challenge and be a chance to gain useful experience.

Although the Rabbit year is a generally positive time for financial matters, the end of the year will be expensive, so if the Monkey is able to save or budget in advance, he will find this helpful. Overall, however, the Monkey will enjoy himself very much in the closing months of the Rabbit year.

The Year of the Dragon starts on 5 February and will be a rewarding one for the Monkey. Inspired by the start of the new millennium and feeling it is time to make more of himself and his abilities, he will look on the year as a time for positive change; indeed, his determination will produce some excellent results.

In his work the Monkey will be given the chance to build on his recent achievements and throughout the year he should look for openings and opportunities to pursue. If none appear, he should seize the initiative and see what he can create for himself. He might try direct approaches to companies he would like to work for, setting out his experience and how he feels he could make a positive contribution, or, alternatively, seek the advice of professional bodies or those currently in the type of position he would like. By taking positive steps, he will obtain useful feedback, some of which, when acted upon, could lead to interesting developments.

The Monkey is certainly blessed with a resourceful nature and this, combined with his determination to make headway, will impress others and be rewarded over the year. Furthermore, the aspects will support and encourage him in his endeavours. While progress can be made at any time during the year, the months from January (the last month of the Rabbit year) to April will prove especially promising.

In carrying out his duties the Monkey should remain alert for pending developments and show a willingness to take on new roles or additional responsibilities. In some cases he could find these will develop in such a way that they lead to a better position or give him experience which he will later be able to profit from. Also with an eye to his future, if there is a skill that he feels would be useful he should take steps to obtain it if at all possible. Again, anything that the Monkey can do to improve himself and develop his capabilities will not only be to his advantage but will also bring him much personal satisfaction.

For those Monkeys seeking work or wanting to switch careers, the Dragon year will see some positive developments. Again, an enterprising approach will be rewarded and by following up all possibilities the Monkey could find some openings for which he is ideally suited, with the first quarter of the year particularly well aspected. He should also promote any ideas that he has, as these too could develop in a pleasing manner. Generally, this is a year which holds much promise for the Monkey, but to make the most of the aspects that prevail, he does need to act and make the most of his considerable abilities.

The Monkey will enjoy a modest improvement in his financial situation over the year but it would be in his interests to remain conservative in his spending. Without some control over his purse strings he could find that money earned could all too easily be money spent. Also, where large purchases are concerned, especially for his accommodation, the Monkey would do well to investigate the ranges and options available rather than act too hastily. By taking his time and waiting for sales and other favourable buying opportunities, he could save unnecessary outlay as well as obtain something more suitable than if he were to rush his purchase. While the Monkey may feel luck is with him over the year, he should not let this lead him into taking undue risks. If he is to avoid problems, money matters do need to be handled with care and fore-thought.

The Monkey can, however, look forward to an active and pleasing personal life. For the unattached Monkey, romance and new friendships could sometimes arise through a chance encounter or a meeting with a former acquaintance. The prospects for an important and often long-lasting relationship being formed in the year 2000 are certainly promising. Any Monkey who may have experienced some recent sadness or who feels alone should look to the start of the new millennium as the beginning of a new phase in his life and should make a concerted effort to go out more and meet others. Positive action on his part can do much to bring about a significant upturn in his fortunes.

Generally, the Monkey's relations with others will go well in the year 2000, and he will not only be heartened by the interest and support he receives, but will also take much satisfaction in helping those around him and in playing a full part in joint activities and projects. His family life, although busy, will be rewarding, while on a social level he can look forward to spending many agree-able occasions in the company of friends, making new acquaintances and attending a variety of often interesting social events.

The Monkey will also get much satisfaction from the time he spends on his own hobbies and interests. He could find it useful to contact fellow enthusiasts, either through a club, society, or, if he is able, over the Internet. This will not only increase his knowledge and enthusiasm, but will also lead to some useful contacts. Again, the Dragon year will do much to support the Monkey in his activities and efforts to further himself.

For many Monkeys travel may not figure too prominently over the year, but to compensate for this, the Monkey will get much enjoyment from outings and visiting places of local interest. Some trips arranged as a treat and at short notice could prove especially pleasurable. For those Monkeys who are keen gardeners, sports enthusiasts or walkers, the year will certainly hold some satisfying times.

In most respects this will be a positive year for the Monkey and by pursuing his aims and promoting himself, he will achieve a considerable amount and do much to improve upon his present position. But, as he himself recognizes, the onus to bring this about does rest with him. However, the Monkey is resourceful, skilled and has a winning way with others, and all this will combine to help make this a splendid, progressive and favourable year for him.

As far as the different types of Monkey are concerned, this will be a pleasing year for the *Metal Monkey*. His personal life is especially well aspected, with romance and new friendships bringing considerable happiness. The spring and summer will be particularly favourable for personal matters, with some Metal Monkeys getting engaged or married at this time. Any Metal Monkey who may be feeling lonely over the year, perhaps because of having to move to a new area, would really find it worth his while to make the effort to go out, join in with group activities and meet others. This is a splendid year for social matters and the Metal Monkey will not only enjoy himself but will also establish some new and important friendships. He can also look forward to receiving valuable support from his family over the year, especially when facing periods of change and uncertainty. Although he may feel sure in his own mind about what to do or where his future may lie, he should listen carefully to the views of those more senior to him, who speak with his interests so much at heart. While he will undoubtedly benefit from the support and advice he receives, he can also reciprocate by assisting someone older than himself who also needs help or guidance. The time he is able to give, together with his kind and considerate manner, will be greatly appreciated. With what promises to be an active personal life, the Metal Monkey will need to exercise care when dealing with finance and watch his level of spending. Wherever possible he should plan for large and forthcoming expenses as well as make adequate provision for any obligations that he has to meet. The time he spends managing his finances will certainly be to his advantage and could prevent difficulties arising at a later date. As far as his work is concerned, the year will produce some interesting developments. The Metal Monkey usually has a clear idea of what he wants to do, and while such a sense of purpose will allow him to achieve much over the years, for now he does need to show a certain flexibility. When openings and opportunities arise, particularly those that would help him add to his skills and experience, he should take advantage of them, even though they may not quite fit in with his current aims. In the year 2000 the Metal Monkey will find it is better to benefit from present opportunities rather than wait for openings that might be still some distance in coming. Also, he could find that a position he is offered, even though it may be different from what he wanted, will allow him to discover skills and strengths he did not really appreciate he had, and if developed, these could help him to later success. For those Metal Monkeys in education, this will prove a valuable year. By working consistently and applying themselves to their studies, they can look forward to some pleasing results. Also, with the year so favouring personal development, if there is a subject or qualification that the Metal Monkey feels could be useful to him, he should follow it up. As he will find, what he learns, starts or accomplishes in the year 2000 will often have a significant bearing on his future. In almost all respects this will be a highly favourable year for the Metal Monkey, but with the year containing so much activity, there could be the temptation for him to neglect his own well-being. To avoid this, it really would be in his interests to make sure he has a well-balanced diet and does not become overtired by engaging in countless activities all at the same time. If he wishes to remain on top form and to enjoy the year as much as he can, he must give due consideration to his own needs. This warning apart, this will be a truly positive year for the Metal Monkey. He knows he has it in him to make much of his life and in the Dragon year he will certainly set himself on the track that will lead him to future success.

This will be a satisfying year for the *Water Monkey* with most areas of his life bringing pleasure. With his wide interests and many good friends, the Water Monkey is rarely at a loss for things to do and, as the year starts, he would do well to give some thought to what he does actually want to accomplish over the year. This includes arranging any breaks and holidays that he may wish to take or following up long-standing invitations to visit friends or relations. In addition, if there has been something that he has had in mind for some time he should look at the feasibility of carrying this out and discuss his ideas with others. By being forthcoming he will find those around him, who think so highly of him, will be keen to assist. Although some of the Water Monkey's ideas will concern his own personal interests, others will involve his home and for many this will include mounting an 'efficiency drive' and sorting out paperwork and belongings and generally tidying up certain areas. Although this may take the Water Monkey longer than he envisaged, he will be pleased with how organized his home has become. In addition many Water Monkeys will also carry out some practical projects, particularly in redesigning and redecorating certain rooms. While again this may be a lengthy and disruptive process, what the Water Monkey achieves will bring both him and those around him much pleasure. In view of all the attention he will give to his home, the Water Monkey may also take the opportunity to buy new furnishings and equipment, but in this he would do well to take his time, check the ranges on offer and ensure that any equipment he buys will meet his present and likely future requirements. Major purchases should not be rushed. The Water Monkey should also check the terms and obligations of any new agreement that he enters into.

Although he is usually astute in these matters, this is not a year for complacency. In addition to the satisfaction household projects will bring, the Water Monkey's domestic life will contain many pleasing occasions. He will delight in the progress of those very dear to him and will have several good reasons for a celebration over the year. His social life will also go well and he can look forward to attending a range of interesting events as well as spending many agreeable hours with friends both old and new. Any Water Monkey who may have experienced some recent sadness or be feeling alone really should make the effort to go to places where he can meet others. By making the effort he can establish what can become some very good friendships. Those Water Monkeys born in 1992 will have an interesting year and will take particular delight in following up a new interest which captures their imagination. However, while the young Water Monkey will make useful progress with his schoolwork, there could be some areas in which he does not feel so confident and these may give rise to concern. At demanding times the Water Monkey should be encouraged to ask for help, as those around him will do much to reassure and instruct him and build his confidence. Generally, though, this will be a fulfilling year for the Water Monkey and by deciding upon his activities and making an effort to realize some of his aspirations, he will accomplish a great deal as well as enjoy the company and support of those around him. In almost all respects this will be a favourable and positive year.

This will be an important year for the *Wood Monkey* and during the course of it he will take some decisions and carry out plans which will have a major bearing on his future. Some of these may be ones he has had in mind for a while, but he will feel that this is the right time to take action. Many Wood Monkeys who have been considering moving will now decide to go ahead and will actively start to look at locations and suitable accommodation. Initially this may prove a long-winded process, but, often by chance, they will find something that meets their requirements perfectly and the moving process will then gather a momentum all of its own. Alternatively, many of those who remain where they are will undertake some major projects on their accommodation. Again, while these will take some while to plan and organize, once started, a period of intense and often disruptive work will commence. The end result will, however, bring the Wood Monkey considerable pleasure as well as do much to enhance his home. For those Wood Monkeys who carry out the practical work themselves, though, care is needed when using dangerous tools, moving heavy items or tackling complex tasks. If in doubt, the Wood Monkey should seek help and at all times he should follow the recommended safety procedures. Accommodation-wise, almost all Wood Monkeys will see some important changes taking place and will be pleased with what they accomplish, despite the often considerable disruption. Another area which the Wood Monkey will give much thought to over the year is his own personal interests. Again, there may have been subjects intriguing him recently; during this year he should take the time to satisfy his curiosity. Some of what he takes up now will be different from anything he has done before, but he will enjoy and feel stimulated by the challenge it gives. Indeed, the Wood Monkey, with his inquisitive nature, always enjoys experimenting and adding to his knowledge, and the Dragon year will give him every chance to do this. In addition to the pleasure his interests (especially new ones) will bring, the Wood Monkey will also give some consideration to his own well-being, particularly if he is sedentary for much of the day. Many Wood Monkeys will start to exercise more, perhaps by taking up additional walking, cycling, swimming or some other suitable activity. By taking action, they will start to feel much better in themselves. For those who may not have given their physical state much attention in recent years, it would, though, be strongly advisable for them to seek proper medical guidance first. As far as the Wood Monkey's work is concerned, the year will see some interesting developments. For the Wood Monkey who is seeking work or who is particularly keen to move on from his present situation, there will be some excellent opportunities. Often these will present duties quite different from what the Wood Monkey is used to, but he will enjoy rising to the challenges set him and will acquit himself well. Some Wood Monkeys will, of course, decide to continue in their present role, but even they will not be unmoved by the events of the Dragon year. Changes could occur as the result of personnel moves or the implementation of new procedures, but by adapting and showing a willingness to be flexible, the Wood Monkey can benefit from what takes place, often by being given greater responsibilities, being rewarded for past efforts or being offered other opportunities. Also, if he has any ideas which he wishes to advance, he should do so. The year does favour enterprise and many Wood Monkeys will find their ideas and proposals well received, with some developing in a pleasing manner. The Wood Monkey will also be encouraged by the support that he receives from his family and friends in the year 2000. However, with some of the more ambitious ventures he is involved in, he does need to remain mindful of all the advice he receives as well as ask for assistance at busy times. In addition, he should resist the temptation of becoming so preoccupied in his work and own activities that they start to encroach on his domestic and social life. Over the year this can provide him with real pleasure, but, as with all things, to enjoy and benefit from it does requires input from the Wood Monkey himself. Wood Monkeys, heed this warning! Overall, however, this will be a year of positive change and while some parts will see moments of intense activity and upheaval, the Wood Monkey will be pleased with how his plans work out. In much of what he does, luck and the supporting aspects will serve him well.

This will be a year for the *Fire Monkey* to enjoy, one which will give him the opportunity to try out ideas, realize ambitions and show others his considerable potential. The exciting trends of the year will become apparent almost as soon as the Dragon year starts, making this an important, constructive and fulfilling time. In his work, the Fire Monkey will be able to make some important gains and build on his experience. As he will find, change is in the air and many Fire Monkeys will find themselves ideally placed to benefit from the opportunities that arise. Indeed, the Fire Monkey has always been quick to spot the potential of developing situations and this ability will serve him well in his work over the year. When new situations arise, whether caused by someone leaving, new plans being introduced or changes under consideration, the Fire Monkey should think of ways in which he could turn the situation to his advantage. By showing a willingness to take on new responsibilities and making constructive suggestions, he will find his initiative and enterprise will be recognized and as a result many Fire Monkeys will be offered more rewarding duties and will considerably enhance their position. Those seeking work should also remain persistent and many will succeed in obtaining a position which has excellent potential. The first quarter of the year will be especially positive for work matters. This is also a favourable year for the Fire Monkey to promote any ideas that he may have been considering recently. While some may fall on stony ground, others could take off in a pleasing manner. Again, it is the Fire Monkey's willingness to take action that will produce so many of the results he will enjoy over the year. However, while work-wise this will be a positive year, the Fire Monkey should not let his good fortune and any financial improvement he enjoys tempt him into risky or highly speculative moves. To push his luck too far could lead to him regretting his actions. If tempted by any venture or investment, he would do well to investigate it thoroughly before proceeding. This is a year for financial caution and also a certain restraint as far as his general level of spending is concerned. The Fire Monkey can, however, look forward to an active and rewarding domestic life over the year. He will delight in the success and progress enjoyed by a younger relation and will offer advice, encouragement and general assistance to various family members. As always, others will value his positive contributions and the Fire Monkey himself will be heartened by the interest shown towards his own activities. He will, though, find some parts of the year particularly busy, especially around the months of May and September, and at this, or indeed any other active time, he would find it helpful to restrict his activities and concentrate on his priorities. This includes not starting or becoming involved in too many practical undertakings at any one time. Occasionally the Fire Monkey's willing spirit does get the better of him and at busy times it would be in his interests to limit his commitments, especially when he already has much to do. If not, he could find the free time he so values all but gone. In addition to the fulfilment the Fire Monkey's domestic life will bring, his social life too is well aspected and he can look forward to having some agreeable times with his friends as well as widening his social circle. On a personal level the Fire Monkey will be in fine form and for those unattached or seeking friends some new and significant friendships could develop during the course of the year. As the Fire Monkey will find in the year 2000, once he has decided upon something, whether it concerns his career, social life or any of his other ideas, he will, by his own efforts, achieve some interesting and worthwhile results. In almost all respects this will be a positive and progressive year.

This will be a satisfying year for the *Earth Monkey* and one which will allow him to usefully build on his experience as well as develop some of his ideas. The Earth Monkey will feel inspired by the start of the new millennium and will find himself setting about his activities with renewed vigour, more determined than ever to make the most of himself and the year. In his work constructive developments are indicated. Although the Earth Monkey will already have achieved a great deal, many will still feel they are not using their abilities to the fullest and over the year they will make every effort to improve on their present position. Some will seek progression within their present organization while others will decide to change to a different type of job, relishing the challenge this will give. In either case, opportunities will arise that would be worth the Earth Monkey pursuing, especially in the early months of the year and again in September and October. In addition to following up any vacancies that interest him, the Earth Monkey should show a willingness to take on new responsibilities and undertake further training as well as speak to those able to advise on career opportunities. By taking the initiative he will not only be given useful advice but will also be alerted to possibilities he may not have considered. Others will also often put in a good word for him and this again will be to his advantage. Those Earth Monkeys seeking work should remain similarly active in their quest. Not only should they follow up any openings they see but they should also look at different ways in which they can use their skills and widen the scope of positions they try for. Their determined attitude will be rewarded and once given their chance they will quickly impress. This in turn will lead to further progress, often within a comparatively short space of time. In addition to what he achieves in his work, the Earth Monkey should advance any ideas he has. As a creative thinker he often comes up with enterprising notions, and again by following some of these through he could find them developing in an encouraging manner. This will also be a favourable year for the Earth Monkey's personal life, with his family and friends providing valuable support and encouragement. However, his domestic life will be busy, with many calls upon his time together with all the usual chores and household projects. To avoid putting himself under too much pressure, the Earth Monkey should resist the temptation to become involved in too many projects at once and will find it better to concentrate on one or just a few – and get them finished – rather than spread his energies too widely. Also if, in view of all his other activities, he commits himself to too much, he could find that some of the time he has set aside for his hobbies, interests and other recreational pursuits will disappear. In the year 2000 the Earth Monkey should aim to strike a balance between all of his activities. While travel opportunities may be limited, he should still aim to take a proper break or holiday over the year and will find the change of scene and rest this gives both beneficial and enjoyable. Any Earth Monkey who may have had some sadness or misfortune to bear recently should look at the start of the new millennium as a time to focus on the present and future rather than dwell too much on what has gone before. By deciding to seek an upturn in their situation, whether through making new friends, a new romance, a change of residence or any other new project, these Earth Monkeys will, by their own effort and desire, bring about some positive change. In almost all respects, this is a year of opportunity for the Earth Monkey and with his personable manner and many talents, he is well placed to benefit from the many opportunities available.

FAMOUS MONKEYS

Gillian Anderson, Francesca Annis, Michael Aspel, Mike Atherton, J. M. Barrie, David Bellamy, Jacqueline Bisset, Victor Borge, Julius Caesar, Johnny Cash, Jacques Chirac, Chelsea Clinton, Joe Cocker, Colette, John Constable, Alistair Cooke, David Copperfield, Joan Crawford, Leonardo da Vinci, Timothy Dalton, Bette Davis, Phil de Glanville, Danny De Vito, Bo Derek, Jonathan Dimbleby, Celine Dion, Jason Donovan, Michael Douglas, Mia Farrow, Carrie Fisher, F. Scott Fitzgerald, Ian Fleming, Dick Francis, Fiona Fullerton, Paul Gauguin, Mika Häkkinnen, Jerry Hall, Tom Hanks, Stephen Hendry, Martina Hingis, Harry Houdini, P. D. James, Pope John Paul II, Lyndon B. Johnson, Buster Keaton, Edward Kennedy, Nigel Kennedy, Don King, Gladys Knight, Patti LaBelle, Leo McKern, Walter Matthau, Kylie Minogue, Jack Nicklaus, Jana Novotna, Peter O'Toole, Anthony Perkins, Robert Powell, Lisa Marie Presley, Debbie Reynolds, Tim Rice, Little Richard, Mickey Rooney, Diana Ross, Boz Scaggs, Gerhard Schröder, Michael Schumacher, Tom Selleck, Omar Sharif, Wilbur Smith, Rod Stewart, Jacques Tati, Elizabeth Taylor, Dame Kiri Te Kanawa, David Trimble, Harry Truman, the Duchess of Windsor.

22 JANUARY 1909 ～ 9 FEBRUARY 1910   *Earth Rooster*

8 FEBRUARY 1921 ～ 27 JANUARY 1922   *Metal Rooster*

26 JANUARY 1933 ～ 13 FEBRUARY 1934   *Water Rooster*

13 FEBRUARY 1945 ～ 1 FEBRUARY 1946   *Wood Rooster*

31 JANUARY 1957 ～ 17 FEBRUARY 1958   *Fire Rooster*

17 FEBRUARY 1969 ～ 5 FEBRUARY 1970   *Earth Rooster*

5 FEBRUARY 1981 ～ 24 JANUARY 1982   *Metal Rooster*

23 JANUARY 1993 ～ 9 FEBRUARY 1994   *Water Rooster*

THE
ROOSTER

THE PERSONALITY OF
THE ROOSTER

A wise man will make more opportunities than he finds.

Francis Bacon: a Rooster

The Rooster is born under the sign of candour. He has a flamboyant and colourful personality and is meticulous in all that he does. He is an excellent organizer and wherever possible likes to plan his various activities well in advance.

The Rooster is highly intelligent and usually very well read. He has a good sense of humour and is an effective and persuasive speaker. He loves discussion and enjoys taking part in any sort of debate. He has no hesitation in speaking his mind and is forthright in his views. He does, however, lack tact and can easily damage his reputation or cause offence by some thoughtless remark or action. The Rooster also has a very volatile nature and he should always try to avoid acting on the spur of the moment.

The Rooster is usually very dignified in his manner and conducts himself with an air of confidence and authority. He is adept at handling financial matters and, as with most things, he organizes his financial affairs with considerable skill. He chooses his investments well and is capable of achieving great wealth. Most Roosters save or use their money wisely, but there are a few who are the reverse and are notorious spendthrifts. Fortunately, the Rooster has great earning capacity and is rarely without sufficient funds to tide himself over.

Another characteristic of the Rooster is that he invariably carries a notebook or scraps of paper around with him. He is constantly writing himself reminders or noting down important facts lest he forgets – the Rooster cannot abide inefficiency and conducts all his activities in an orderly, precise and methodical manner.

The Rooster is usually very ambitious, but can be unrealistic in some of what he hopes to achieve. He occasionally lets his imagination run away with him and while he does not like any interference from others, it would be in his own interests if he were to listen to their views a little more often. He also does not like criticism and if he feels anybody is doubting his judgement or prying too closely into his affairs, he is certain to let his feelings be known. He can also be rather self-centred and stubborn over relatively trivial matters, but to compensate for this he is reliable, honest and trustworthy, and this is very much appreciated by all who come into contact with him.

Roosters born between the hours of five and seven, both at dawn and sundown, tend to be the most extrovert of their sign, but all Roosters like to lead an active social life and enjoy attending parties and big functions. The Rooster usually has a wide circle of friends and is able to build up influential contacts with remarkable ease. He often belongs to several clubs and societies and involves himself in a variety of different activities. He is particularly interested in the environment, humanitarian affairs and anything affecting the welfare of others. The Rooster has a very caring nature and will do much to help those less fortunate than himself.

He also gets much pleasure from gardening and, while he may not always spend as much time in the garden as he would like, his garden is invariably well kept and extremely productive.

The Rooster is generally very distinguished in his appearance and if his job permits, he will wear an official uniform with great pride and dignity. He is not averse to publicity and takes great delight in being the centre of attention. He often does well at PR work or any job which brings him into contact with the media. He also makes a very good teacher.

The female Rooster leads a varied and interesting life. She involves herself in many different activities and there are some who wonder how she can achieve so much. She often holds very strong views and, like her male counter-part, has no hesitation in speaking her mind or telling others how she thinks things should be done. She is supremely efficient and well organized and her home is usually very neat and tidy. She has good taste in clothes and usually wears smart but very practical outfits.

The Rooster usually has a large family and as a parent takes a particularly active interest in the education of his children. He is very loyal to his partner and will find that he is especially well suited to those born under the signs of the Snake, Horse, Ox and Dragon. Provided they do not interfere too much in the Rooster's various activities, the Rat, Tiger, Goat and Pig can also establish a good relationship with him, but two Roosters together are likely to squabble and irritate each other. The rather sensitive Rabbit will find the Rooster a bit too blunt for his liking, and the Rooster will quickly become exasperated by the ever-inquisitive and artful Monkey. He will also find it difficult to get on with the anxious Dog.

If the Rooster can overcome his volatile nature and exercise more tact, he will go far in life. He is capable and talented and will invariably make a lasting – and usually favourable – impression almost everywhere he goes.

THE FIVE DIFFERENT TYPES OF ROOSTER

In addition to the 12 signs of the Chinese zodiac, there are five elements and these have a strengthening or moderating influence on the sign. The effects of the five elements on the Rooster are described below, together with the years in which the elements were exercising their influence. Therefore all Roosters born in 1921 and 1981 are Metal Roosters, those born in 1933 and 1993 are Water Roosters, and so on.

Metal Rooster: 1921, 1981

The Metal Rooster is a hard and conscientious worker. He knows exactly what he wants in life and sets about everything he does in a positive and determined manner. He can at times appear abrasive and he would almost certainly do better if he were more willing to reach a compromise with others rather than hold so rigidly to his firmly held beliefs. He is very articulate and most astute when dealing with financial matters. He is loyal to his friends and often devotes much energy to working for the common good.

Water Rooster: 1933, 1993

This Rooster has a very persuasive manner and can easily gain the co-operation of others. He is intelligent, well read and gets much enjoyment from taking part in discussions and debates. He has a seemingly inexhaustible amount of energy and is prepared to work long hours in order to secure what he wants. He can, however, waste much valuable time worrying over minor and inconsequential details. He is approachable, has a good sense of humour and is highly regarded by others.

Wood Rooster: 1945

The Wood Rooster is honest, reliable and often sets himself high standards. He is ambitious, but also more prepared to work in a team than some of the other types of Rooster. He usually succeeds in life, but does have a tendency to get caught up in bureaucratic matters or attempt too many things all at the same time. He has wide interests, likes to travel and is very considerate and caring towards his family and friends.

Fire Rooster: 1957

This Rooster is extremely strong-willed. He has many leadership qualities, is an excellent organizer and is most efficient in his work. Through sheer force of character he often secures his objectives, but he does have a tendency to be very forthright and not always consider the feelings of others. If the Fire Rooster can learn to be more tactful he can often succeed beyond his wildest dreams.

Earth Rooster: 1909, 1969

This Rooster has a deep and penetrating mind. He is extremely efficient, very perceptive and is particularly astute in business and financial matters. He is also persistent and once he has set himself an objective, he will rarely allow himself to be deflected from achieving his aim. The Earth Rooster works hard and is held in great esteem by his friends and colleagues. He usually enjoys the arts and takes a keen interest in the activities of the various members of his family.

PROSPECTS FOR THE ROOSTER IN THE YEAR 2000

The Chinese New Year starts on 5 February 2000. Until then, the old year, the Year of the Rabbit, is still making its presence felt.

The Year of the Rabbit (16 February 1999 to 4 February 2000) will have been a variable one for the Rooster. While not everything will have gone as well as he would have liked, there will still have been aspects of the year which will have brought him real pleasure. His prospects will noticeably improve during the last quarter of the Rabbit year, with this improvement carrying on into the next, more favourable Chinese year.

As far as his personal life is concerned, this will be an active time for the Rooster and he will find himself in great demand. As well as socializing a great deal he will also enjoy helping to arrange some events, particularly with the approach of Christmas and the celebrations for the new millennium. His flair for organizing, attention to detail and convivial manner will be much appreciated, with the end of the year bringing him considerable pleasure and satisfaction.

However, the last quarter of the Rabbit year will be an expensive time and the Rooster would do well to make some provision for the outlay he will be making. While some Roosters can be meticulous in managing their financial affairs, others can be notorious spendthrifts and without some control over their purse strings these Roosters could find their resources considerably depleted come the year 2000. In the Rabbit year matters of finance can prove problematical and all Roosters need to exercise care in this area.

Most Roosters will have been able to make steady progress in their work, however, although the best results will have come – and will continue to come – from concentrating on areas which draw on the Rooster's experience and expertise rather than from trying anything too diverse, new or ambitious. The Rooster should also look to the Rabbit year as a time to add to his skills and if in the remaining months he has the opportunity to undergo any training, he should seize the chance. What he learns or accomplishes at this time will serve him well in the forthcoming year.

The Year of the Dragon starts on 5 February and is one in which the Rooster will enjoy considerable success. Although over recent years he has taken pride in some of his accomplishments, he will also feel partly unfulfilled. He knows he is capable of a great deal and there will have been occasions when he will have felt he has not made the most of his talents or that his progress could be greater. Accordingly in the first year of the new millennium he will set about his activities with renewed resolve, focusing on his goals and planning his activities with consummate skill. As a result of his determined efforts, this will be a year he will enjoy and one in which he will prosper.

To make the most of the year the Rooster should, if he has not already done so, map out what it is he hopes to accomplish. His goals may involve his work or his domestic and social life, but whatever he wants to achieve, by giving it some thought in advance he will find the year that much more productive and fulfilling.

Especially well aspected are work matters and the Rooster should aim to build on his skills and seek out opportunities that would help him to make the progress he desires. By going after his goals and drawing on his strengths, he will make impressive headway.

Over the year the Rooster will have chances to take on greater and more fulfilling responsibilities, switch to a completely different job or obtain promotion. However, to benefit from the favourable aspects, he needs to remain alert for openings as well as be prepared to take the initiative. The Rooster is renowned for being a doer and in the year 2000 he will certainly do, in style and with considerable success.

Those Roosters seeking work will also fare well and should not only pursue any vacancies that interest them but also think of different ways in which they can develop their experience. With some enterprising thinking they could come up with possibilities that would be worth exploring and which, once followed, could yield some interesting openings and even set them off on a new career. As so many Roosters will find, the Dragon year will offer the opportunities they have long been seeking, opportunities that will inspire them and which will hold interesting prospects.

Over the year the Rooster should also promote any ideas he has and could find that some of these will develop in an encouraging manner. The Dragon year is one of enterprise and for those who are prepared to be forward in expressing their ideas and making constructive suggestions, a favourable response could await.

The Rooster can look forward to a noticeable improvement in his finances during the year, either through an increase in salary, as a gift or from some other source. However, this improvement will not show until the second half of the year and for the first few months of 2000 the Rooster will need to be restrained in his spending and budget accordingly – especially as he may also still be facing large expenses from the Rabbit year! When his financial situation does improve, he should aim to manage his money carefully, setting some of it aside for specific purposes. These could be home improvements, equipment, transport or holidays as well as savings, but whatever his plans, the Rooster will find that with forethought he will be putting his money to more effective use.

The Rooster's personal life will bring him much pleasure over the year and he can look forward to some enjoyable and meaningful times with both family and friends. However, his domestic life will be a fairly busy one, with those close to him being involved in a range of different activities. As always, the Rooster will show a caring interest in what they do and his views, advice and help will often be sought and appreciated. He will also busy himself with various household projects, some of which he may have had in mind for some time. Although some of these may prove more complex than anticipated, the Rooster will be pleased with the end result, especially if it improves the decor and comfort of his accommodation. Many Roosters are keen gardeners and will take great delight in altering and adding new features to their garden over the year. Once again, the Rooster's desire to set his ideas in motion will lead to some heartening results.

The Rooster can also look forward to many congenial times with his friends and to attending a variety of interesting social events, with the late summer being an especially active time. For the unattached Rooster or for those seeking new friends, there will be excellent opportunities to meet others and during the year 2000 many Roosters will build up some new and long-standing friendships. Affairs of the heart are superbly aspected, with many unattached Roosters getting engaged or married over the year.

The Rooster's hobbies and interests will also bring him much satisfaction and while he will face many demands on his time, he should ensure that he allows himself enough time to pursue these. Also, if there is an interest he would like to develop further or a new one he is keen to take up, he should aim to do so. His interests really can lead to some fulfilling times as well as provide him with a valuable break from his usual preoccupations.

The Rooster will also enjoy any travelling he undertakes over the year. Again, he would find it helpful to give some thought in advance to where he would like to go. Many

Roosters can look forward to visiting some truly interesting and in some cases awe-inspiring destinations.

As far as the Chinese years are concerned, the Dragon year is one of the best for the Rooster and most areas of his life will see pleasing developments. However to benefit from the auspicious aspects the Rooster does need to decide upon his objectives early on and then work purposefully towards them. Given his abilities and fondness for planning, he will usually be content to do this. The main point that he needs to watch is to avoid overcommitting himself at any one time and becoming so preoccupied with a certain activity that it distracts him from other equally important ones. Neither should he become too impatient for results. He will get results, but not always as quickly as he would like! Overall, there is a tremendous amount in his favour and almost all Roosters will prosper, progress and greatly enjoy themselves over the year.

As far as the different types of Rooster are concerned, this will be a significant year for the *Metal Rooster*. Full of bright ideas and always keen to give of his best, he will look to the Dragon year as a time for progress, opportunity and making more of himself. He will certainly meet with considerable success. However, he should also be realistic in what he attempts and seeks. The Metal Rooster may hold great ambitions but some of these do require experience he does not yet possess and, as he himself knows, there are plenty of years ahead in which to achieve all his aspirations and more. In the Dragon year the Metal Rooster should concentrate on building a base and gaining the experience he needs. There will be particularly positive developments as far as his work is concerned and, whether he is in a job or seeking one, the year will produce some excellent openings for him to pursue. For many Metal Roosters, one opportunity successfully grasped will lead to others. A large number of Metal Roosters will change the nature of what they do at least once over the year, improving their position and taking on more interesting, challenging and often more remunerative duties. Also, with his future in mind, if the Metal Rooster feels there are certain skills or qualifications he needs, this would be an excellent time to see whether he can obtain them. This is also an important year for those Metal Roosters in education. By setting about their studies and revision in a systematic way, they will obtain some impressive results. This will require a certain self-discipline, but the effort and sacrifices made will be well rewarded. Another positive area concerns the Metal Rooster's personal life, with his relations with others bringing much happiness. Many Metal Roosters will form new and important friendships over the year, with some getting engaged or married, such are the auspicious aspects that prevail. The summer will be an especially active time and for those currently unattached, a chance meeting is likely to prove significant. Again, the Dragon year will be responsible for some exciting times in the Metal Rooster's life, many of which will help to shape his future. However, with so much of importance happening, if the Metal Rooster has any concerns, whether personal, professional or financial, he should not hesitate to seek the views of those around him, especially his family. Many times they can do much to assist and advise, and it is important for the Metal Rooster to remember that he does have others he can turn to. As far as financial matters are concerned, many Metal Roosters will have started the year in a rather precarious state and will need to watch their outgoings carefully, particularly in the first few months of the Dragon year. Their financial situation will improve over the year but at all times the Metal Rooster should aim to be prudent and careful, remembering money borrowed or credit received will need to be repaid, sometimes with hefty interest. Fortunately many Metal Roosters are adept in financial matters, but care and watchfulness are needed, especially with the active personal life the Metal Rooster will lead and the accommodation expenses he will face. In addition, the Metal Rooster needs to be vigilant with forms and any important correspondence he receives. If he has doubts or uncertainties, he should check. To take risks or take too long over a reply could result in problems. These warnings apart, this will be a truly splendid year for the Metal Rooster. There will be interesting opportunities for him in his work which will do much to prepare the way for his longer term aspirations, while personally, the Dragon year will bring him much happiness, with love and romance figuring prominently. The first year of the new millennium will prove a memorable one, with many positive and far-reaching benefits.

The *Water Rooster* likes to live life to the full and almost always ensures that he has a range of interesting activities to enjoy. The Dragon year will particularly delight him. He will take considerable pleasure from his interests and hobbies and some Water Roosters will find that plans or projects started in the previous year will now have a successful outcome. In addition to his existing activities it would be worth the Water Rooster considering realizing any other goals he may have. These could include travelling to destinations he has long wanted to see, starting new projects in his home or garden, following up a subject that has been intriguing him or making a special effort to realize one of his longer-term ambitions. He would do well to discuss his plans with others, as he will find that those around him can prove instrumental in helping him secure some of his aims. In order for them to do this, however, the Water Rooster does need to be forth-coming. Generally, the year holds considerable potential for him, but it rests with him to decide upon his objectives and then actively pursue them. The one cautionary note that does need to be sounded is that the Water Rooster should take care if he tackles anything strenuous and should not proceed without the necessary help or prepara-tions. To launch into an energetic task for which he is ill-prepared or to lift heavy weights without assistance could result in strains and other problems, and despite the Water Rooster's enthusiasm, he must remain respectful of his well-being and physical condition. One particularly well-aspected area, however, is travel and the Water Rooster will thoroughly enjoy the journeys he goes on and some of the places he sees. Some Water Roosters will also delight in pursuing a particular theme over the year, perhaps looking at various aspects of local or family history, visiting museums in their region or following up some other common link. This will make some of their outings all the more meaningful. The Water Rooster will also get much satisfaction from passing on some of his experience and knowledge, either by meeting those who share his interests or by writing something down. The Water Rooster is an effective communicator and others will often show great respect for what he has to say. His domestic and social life will provide him with much pleasure over the year and he can look forward to many memorable times with both family and friends. He will particularly enjoy those activities he can share. Generally, throughout the year, the Water Rooster will truly value the support and companionship of others. He will also be proud of the achievements of a younger relation and while he may not wish to appear interfering, if there is any advice he wants to pass on or he feels he can help in any way, he should do so. His interest, care and sincerity will be truly valued. Any Water Rooster who is hoping to build up his social life and make new friends, perhaps because he has recently moved, should take positive steps to meet others. Joining a club or special interest group may help. By taking the initiative, lonely Water Roosters will soon strike up some new friendships and will bring about a noticeable improvement in their social and personal life. Financial matters are also well aspected over the year, with some Water Roosters receiving an appreciable sum, either from a maturing policy or investment or as a gift. While this upturn will be welcome, the Water Rooster should give serious thought to what he should do with any additional sum he receives. Without care he could find himself succumbing to too many immediate temptations rather than putting his money to better purpose. In almost all respects, however, the aspects of the Dragon year will support the Water Rooster well, with his personal life, interests and travel bringing him particular satisfaction.

This will be a satisfying year for the *Wood Rooster* and one which will see positive developments in many areas of his life. His personal interests and work are particularly well aspected and the year will give him the chance to develop ideas and put his skills to good use. Almost as soon as the Dragon year starts, the Wood Rooster will feel more inspired than he has of late and will have added determination to go after his aims and aspirations. As a result, he will accomplish a considerable amount. Some particularly pleasing developments are possible in his work. Whether in work or seeking work, the year will bring the Wood Rooster the opportunity to draw on his experience, to take on new duties and find more fulfilment. Some of the opportunities will arise in a rather unusual manner, perhaps through a tip, recommendation or bright idea, but they will nevertheless hold considerable potential. The Wood Rooster will enjoy rising to the challenge they present and, again feeling more motivated and inspired, will impress others and be given every encouragement. This really is a year in which he can make more of himself and he should seize any chances offered. This also applies to those Wood Roosters who might have opted for early retirement – by following up an idea or setting themselves a new challenge they can make this a rewarding and fulfilling time. This is also a positive year for financial matters, with the Wood Rooster seeing an appreciable upturn in his situation. However, he should not let his good fortune tempt him to spend too readily and when he is contemplating purchases – especially items of home furnishing and equipment – he will find it more satisfying to take his time shopping around than to proceed too hastily. This way he will be able to make some excellent purchases and find items more suitable to his needs. In addition, if the Wood Rooster finds himself with any funds he does not immediately need, he would do well to consider making some savings rather than letting his money 'burn a hole in his pocket'. With good management he can fare well in financial matters and end the year in a much improved situation. He will also enjoy the travelling that he undertakes and all Wood Roosters should aim to take a break or holiday during the year, perhaps visiting a favourite destination or a place they have long wanted to see. If he receives an invitation to visit friends or relations he has not seen for some time, the Wood Rooster should again consider taking this up; such a reunion will lead to some truly enjoyable times. He can also look forward to an active domestic and social life over the year. He will find himself much in demand with others and will spend considerable time advising those around him as well as occupying himself with projects in his home and garden. Admittedly, there will be occasions when he will feel under pressure, but by prioritizing his tasks and asking for assistance at appropriate times, he will be satisfied with what he is able to accomplish. There will be good cause for a family celebration during the year and the Wood Rooster will enjoy helping to arrange it. This will also be an active year for social matters, with many agreeable occasions spent with friends. The Wood Rooster is likely to widen his social circle as well as attend a variety of often interesting social events. The Dragon year is one of the most rewarding years for him and by deciding what he wants and channelling his efforts accordingly, he will enjoy some pleasing results. Good luck and good fortune will accompany him in much of what he does.

This is the year the *Fire Rooster* has been waiting for! It is a year of opportunity and one in which his experience and past endeavours will be recognized and rewarded. For some time the Fire Rooster will have been making steady progress and impressing those around him, but in his view he is still not realizing his full potential or achieving all he would like. However, almost as soon as the Dragon year starts, this will change. Several events around the turn of the year will inspire and motivate the Fire Rooster and strengthen his resolve to make more of himself. His determination, faith in himself and buoyant spirit will propel him forward to new achievements. As soon as the year starts the Fire Rooster should think seriously about what he wants to accomplish, discuss his thoughts with those around him, including those with the necessary experience, and then take positive action to secure his aims. By taking the initiative, following up ideas and investigating any available opportunities, he will make splendid headway and he should leave no stone unturned in his quest for improvement and progress. From January (the last month of the Rabbit year) to mid-April exciting developments could take place in his work, providing him with an excellent chance to display his worth and find greater fulfilment in what he does. It is also a favourable year for the Fire Rooster to promote any ideas he has, particularly any he may have been considering for some time. In many cases he will be considerably encouraged by the response and some of his ideas could develop in a significant manner over the course of the year. The progress that the Fire

Rooster makes will also lead to an improvement in his financial situation, although he will not really benefit from this until later in the year. This upturn will encourage many Fire Roosters to carry out projects on their home or move altogether. Where major decisions involving finance are concerned, however, the Fire Rooster should take his time and consider all the implications and consequences of his plans rather than act too swiftly. Those who decide to move will find that it may take some time before they are able to locate a place that meets their requirements, but their patience will be well rewarded. With his upturn in fortune, the Fire Rooster would do well to consider saving or investing any funds he may not immediately need, as in time a carefully chosen policy or investment could develop into a valuable asset. In view of the activity in other areas of his life, he may find the time that he has for his own hobbies is limited, but it is important he does not neglect these. Not only will they bring him pleasure but they will also help him to unwind and take his mind off his usual concerns. If the Fire Rooster has been thinking of taking one of his interests further, perhaps even setting it on a semi-professional basis, he should aim to extend his skills and, if appropriate, promote what he does. For Fire Roosters with creative and practical interests, the Dragon year could prove significant. As far as his relations with others are concerned, this too will be a favourable year for the Fire Rooster. He will be heartened by the support and encouragement he is given as well as enjoy many happy occasions with his loved ones. There will also be some family news over the year which will truly delight him. This could include the engagement or marriage of a close relation or the birth of a grandchild, but whatever the event, it will certainly help to make the Dragon year all the more memorable. However, while his personal life will bring him much contentment, there will be many demands upon the Fire Rooster's time, together with numerous household matters requiring his attention. In view of this, it is important he seeks assistance if he feels he has too much to cope with or faces a mountain of tasks. Help will be readily forthcoming, but the Fire Rooster must ask for it! He can look forward to a rewarding social life over the year and will enjoy meeting old friends as well as making new ones. The unattached Fire Rooster could even find a chance encounter transforms his life! The Year of the Dragon is a powerful and significant one and will give the Fire Rooster the chances he has long been waiting for. He has the talent, the personality and drive to go far in life, and for the determined Fire Rooster, the year can turn out to be spectacularly successful.

This will be an exciting and fulfilling year for the *Earth Rooster*. His personal life in particular will bring him much happiness and he can look forward to many meaningful times with his loved ones and encouraging those around him. The year will also contain several occasions which will fill him with real pride, especially in the progress of some of those dear to him. In addition, he will find that joint interests will bring much satisfaction to all concerned. Indeed, throughout the year, the Earth Rooster should encourage others to play a full part in household activities and projects as well as share in mutual hobbies and interests. This will help maintain the spirit of closeness he so values and where practical projects are concerned, the pooling of talents and skills will lead to better results. The Earth Rooster will also do much to assist a more senior relation over the year and his efforts will be greatly appreciated. The Earth Rooster may not always be aware of just how much he means to those around him but his importance and the love they have for him will certainly be evident during the year. In addition to a gratifying domestic life, the Earth Rooster will enjoy a pleasing social life. Admittedly, it may not have the pace and activity of some years, and other commitments may lead the Earth Rooster to cut back on his level of socializing, but he can still look forward to some enjoyable occasions with his friends and to attending some interesting social events. There will also be opportunities to make new friends and acquaintances, with one new friendship becoming particularly helpful in the future. The year will also see some positive developments in the Earth Rooster's work. As the year starts, many Earth Roosters will resolve to make a determined effort to improve their position and make more effective use of their experience. In this they will enjoy considerable success. Throughout the year the Earth Rooster should look out for any opportunities which are in line with his long-term aspirations, as well as make enquiries to appropriate companies and organizations. His initiative, experience and persistence will pay off and almost all Earth Roosters will be able to improve on their present position over the year as well as prepare the way for greater successes in the future. This also applies to those Earth Roosters who are considering switching careers or are currently seeking work. The Dragon year offers considerable promise and is a time when the Earth Rooster should commit himself to a course of positive action to get what he wants. He would also do well to take advantage of any courses or training he is offered, and if there is a subject or skill that he feels could be useful, he should follow it up. He may extend his computer knowledge, take up a language, improve his business or office skills, or devote time to something specific to his line of work, but whatever the Earth Rooster learns at this time will not only prove useful but will also be personally satisfying. As far as financial matters are concerned, however, this will be a mixed year. Many Earth Roosters will start it facing some large bills and for the first few months will need to budget carefully and be restrained in their outgoings. Their situation will improve as the year progresses, but again there could be further large expenses to meet, especially connected with home equipment or furnishings, transport and general accommodation costs. In view of this, the Earth Rooster should continue to watch what he spends and could find it helpful to maintain a set of accounts and so keep abreast of his situation. With careful financial management, he should be able to avoid problems and indeed enjoy the improvement in income he will receive, but this is a year when vigilance will repay. Overall, this will be a positive and progressive year for the Earth Rooster and by making the most of its opportunities he will make significant headway. In addition, his personal life will bring him much happiness.

FAMOUS ROOSTERS

Adamski, Kate Adie, Francis Bacon, Dame Janet Baker, Severiano Ballesteros, Dennis Bergkamp, Enid Blyton, Sir Dirk Bogarde, Barbara Taylor Bradford, Richard Briers, Michael Caine, Jasper Carrott, Enrico Caruso, Christopher Cazenove, Jean Chrétien, Eric Clapton, Joan Collins, Rita Coolidge, Daniel Day Lewis, Sacha Distel, the Duke of Edinburgh, Ernie Els, Gloria Estefan, Nick Faldo, Mohamed al Fayed, Bryan Ferry, Errol Flynn, Benjamin Franklin, Dawn French, Stephen Fry, Paul Gallico, David Gower, Steffi Graf, Melanie Griffith, Richard Harris, Deborah Harry, Goldie Hawn, Katherine Hepburn, Michael Heseltine, Glenn Hoddle, Quincy Jones, Diane Keaton, Dean Koontz, Bernhard Langer, D. H. Lawrence, Martyn Lewis, David Livingstone, Ken Livingstone, Jayne Mansfield, Steve Martin, James Mason, W. Somerset Maugham, Paul Merton, Bette Midler, Van Morrison, Willie Nelson, Paul Nicholas, Barry Norman, Kim Novak, Yoko Ono, Dolly Parton, Michelle Pfeiffer, Priscilla Presley, Mary Quant, Nancy Reagan, Joan Rivers, Bobby Robson, Paul Scofield, Jenny Seagrove, Sir Harry Secombe, George Segal, Carly Simon, Britney Spears, Johann Strauss, Sir Peter Ustinov, Richard Wagner, Neil Young.

10 FEBRUARY 1910 ～ 29 JANUARY 1911   *Metal Dog*

28 JANUARY 1922 ～ 15 FEBRUARY 1923   *Water Dog*

14 FEBRUARY 1934 ～ 3 FEBRUARY 1935   *Wood Dog*

2 FEBRUARY 1946 ～ 21 JANUARY 1947   *Fire Dog*

18 FEBRUARY 1958 ～ 7 FEBRUARY 1959   *Earth Dog*

6 FEBRUARY 1970 ～ 26 JANUARY 1971   *Metal Dog*

25 JANUARY 1982 ～ 12 FEBRUARY 1983   *Water Dog*

10 FEBRUARY 1994 ～ 30 JANUARY 1995   *Wood Dog*

T H E
DOG

THE PERSONALITY OF THE DOG

Above all things, never think that you're not good enough
yourself. A man should never think that. My belief is that
in life people will take you very much at your own reck-
oning.

Anthony Trollope: a Dog

The Dog is born under the signs of loyalty and anxiety. He
usually holds very firm views and beliefs and is the cham-
pion of good causes. He hates any sort of injustice or unfair
treatment and will do all in his power to help those less
fortunate than himself. He has a strong sense of fair play
and will be honourable and open in all his dealings.

The Dog is very direct and straightforward. He is never
one to skirt round issues and speaks frankly and to the
point. He can also be stubborn, but he is more than
prepared to listen to the views of others and will try to be
as fair as possible in coming to his decisions. He will
readily give advice where it is needed and will be the first
to offer assistance when things go wrong.

The Dog instils confidence wherever he goes and there
are many who admire him for his integrity and resolute
manner. He is a very good judge of character and can often
form an accurate impression of someone very shortly after
meeting them. He is also very intuitive and can frequently
sense how things are going to work out long in advance.

Despite his friendly and amiable manner, the Dog is not
a big socializer. He dislikes having to attend large social
functions or parties and much prefers a quiet meal with

friends or a chat by the fire. He is an excellent conversationalist and is often a marvellous raconteur of amusing stories and anecdotes. He is also quick-witted and his mind is always alert.

The Dog can keep calm in a crisis and although he does have a temper, his outbursts tend to be short-lived. He is loyal and trustworthy, but if he ever feels badly let down or rejected by someone, he will rarely forgive or forget.

The Dog usually has very set interests. He prefers to specialize and become an expert in a chosen area rather than dabble in a variety of different activities. He usually does well in jobs where he feels that he is being of service to others and is often suited to careers in the social services, the medical and legal professions and teaching. The Dog does, however, need to feel motivated in his work. He has to have a sense of purpose and if ever this is lacking he can quite often drift through life without ever achieving very much. Once he has the motivation, however, very little can prevent him from securing his objective.

Another characteristic of the Dog is his tendency to worry and to view things rather pessimistically. Quite often his worries are totally unnecessary and are of his own making. Although it may be difficult, worrying is a habit which the Dog should try to overcome.

The Dog is not materialistic or particularly bothered about accumulating great wealth. As long as he has the necessary money to support his family and to spend on the occasional luxury, he is more than happy. However, when he does have any spare money he tends to be rather a spendthrift and does not always put his money to its best use. He is also not a very good speculator and would be advised to seek professional advice before entering into any major long-term investment.

The Dog will rarely be short of admirers, but he is not an easy person to live with. His moods are changeable and his standards high, but he will be loyal and protective to his partner and will do all in his power to provide them with a good and comfortable home. He can get on extremely well with those born under the signs of the Horse, Pig, Tiger and Monkey, and can also establish a sound and stable relationship with the Rat, Ox, Rabbit, Snake and another Dog, but will find the Dragon a bit too flamboyant for his liking. He will also find it difficult to understand the creative and imaginative Goat and is likely to be highly irritated by the candid Rooster.

The female Dog is renowned for her beauty. She has a warm and caring nature, although until she knows someone well she can be both secretive and very guarded. She is highly intelligent and despite her calm and tranquil appearance she can be extremely ambitious. She enjoys sport and other outdoor activities and has a happy knack of finding bargains in the most unlikely of places. She can also get rather impatient when things do not work out as she would like.

The Dog usually has a very good way with children and can be a loving and doting parent. He will rarely be happier than when he is helping someone or doing something that will benefit others. Providing he can cure himself of his tendency to worry, he will lead a very full and active life – and in that life he will make many friends and do a tremendous amount of good.

THE FIVE DIFFERENT TYPES
OF DOG

In addition to the 12 signs of the Chinese zodiac, there are five elements and these have a strengthening or moderating influence on the sign. The effects of the five elements on the Dog are described below, together with the years in which the elements were exercising their influence. Therefore all Dogs born in 1910 and 1970 are Metal Dogs, those born in 1922 and 1982 are Water Dogs, and so on.

Metal Dog: 1910, 1970
The Metal Dog is bold, confident and forthright, and sets about everything he does in a resolute and determined manner. He has a great belief in his abilities and has no hesitation about speaking his mind or devoting himself to some just cause. He can be rather serious at times and can become anxious and irritable when things are not going according to plan. He tends to have very specific interests and it would certainly help him to broaden his outlook and become more involved in group activities. He is extremely loyal and faithful to his friends.

Water Dog: 1922, 1982
The Water Dog has a very direct and outgoing personality. He is an excellent communicator and has little trouble in persuading others to fall in with his plans. He does, however, have a somewhat carefree nature and is not as disciplined or as thorough as he should be in certain

matters. Neither does he keep as much control over his finances as he should, but he can be most generous to his family and friends and will make sure that they want for nothing. The Water Dog is usually very good with children and has a wide circle of friends.

Wood Dog: 1934, 1994

This Dog is a hard and conscientious worker and will usually make a favourable impression wherever he goes. He is less independent than some of the other types of Dog and prefers to work in a group rather than on his own. He is popular, has a good sense of humour and takes a very keen interest in the activities of the various members of his family. He is often attracted to the finer things in life and can get much pleasure from collecting stamps, coins, pictures or antiques. He also prefers to live in the country rather than the town.

Fire Dog: 1946

This Dog has a lively, outgoing personality and is able to establish friendships with remarkable ease. He is an honest and conscientious worker and likes to take an active part in all that is going on around him. He also likes to explore new ideas, and providing he can get the necessary support and advice, he can often succeed where others have failed. He does, however, have a tendency to be stubborn. Providing he can overcome this, the Fire Dog can often achieve considerable fame and fortune.

Earth Dog: 1958

The Earth Dog is very talented and astute. He is method-ical and efficient and is capable of going far in his chosen profession. He tends to be rather quiet and reserved but has a very persuasive manner and usually secures his objectives without too much opposition. He is generous and kind and is always ready to lend a helping hand when it is needed. He is also held in very high esteem by his friends and colleagues and he is usually most dignified in his appearance.

PROSPECTS FOR THE DOG IN THE YEAR 2000

The Chinese New Year starts on 5 February 2000. Until then, the old year, the Year of the Rabbit, is still making its presence felt.

The Year of the Rabbit (16 February 1999 to 4 February 2000) will have been a favourable one for the Dog and to get the most from what remains of it, he should give some thought to what he wants accomplish. Otherwise he could find himself flitting from one activity to another and not making the best use of his time.

The Dog's personal life will be particularly active, with much to arrange and fit in. Again, the Dog should decide on his priorities and concentrate on them, asking for addi-tional support whenever necessary. He should also aim to keep his commitments to a manageable level. Admittedly, this may mean that some projects and tasks, particularly household, have to be temporarily postponed, but this would be better than being under too much pressure when there is, after all, so much to do and enjoy.

The Dog will find himself in great demand as the year ends, with parties, get-togethers and social events to attend, as well as Christmas and the celebrations for the new millennium. He will also receive invitations to visit family and friends who may live some distance away and any of these that he is able to accept could result in some particularly pleasurable occasions. Similarly, any travel that the Dog is able to undertake at this time will go well.

The Rabbit year is also a positive one for work matters and the Dog will have done much to impress others and add to his experience during the course of it. Any Dog who is currently looking for work or is particularly keen to make further headway should actively follow up any opportunities in the closing months of the year. By working determinedly, these Dogs can make additional progress.

As far as finance is concerned, the last months of the Rabbit year will, though, be an expensive time for the Dog, particularly with his personal life being so active. In view of this, it would certainly be in his interests to keep a watchful eye on his spending and, if possible, try to spread some of his costs out.

Overall, the last months of the Rabbit year will be active but very enjoyable for the Dog.

The Year of the Dragon starts on 5 February and will be a challenging one for the Dog. Not everything will go as smoothly as he would like and he could have to modify some of his plans. However, while the Dragon year may not be the easiest for the Dog, it can still have a significant bearing on his future.

Many Dogs will have made useful progress in their work over the last 12 months and they should now aim to consolidate these gains and, if they have taken on a new position or duties, familiarize themselves with them. Throughout the year, the Dog should also keep himself informed of any proposals or changes under consideration and show willingness to adapt to new situations. Although he may have misgivings about some of the developments taking place, this is very much a year in which he should proceed carefully and tactfully and not 'rock the boat'. The Dog could also find himself being given some challenging tasks over the year. By rising to these, daunting though they may be, he will impress others and add to his experience, both of which will be to his future advantage. Workwise this may be a testing year but it holds considerable long-term benefits!

During the year the Dog would also find it helpful to give some thought to how he would like his career to develop. By discussing his ideas with those able to advise he may well find himself becoming better focused on the direction he should take and the type of opportunities he needs to follow up. Also, if he feels he requires further skills or experience, he should try to obtain this now. The Dragon year is very much a time for preparing the way for the advances he will make in 2001 and beyond.

This also applies to those Dogs seeking work. If they are eligible for any training courses they should actively follow these up; indeed, they will sometimes find that a position will result from some additional training they have undertaken. However, whether training is possible or not, these Dogs should remain alert for openings over the year and will find that a position offered them now has the potential to develop well in the future.

Admittedly, there will be occasions when the Dog, whether in work or seeking work, will get despondent in face of the struggle involved in getting what he wants, but there are good reasons for him to take heart. The awkward elements of the year are but a passing phase and by facing the challenges before him and persisting with his aims, he can do much to turn the situation to his future advantage. As has so often been shown in the past, before a period of success there is often a time of adjustment, preparation and even setback, and this is how it will be for the Dog. He will emerge from the Dragon year far more focused on his next objectives and having learnt a great deal.

At demanding times, the Dog would also find it helpful to remember that there are many around him who are able to offer advice and he should not hesitate to avail himself of their support. He will often find that others will be able to put his mind at ease or offer constructive help. The one thing he should avoid is brooding over any awkward situation on his own and thereby increasing his own burden. As he will find, a worry shared *is* a worry halved.

The Dog will also need to exercise care in financial matters throughout the year and should watch his level of outgoings in particular. This is not a year for taking risks, stretching his resources too far or getting involved in matters or investments which he has not fully investigated. If in doubt, he should seek guidance. Similarly, paperwork concerning tax and other important matters needs careful attention. To take risks or delay a response could be to the Dog's detriment.

Although much of the foregoing has been of a cautionary nature, provided the Dog proceeds with care he can do much to prevent problems from arising or minimize the effects of any that do occur.

However, while there will be difficult moments for the Dog during the year 2000, there will also be times of real pleasure and fulfilment. Some of these could come about as a result the Dog's own interests and it is important that he sets time aside for these. They will not only take his mind off his usual preoccupations but will also help him to relax and unwind. He could take particular delight in making and designing certain items, in some sort of craftwork or even in taking up something entirely new. By doing something rewarding with his spare time, whatever it may be, the Dog can look forward to some truly satisfying moments.

He should also ensure that he takes a proper break or holiday over the year. Again, he will not only benefit from the rest this gives but, with travel being favourably aspected, he will also thoroughly enjoy some of the places he visits, especially those which are off the usual tourist map.

The Dog's relations with those close to him will also bring him happiness over the year. In addition to the sterling support he will receive, he will find that joint activities and mutual interests will lead to some pleasing occasions. These may include tackling any household projects that the Dog may have been contemplating. He will find that some of these, notably those that add to the decor and comfort of his home, will be appreciated by all concerned.

The Dog will, as always, take a caring interest in the activities of those around him over the year, with his advice being greatly valued. However, while his domestic life will generally go well, in view of some of the pressures he will face over the year, he must not take his anxieties out on others. To help prevent this, he would find it helpful to discuss any concerns he might have rather than dwell upon them.

The Dog's social life will be pleasant and he can look forward to many agreeable times with his friends. There will also be opportunities to add to his friends over the year, but where matters of the heart are concerned, the Dog should let any new friendship form gradually and in its own time rather than act too hastily. He will find this will help to put the relationship on a more secure base by allowing each the chance to get to know the other better. Over the months ahead new relationships can develop in a promising manner, but care is needed in the early stages.

Although the Dragon year will bring its pressures and testing situations, the Dog will learn a great deal from it, including where his real interests and strengths lie, and also gain valuable experience. All this will do much to prepare for the progress and success he will soon enjoy in the Year of the Snake.

As far as the different types of Dog are concerned, this will be an important year for the *Metal Dog*. Although he may face problems with some of his activities over the year, what he accomplishes, together with some of the decisions he takes, will have a significant bearing on his future. Indeed, for some Metal Dogs, the Dragon year will mark a turning-point in their lives and will usher in the changes necessary for their future progress. In his work the Metal Dog will need to proceed with care. Although he will continue to impress others with his diligent manner, there could be events that will cause him concern. These could be the results of changes in personnel or the introduction of new plans. The Metal Dog should watch changing situations carefully and show some flexibility in his attitude rather than appearing too intransigent. The developments that take place will also cause him to look closely at his own work and many Metal Dogs will be tempted to make a change, either trying for promotion or a new job or even switching to a different career altogether. However, this will not be easy and could take some time to put into effect. Also, before taking any precipitous action, the Metal Dog should give serious thought to just how he would like his career to develop. He would find it helpful to discuss his options with those qualified to advise or currently engaged in the type of position he is considering. Although the Metal Dog may be desirous of a change, he must not embark on anything too hurriedly or expect quick results. However, once he has decided how he wishes to proceed, he should seek out opportunities and persist in following these up. Eventually many Metal Dogs will get what they want, but it will take considerable determination on their part. Those Metal Dogs who start the Dragon year seeking work should also remain active in pursuing any opportunities they see, but again should consider how they would like their longer term future to develop. If they are able to undergo any training that would help them towards their ultimate objectives, this would be to their advantage, and approaches to relevant organizations and professional bodies could bring useful leads and advice. Many Metal Dogs will find that the Dragon year will be one in which their career takes a different and often more exciting course. During it, however, the Metal Dog will need to exercise care in financial matters. Several times during the year he will face large expenses, especially related to accommodation and travel, and it is important he makes allowances for these and keeps a watchful eye on his financial situation. The time he takes in managing his finances will certainly help to avert problems and lead to him making more effective use of his money. The Metal Dog's personal life will be fairly active over the year and he will do much to help and advise others. His care, sound judgement and considerate manner will be greatly valued. However, with his own activities and the interests of others, plus the usual household matters, there will be occasions when the Metal Dog will despair of all he has to do. At such times he could find it helpful to set priorities and avoid becoming involved in too many projects at once. Admittedly, this may mean he does not accomplish all he would like, but better this than placing himself under too much strain. However busy the Metal Dog's personal life will be, the year will contain some truly happy occasions with both family and friends and he will be considerably heartened by the love and affection he is shown and the support he receives. The Metal Dog should also make sure that he devotes time to his recreational activities, as they do help him relax and unwind. He should take advantage of any opportunity he gets to go away for a holiday or break and will benefit from the change of scene. Although the Dragon year may bring its challenging moments, these will often cause the Metal Dog to reflect on his current situation and make some changes. By doing this, he can do much to improve his prospects and set himself on course to enjoy the more favourable and progressive times that await over the next few years.

This will be an important year for the *Water Dog*. Many Water Dogs will start the year with high hopes and often set ideas about what they want to achieve. Some of these hopes, particularly those concerning the Water Dog's personal life, will come to fruition, but in other areas there could be disappointment and the Water Dog could have to review some of his plans. This may especially be the case in work matters. Although the Water Dog is keen to use his skills and qualifications to the best advantage and has ideas he is keen to try out, putting his hopes into practice may prove more difficult than he anticipated. Sometimes this could be because of the conditions that prevail but there will also be some Water Dogs who are aiming for positions without having the necessary experience or training behind them. In the year 2000 it is important that the Water Dog keeps his goals at realistic levels; he is still at a young age and there is plenty of time for him to attain all he wants. In the meantime he should aim to build up his experience and, whether in work or seeking work, should take advantage of any openings that may be offered, even though they may be different from those he was hoping for. All the time he will be learning and gaining experience, and indeed, some Water Dogs will discover skills and strengths they did not know they had and will find a vocation for which they are ideally suited. The year may contain its disappointments, but it will also have some far-reaching benefits and all Water Dogs should show a willingness to make the most of the situations that prevail. Many of those Water Dogs in education will face important exams over the year and to help them achieve the best results they should set about their studies in a systematic and disciplined way, not leaving project work or revision to the last moment! As an incentive, the young Water Dog could find it helpful to keep his future goals in mind, knowing that what he achieves now can do much to help his prospects. He should also take advantage of any vocational training that he may be eligible for and if there is a skill which he thinks may be useful, he should investigate ways he can obtain this. Again, what he accomplishes now can prove important in the long term. In financial matters, however, the year calls for care. There will be many temptations to spend, but throughout the year the Water Dog should exercise some restraint and think hard before proceeding with any large purchase or commitment that his income may not be able to stand. This is very much a year in which to keep control of the purse strings. As far as the Water Dog's relations with others are concerned, this will prove an interesting year. On a social level he can look forward to many enjoyable occasions in the company of friends and to attending various parties and events. Many Water Dogs will add to their social circle and romance will certainly figure prominently, particularly in the second half of the year. However, while his social life will go well, the Water Dog's domestic life can sometimes prove awkward and several times he could find himself at variance with family members. At such times the Water Dog should try to reach an understanding with those around him, explaining his own viewpoint as well as listening to those of others in order to avoid any tensions and disagreements. The Water Dog should also bear in mind that while he may not agree with all he is told by those around him, they do genuinely care about him and speak with his best interests at heart. Water Dogs, take note and make a special effort to preserve the normally good relations with family members! However, while care and consideration will certainly be needed in the Water Dog's home life, there will also be times of joy and great pleasure. These could include not only delight in his own progress (particularly academic), but also some happy and memorable family occasions. Travel, too, will appeal to many Water Dogs over the year and they will thoroughly enjoy any chance they get to visit new destinations. Overall, this will be a variable year for the Water Dog. Although not all his activities may work out as he would like, the year will still contain some pleasant times, especially on a social level. Also, the experience the Water Dog obtains, together with the skills and qualifications he acquires, will help towards the success he will enjoy in future years.

This will be a reasonable year for the *Wood Dog*, although he will need to exercise care with certain of his activities. One of the more awkwardly aspected areas of the year concerns paperwork and when the Wood Dog receives any important correspondence or forms, especially related to finance and tax, he needs to deal with them promptly and carefully. If he has any uncertainties over what is being asked or required, he should seek clarification. To take risks or be too dilatory in his response could be to his detriment and even cost. Also, many Wood Dogs will make some large purchases over the year, particularly connected with home entertainment and furnishings, and again they should deal with the transaction carefully, making sure they read the small print, terms of guarantee and, if buying on credit, conditions of repayment. Wood Dogs, take note – be thorough and vigilant and do keep receipts, guarantees and agreements safe in case they are required later. More positively aspected are the Wood Dog's own personal interests and he will find the time he spends on these particularly rewarding. Those Wood Dogs whose interests are artistic or creative can look forward to some particularly pleasing results and would do well to show what they produce to others, even perhaps considering entering an appropriate competition. They will be greatly encouraged by the response and inspired to develop their interest further. The Wood Dog would also do well to contact others who share his interests. By meeting and conversing with fellow enthusiasts, he will gain much useful information as well as make some new friends and acquaintances. Outdoor activities will also bring pleasure over the year, and for the keen gardener or those Wood Dogs who follow sport or enjoy travel the year will contain many satisfying moments. However, a word of warning: any Wood Dog who is a gardening or do-it-yourself enthusiast does need to be careful when moving heavy weights. When tackling strenuous tasks he would be wise to seek assistance, otherwise a resultant strain could cause him considerable discomfort. The Wood Dog's social life will go well, however, and over the year he can look forward to some agreeable occasions in the company of his friends and to attending various social events. Any Wood Dog who may be feeling lonely or dispirited should make every effort to go out more. By taking positive action these Wood Dogs really can do much to bring about an improvement in their social life. On a domestic level, the Wood Dog will take a fond interest in the activities of those around him as well as value the support he receives. With some of the more awkward matters he has to deal with, he should not hesitate to speak of his concerns to others rather than keep them to himself. Although he may sometimes feel that others do not want to hear of his problems, this is not the case and in the Dragon year the Wood Dog will find that those dear to him can do much to put his mind at ease and even sort out worrying matters. Help, advice and support are all there within his family and close friends and, at difficult times, the Wood Dog should not hesitate to avail himself of their assistance. Similarly, if any domestic or personal matter should give him concern, he should raise it rather than keep it to himself. By doing so, he could find that his worries are misplaced or that once the matter is out in the open it can be discussed and dealt with. The Wood Dog's family does mean a great deal to him and the care and affection he is shown will hearten him over the year. Although the Dragon year will have its difficult moments, it will still contain many happy occasions, and the Wood Dog's interests and relations with others will bring him real pleasure. By dealing with important paper-work efficiently and seeking help when any problems do arise, he can do much to overcome or minimize the more awkward aspects that prevail. From late summer onwards, his fortunes will gradually pick up, with the second half of the year being much better than the first.

The *Fire Dog* possesses a wonderful sense of purpose and is always keen to make the most of himself and his abilities. However, despite his best endeavours, not all that he does over the year will work out as he would like and he could find some of his plans have to be altered or postponed. Some of the year will indeed prove testing, but there will also be a positive side to this. Some of the events will turn out to be 'blessings in disguise', causing the Fire Dog to reconsider some of his existing ideas and come up with stronger ones. In addition, some of what happens will give rise to new opportunities and the Fire Dog, with his enterprising and determined spirit, can often turn these to his advantage. In his work he will, though, need to remain alert to all that is going on, take note of the views of others and be prepared to adapt to new situations. During the year several important changes will take place which will affect his duties, and despite his unease, the Fire Dog should aim to make the best of the situations in which he finds himself. Some Fire Dogs will find that new opportunities will become available for them to pursue while others may feel that they will benefit from a change and will decide to seek fresh challenges. These and any other Fire Dogs looking for work should actively follow up any suitable openings and also be adventurous in what they try for. By widening the scope of their quest, they will find it becomes more productive, and once in a position, they will quickly learn new skills and feel more inspired by the tasks and challenges before them. The Dragon year does indeed look well on the enterprising, and while not an easy year for the Fire Dog, his endeavours will often be to his long-term advantage. The Fire Dog will, though, need to exercise care with his finances, particularly as he will want to make some major purchases for his accommodation over the year as well as set some money aside for travel, his interests and some general family expenses. In view of this, the Fire Dog should budget carefully and keep a watchful eye on his outgoings. As far as his family life is concerned, this will be a busy year. As always the Fire Dog will take a caring interest in the activities of those around him, with both younger and more senior relations often seeking his help. Sometimes providing this will take up much of the Fire Dog's time, but any assistance he is able to give will be truly valued. While, as in any year, a few family problems and differences of opinion will emerge, there will still be much that will bring the Fire Dog considerable happiness, with the summer being an especially pleasing time for family matters. The Fire Dog's social life will also bring him contentment and he will greatly enjoy meeting up with his friends. An older and close friend will prove especially important over the year, offering advice and information which will prove pertinent and helpful. In view of the often busy nature of the year, it is important that the Fire Dog sets time aside for his own hobbies and interests, as these will help him to rest and unwind, and that he also pays some attention to his well-being. This includes making sure he eats a balanced diet as well as gets sufficient exercise. Although this is something some Fire Dogs may prefer to gloss over, any attention to their own welfare will certainly be to their advantage. Generally, although this may not be the smoothest of years, it will help to prepare the way for the more progressive times the Fire Dog is soon to enjoy.

This will be an active year for the *Earth Dog* with much happening in his life. However, while some of the year will be demanding, by setting about his activities in his usual efficient manner and keeping his commitments to a manageable level, he will cope well with the pressures placed upon him and will emerge from the year with much to his credit. One of the busiest areas will be his domestic life, where there will be many matters requiring his attention. In particular the Earth Dog will do much to assist those around him, and the time he spends on others, together with his kindnesses and considerate nature, will be truly valued. Indeed, the Earth Dog may not quite realize just how much he means to so many, but his importance will certainly become evident as the year unfolds. Some of the domestic matters with which he is involved will be occasions of much happiness – including some kind of celebration – but there will also be a few problems and worries. At difficult times the Earth Dog's personable manner will be of great help, and should any differences of opinion arise, he should use his skills to seek a solution or compromise rather than letting the matter continue and sour the atmosphere. Also, at busy times, the Earth Dog should set himself priorities as well as ask for additional assistance. While he may have a willing nature, he must not overload himself with household tasks when these can often be shared out. The Earth Dog will also be keen to complete some practical projects on his home over the year, but he should allow plenty of time for these and should avoid becoming involved in too many activities at the same time. Again, prioritizing will help, even though this may mean delaying some of his plans. In view of the active nature of his home life, the Earth Dog may find he does not have as much time for his interests or socializing as he would like. However it is vital he does not neglect these activities. Not only will they allow him to have a break from his usual concerns, but also time spent in the company of his friends and pursuing his interests will bring him considerable pleasure. In addition, he will receive several invitations to social events and while he may be in two minds about going to some of these, by doing so he will find that they turn out to be splendid and often memorable occasions. Although the Dragon year will be a demanding one for the Earth Dog, it is important that he balances his various activities and gives himself time to relax and enjoy himself. He should also ensure that he takes a proper holiday or break over the year; again, this will do him much good and travel is well aspected. As far as the Earth Dog's work is concerned, this will be a reasonable year, although his level of progress may not always meet with his high expectations. As with other Dogs, the Earth Dog should keep himself informed of developments in the workplace and show himself willing to adapt. Some of the year will prove frustrating for him, particularly as he will not always be able to secure the results he desires, but by giving of his best and working steadily, he will be well placed to make more substantial headway in future years. Whether in work or seeking work, the Earth Dog should also take advantage of any opportunity to add to his skills. Again, this will do much to further his prospects, and for those looking for work, some new opportunities could arise as a result of some training undertaken. As far as financial matters are concerned, the Earth Dog should not encounter any undue problems over the year, although it would be in his interests to make allowance for forthcoming expenses such as travel, holidays and, for some, a wedding in the family. Again, the Earth Dog's methodical nature will be to his advantage and with careful management he should be able to end the year in an improved financial situation. Although the year will be demanding, by using his time well and giving of his best, the Earth Dog will do much to prepare the way for his future advances and towards the end of 2000 and throughout 2001, he will reap the rewards of his patience and effort.

FAMOUS DOGS

André Agassi, Jane Asher, Zoë Ball, Brigitte Bardot, Gary Barlow, Dr Christiaan Barnard, Candice Bergman, David Bowie, Michael Buerk, George W. Bush, Kate Bush, Max Bygraves, Naomi Campbell, Mariah Carey, King Carl Gustaf XVI of Sweden, José Carreras, Paul Cézanne, Cher, Sir Winston Churchill, Petula Clark, Bill Clinton, Leonard Cohen, Robin Cook, Jamie Lee Curtis, Charles Dance, Claude Debussy, Dame Judi Dench, Frankie Dettori, Blake Edwards, Sally Field, Joseph Fiennes, Robert Frost, Ava Gardner, Judy Garland, George Gershwin, Lenny Henry, O. Henry, Patricia Hodge, Victor Hugo, Barry Humphries, Holly Hunter, Michael Jackson, Al Jolson, Felicity Kendal, Sue Lawley, Maureen Lipman, Sophia Loren, Joanna Lumley, Shirley MacLaine, Madonna, Norman Mailer, Winnie Mandela, Barry Manilow, Rik Mayall, Golda Meir, Freddie Mercury, Liza Minnelli, David Niven, Gary

Numan, Sydney Pollack, Elvis Presley, The Artist formerly known as Prince, George Robertson, Paul Robeson, Linda Ronstadt, Gabriela Sabatini, Sade, Carl Sagan, Susan Sarandon, Jennifer Saunders, Claudia Schiffer, Norman Schwarzkopf, Dr Albert Schweitzer, Alan Shearer, Clare Short, Sylvester Stallone, Robert Louis Stevenson, Sharon Stone, Jack Straw, David Suchet, Donald Sutherland, Chris Tarrant, Mother Teresa, Voltaire, Paul Weller, Prince William, Shelley Winters.

30 JANUARY 1911 ∿ 17 FEBRUARY 1912		*Metal Pig*
16 FEBRUARY 1923 ∿ 4 FEBRUARY 1924		*Water Pig*
4 FEBRUARY 1935 ∿ 23 JANUARY 1936		*Wood Pig*
22 JANUARY 1947 ∿ 9 FEBRUARY 1948		*Fire Pig*
8 FEBRUARY 1959 ∿ 27 JANUARY 1960		*Earth Pig*
27 JANUARY 1971 ∿ 14 FEBRUARY 1972		*Metal Pig*
13 FEBRUARY 1983 ∿ 1 FEBRUARY 1984		*Water Pig*
31 JANUARY 1995 ∿ 18 FEBRUARY 1996		*Wood Pig*

THE
PIG

THE PERSONALITY OF THE PIG

Sow a thought and you reap an act;
Sow an act and you reap a habit;
Sow a habit and you reap a character;
Sow a character and you reap a destiny.

Ralph Waldo Emerson: a Pig

The Pig is born under the sign of honesty. He has a kind and understanding nature and is well known for his abilities as a peacemaker. He hates any sort of discord or unpleasantness and will do all in his power to sort out differences of opinion or bring opposing factions together.

He is also an excellent conversationalist and speaks truthfully and to the point. He dislikes any form of falsehood or hypocrisy and is a firm believer in justice and the maintenance of law and order. In spite of these beliefs, however, the Pig is reasonably tolerant and often prepared to forgive others for their wrongs. He rarely harbours grudges and is never vindictive.

The Pig is usually very popular. He enjoys other people's company and likes to be involved in joint or group activities. He will be a loyal member of any club or society and can be relied upon to lend a helping hand at functions. He is also an excellent fund-raiser for charities and often a great supporter of humanitarian causes.

The Pig is a hard and conscientious worker and is particularly respected for his reliability and integrity. In his early years he will try his hand at several different jobs, but he is usually happiest where he feels that he is being of service to others. He will unselfishly give up his time for the common good and is highly valued by his colleagues and employers.

The Pig has a good sense of humour and invariably has a smile, joke or whimsical remark at the ready. He loves to entertain and to please others, and there are many Pigs who have been attracted to careers in show business or who enjoy following the careers of famous stars and personalities.

There are, unfortunately, some who take advantage of the Pig's good nature and impose upon his generosity. The Pig has great difficulty in saying 'No' and, although he may dislike being firm, it would be in his own interests to say occasionally, 'Enough is enough.' The Pig can also be rather naïve and gullible; however, if at any stage in his life he feels that he has been badly let down, he will make sure that it will never happen again and will try to become self-reliant. There are many Pigs who have become entrepreneurs or forged a successful career on their own after some early disappointment in life. Although the Pig tends to spend his money quite freely, he is usually very astute in financial matters and there are many Pigs who have become wealthy.

Another characteristic of the Pig is his ability to recover from setbacks reasonably quickly. His faith and his strength of character keep him going. If he thinks that there is a job he can do or he has something that he wants to achieve, he will pursue it with a dogged determination. He can also be stubborn and, no matter how many may plead with him, once he has made his mind up he will rarely change his views.

Although the Pig may work hard, he also knows how to enjoy himself. He is a great pleasure-seeker and will quite happily spend his hard-earned money on a lavish holiday or an expensive meal – for the Pig is a connoisseur of good food and wine – or taking part in a variety of recreational activities. He also enjoys small social gatherings and, if he is in company he likes, can very easily become the life and soul of the party. He does, however, tend to become rather withdrawn at larger functions or when among strangers.

The Pig is also a creature of comfort and his home will usually be fitted with all the latest in luxury appliances. Where possible, he will prefer to live in the country rather than the town and will opt to have a big garden, for the Pig is usually a keen and successful gardener.

The Pig is very popular with the opposite sex and will often have numerous romances before he settles down. Once settled, however, he will be loyal to his partner and he will find that he is especially well suited to those born under the signs of the Goat, Rabbit, Dog and Tiger, and also to another Pig. Due to his affable and easy-going nature he can also establish a satisfactory relationship with all the remaining signs of the Chinese zodiac, with the exception of the Snake. The Snake tends to be wily, secretive and very guarded, and this can be intensely irritating to the honest and open-hearted Pig.

The female Pig will devote all her energies to the needs of her children and her partner. She will try to ensure that they want for nothing and their pleasure is very much her pleasure. Her home will either be very clean and orderly or hopelessly untidy. Strangely, there seems to be no in between with Pigs – they either love housework or detest it! The female Pig does, however, have considerable talents as an organizer and this, combined with her friendly and open manner, enables her to secure many of her objectives. She can also be a caring and conscientious parent and has very good taste in clothes.

The Pig is usually lucky in life and will rarely want for anything. Provided he does not let others take advantage of his good nature and is not afraid of asserting himself, he will go through life making friends, helping others and winning the admiration of many.

THE FIVE DIFFERENT TYPES OF PIG

In addition to the 12 signs of the Chinese zodiac, there are five elements and these have a strengthening or moderating influence on the sign. The effects of the five elements on the Pig are described below, together with the years in which the elements were exercising their influence. Therefore all Pigs born in 1911 and 1971 are Metal Pigs, those born in 1923 and 1983 are Water Pigs, and so on.

Metal Pig: 1911, 1971

The Metal Pig is more ambitious and determined than some of the other types of Pig. He is strong, energetic and likes to be involved in a wide variety of different activities. He is very open and forthright in his views, although he can be a little too trusting at times and has a tendency to accept things at face value. He has a good sense of humour and loves to attend parties and other social gatherings. He has a warm, outgoing nature and usually has a large circle of friends.

Water Pig: 1923, 1983

The Water Pig has a heart of gold. He is generous and loyal and tries to remain on good terms with everyone. He will do his utmost to help others, but sadly there are some who will take advantage of his kind nature and he should, in his own interests, be a little more discriminating and be prepared to stand firm against anything that he does not like. Although he prefers the quieter things in life, he has a wide range of interests. He particularly enjoys outdoor pursuits and attending parties and social occasions. He is a hard and conscientious worker and invariably does well in his chosen profession. He is also gifted in the art of communication.

Wood Pig: 1935, 1995

This Pig has a friendly, persuasive manner and is easily able to gain the confidence of others. He likes to be involved in all that is going on around him and can sometimes take on more responsibility than he can properly handle. He is loyal to his family and friends and he also derives much pleasure from helping those less fortunate than himself. The Wood Pig is usually an optimist and leads a very full, enjoyable and satisfying life. He also has a good sense of humour.

Fire Pig: 1947

The Fire Pig is both energetic and adventurous and he sets about everything he does in a confident and resolute manner. He is very forthright in his views and does not mind taking risks in order to achieve his objectives. He can, however, get carried away by the excitement of the moment and ought to exercise more caution with some of the enterprises in which he gets involved. The Fire Pig is usually lucky in money matters and is well known for his generosity. He is also very caring towards the members of his family.

Earth Pig: 1959

This Pig has a kindly nature. He is sensible and realistic and will go to great lengths to please his employers and secure his aims and ambitions. He is an excellent organizer and is particularly astute in business and financial matters. He has a good sense of humour and a wide circle of friends. He also likes to lead an active social life, although he does sometimes have a tendency to eat and drink more than is good for him.

PROSPECTS FOR THE PIG IN THE YEAR 2000

The Chinese New Year starts on 5 February 2000. Until then, the old year, the Year of the Rabbit, is still making its presence felt.

The Year of the Rabbit (16 February 1999 to 4 February 2000) will have been a positive one for the Pig and in what remains it he will accomplish much as well as greatly enjoy himself. Indeed, with his appreciation of the finer things in life and his sociable nature, the Pig will revel in the social occasions he attends as well as the celebrations for the new millennium. When it comes to celebration, the Pig will certainly do it in style, making the turn of the millennium a truly memorable experience.

As the Pig will find himself very much in demand in the closing months of the year, he could find it difficult to fit in all that he would like. In view of this, he would find it helpful to plan ahead and deal with certain activities, such as correspondence, seasonal shopping and outstanding tasks, in advance. This will often help to relieve some of the pressure from what promises to be a busy December, and with a concerted effort, the Pig will be delighted with just how much he is able to get out of the way before the activity really starts.

For the unattached Pig, or those seeking new friends, the last quarter of the Rabbit year will be a splendid time, with plenty of opportunities to meet others. Romance is especially well aspected and, as so many will find, this really is a promising time for personal matters.

Work too is another positive area and for those Pigs seeking positions or wanting to make further progress, the period from September to the end of November 1999 will hold some interesting opportunities. With his determined and enterprising nature, the Pig will impress others and can, if he wants, make further headway. He will also fare well in financial matters, but with so much social activity, he must allow for considerable outlay at the end of the year. He also needs to keep control of the purse strings; too much impulse buying (a real temptation) could deplete his resources. Also if any Pig receives important and official correspondence or is involved in legal matters at this time, he should proceed with care and, if appropriate, seek advice. If not handled properly, such matters could cause problems.

In virtually all other respects, though, the Rabbit year will be an auspicious time for the Pig and one which he will thoroughly enjoy.

The Year of the Dragon starts on 5 February and will be a reasonable one for the Pig, allowing him to make useful progress and enjoy a pleasing personal life.

As far as his work is concerned, the Pig will have learnt much over the last 12 months and the Dragon year will give him the chance to consolidate his position and put his experience to good use. Those Pigs who have recently taken on new duties should take the time to familiarize themselves with the various aspects of their work and take advantage of any training opportunities that may be offered. There will also be chances for the Pig to improve on his present position, and if he sees openings which he considers himself well suited for, he should actively pursue these. Admittedly, opportunities may not be plentiful, but the ones that do arise could prove excellent for the Pig, providing him with some stimulating challenges and renewing his incentive to give of his best.

Although this will be a generally positive year for work matters, there may be occasions when the Pig feels ill-at-ease with proposals being considered, changes being introduced or the views of his colleagues. At such times he should proceed with care, discretion and tact. If he acts or speaks unwisely, he could find he has undermined some of his earlier good work and he should try to avoid this. At times this year it would be wise for the Pig to think before he speaks!

Those Pigs seeking work or wanting to move from their present position should also remain active in pursuing any openings that they see as well as following up any ideas they have. Their enterprising approach will impress others and will often lead to them obtaining a position which will allow them to put their skills and experience to good use. The months from mid-April to June and September and October could hold some particularly interesting possibilities.

This is also a positive year for financial matters, with many Pigs enjoying an increase in their income or receiving a sum from another source. Indeed, the Pig's money-making abilities will be in fine form over the year, with almost all Pigs being able to improve on their position. However the Pig should aim to use this financial upturn well rather than allow his money to 'burn a hole in his pocket' or succumb to too many expensive whims. He could find it helpful to set a certain amount aside for specific items and expenses as well as saving any money that he does not immediately need. With the aspects supporting the Pig well in financial matters, a carefully chosen investment or savings policy started now could become a useful asset in later years.

The Pig's personal life will also provide him with considerable pleasure. As always, he will play a full part in family life, doing much to assist those around him and engaging in a wide range of family activities. Most of his domestic life will go well and be the source of pride and satisfaction.

However, there could still be matters that lead to a difference of opinion and at such times the Pig should use his skills as a peacemaker and seek a compromise. If not, he could find these disagreements escalate and take the edge off what could otherwise be happy and convivial times. Throughout the Dragon year, the Pig should strive to preserve the congenial atmosphere he so values. This may often require positive input on his part.

Many Pigs will also decide to carry out some practical projects on their home over the year, particularly adding new features, changing the decor and replacing some equipment. Although some of the Pig's plans may take longer to carry out than he anticipated, he will be well satisfied with the finished result. However, where practical tasks are concerned, the Pig does need to allow plenty of time, accept that there will sometimes be considerable disruption and, where applicable, seek the advice of experts. To rush projects, skimp on preparation or not carry out certain tasks properly will only lead to less satisfactory results. This is something the ever-eager Pig should bear in mind!

In addition to the practical projects that he carries out, the Pig will also delight in his own personal interests. Over the year he will find that one of these will develop in an unexpected way, bringing praise for his talents and knowledge and inspiring him to do more. For those Pigs with an interest which allows them to use their creative and practical abilities, this is again a favourable year to extend their skills, perhaps by finding out more about their area of interest or starting a new project. By devoting time to his interests and furthering them in a positive way, the Pig will not only make them more fulfilling but will also find that they will provide him with some truly absorbing times. Also, if there is a new subject or interest that he has been thinking of taking up, this would be a good year in which to do it, perhaps as a 'new millennium's resolution'.

The Pig's social life will bring him much pleasure and he will greatly enjoy the company of friends and the social functions he attends over the year. New friendships, especially of a romantic nature, whether formed in the Rabbit or the Dragon year, will flourish and bring the Pig much happiness. For any Pig who may be living in a new area, feeling lonely or just wishing to make new friends, the Dragon year will certainly bring opportunities to meet others and build up an active social life. However, the initiative to bring this about does rest with the Pig himself. Given his ability to relate so well to others, though, it is something he should not find too difficult! All Pigs will find April and the months from July to late September especially pleasing for social matters.

Generally, this will be a satisfying year for the Pig, with most aspects of his life bringing pleasure. The Dragon year does favour the enterprising, and for those who are willing to make that extra effort, the results of the year can be particularly rewarding. Whether he is determined to improve his lot or is content with the way things are, the Pig will generally fare well in 2000 and, in keeping with his amiable and sociable nature, will enjoy himself, often in the way of his choosing!

As far as the different types of Pig on concerned, this will be a positive year for the *Metal Pig* and will contain interesting developments in many areas of his life. Over the year he will have the opportunity to build on his more recent achievements and make further headway. With his keen mind, his ability to relate so well to others and his considerable talents, the Metal Pig knows he has a good future ahead of him and his self-belief and determined nature will certainly aid his progress. In his work, the Metal Pig will be given every encouragement to develop his skills and will certainly impress those around him. Many times this will lead him to being given additional duties or the chance to move to a different position. This is a time of advance and the Metal Pig really should seize the opportunities that become available, with March, April and late summer seeing some particularly positive developments. There will also be several occasions when the Metal Pig will have the chance to discuss his longer-term prospects with those more senior to him or meet individuals who are engaged in the type of position he would like. By making the most of such meetings he will be given some advice which will prove highly useful over the next few years. Many of those Metal Pigs seeking work will also find their quest for a position rewarded, often in an unexpected but fortuitous way. This could be by hearing of an opening by chance, following up a vague piece of information or through someone's recommendation, but no matter how the opportunity arises, it will enable the Metal Pig to show his potential and he will again impress others. All Metal Pigs, whether in work or seeking work, should also take advantage of any training opportunities they may be offered or use some of their spare time to add to their skills. This may include extending their computer knowledge or taking up some other practical activity. By doing something positive, Metal Pigs will be able to use their time to their future benefit. This will be a favourable year for financial matters, but the Metal Pig should keep a watchful eye over his level of spending and make allowance for regular outgoings. Many Metal Pigs will start the year facing some large bills, particularly with the end of the Rabbit year being so expensive, and before taking on any new financial commitments, they should try to deal with these outstanding matters first. Also, if the Metal Pig has some large purchases in mind, it would be to his advantage to wait for sale times or other attractive buying opportunities rather than to rush into his purchases. This way he could pick up some excellent bargains and save himself considerable outlay. As far as the Metal Pig's domestic life is concerned, this will be a busy and fulfilling year. The Metal Pig will do much to help, advise and encourage those around him, particularly those much younger as well as more senior than himself. His assistance will be greatly appreciated, with the strong regard others have for his abilities being amply justified. He will also be keen to involve others in some of the household projects he has in mind, but should be wary of starting too many all at once. If not, he could find himself under considerable pressure, some of it unnecessary and even self-inflicted. Again, the Metal Pig would do well to plan household projects in advance and make sure he spreads them through the year. He will enjoy any holidays and breaks he takes over the year and will have the opportunity to visit some truly interesting places, both local and some distance away. For those with a thirst for adventure or the unusual, the year should certainly prove satisfying! With the considerable activity in his domestic life plus all the other things he wants to do, the Metal Pig may feel he has to cut down on his social life. However, while sometimes it may prove difficult to meet up with friends as much as he used to, he should still make the effort to go out regularly and not lose contact with the social circle he has built up. For Metal Pigs who may be unattached or seeking friends, there will be many opportunities to get to know others over the year. To help with this, these Metal Pigs might consider joining a local society or group where they are more likely to meet with those of similar age and interests. Such action could have positive and far-reaching benefits! With his talents, drive and personality, the Metal Pig can make much of the Dragon year, but to benefit from the positive aspects, he should plan his activities as well as make the most of the opportunities that the year will bring. For the determined and enterprising Metal Pig, this will indeed be a significant time and one which will often have a favourable bearing on his future.

This will be an active and agreeable year for the *Water Pig*, with most areas of his life containing interesting developments. For the many Water Pigs in education this will be an important year, with some key exams taking place and the selection of subjects for further study. There will be occasions when these Water Pigs will feel under pressure and daunted by what is being asked of them, but by giving of their best, asking at times of difficulty and working steadily, rather than leaving revision and project work to the last moment, they will obtain some pleasing results. Admittedly, this will mean imposing a certain self-discipline, but what the young Water Pigs achieve now will certainly help their prospects later on. Also, when important decisions need to be taken, particularly when considering subjects for more specialist study or vocational training, the Water Pig should be prepared to discuss his options fully with those around him. Again, his decisions will have important long-term implications and he should take his time in coming to them. For those Water Pigs who seek work over the year, whether on a temporary or permanent basis, this will be an interesting year. A position the Water Pig is offered, although maybe different from the type he was originally seeking, will provide him with useful experience and will be a base, albeit initially small, from which he can develop. Indeed, in the year 2000 it will often be a case of establishing himself on the first rung of the ladder – a ladder which he will assuredly climb in the years ahead. As far as financial matters are concerned, the Water Pig will need to proceed carefully. There will be occasions when his resources will not allow him to do all he would like and he will need to decide how best he can use his sometimes limited means. With planning, however, many Water Pigs will be pleasantly surprised at just how successfully they can manage and what a difference some resourcefulness and enterprise can make! The Water Pig is always one who values his relations with others and both his domestic and social life will bring him much happiness over the year. In addition to the support and advice those around him will give, the Water Pig will also enjoy assisting others in his family, including those much older than himself. This will be greatly appreciated. Socially, too, this will be an active year and the Water Pig will enjoy the time he spends with friends and attending numerous parties and other social events. Indeed, in some parts of the year 2000, his personal diary will be very full, especially during the summer months. It is also at this time that he could strike up what will become a particularly meaningful friendship. Another satisfying area will be his own personal interests and although these may sometimes be difficult to fit in with everything else he wants to do, it is important that the Water Pig does not neglect these. They will not only give him a break from his usual preoccupations but will also allow him to get to know others he might not ordinarily meet and to develop skills and other facets of his character. The Water Pig may already have enough to keep him occupied in 2000, but he owes it to himself to devote time to his own interests. Generally, this will be a positive year for him, with his academic and vocational achievements often being to his long-term benefit, while on a personal level, he really will find himself much in demand and enjoying a pleasing and active social life.

An interesting year is ahead for the *Wood Pig*. Inspired by the start of the new millennium, he will feel that the time has now come for him to set himself some new challenges as well as carry out some of his ideas. These will often relate to his own interests and the Wood Pig may either take up a new hobby or add to his existing skills. Whatever he decides upon, he will find this will help to make this a fulfilling and personally rewarding year. Indeed, the Wood Pig has always been one to enjoy a challenge and by giving himself some objectives, he will certainly add some sparkle to the year 2000. He will particularly enjoy using his creative talents and interests such as photography, artwork, writing or some sort of design work could well fire his imagination. These could even extend to some interior or exterior design, with the Wood Pig deciding to alter the look of certain rooms or redesign his garden. He will also involve others in much of what he does and will often find that a project will benefit from the pooling of talents as well as be easier and more fun to complete. However, while the Wood Pig will accomplish a great deal, if any practical project he tackles involves moving heavy weights or using potentially dangerous equipment, he must take care, follow the recommended safety procedures and, if appropriate, get the task carried out by an expert. Despite the generally favourable aspects that prevail, this is just not a year in which he can take risks with his personal safety. Some Wood Pigs will decide to move over the year and the process will take them considerably longer than they envisaged. However, although time-consuming and at times frustrating, those who do move will be pleased with their new accommodation and will feel that the year has not only ushered in a new millennium but also an interesting new phase in their lives. The Wood Pig's domestic life will bring him considerable pleasure and in addition to his involvement in family activities, he will enjoy following the progress of family members. Several times during the year his advice will be sought by those much younger than himself and he will not only be glad to give his views but will also be heartened by the respect and obvious affection shown him. The Wood Pig does indeed hold an important place in the hearts of many and this will become evident over the year. The aspects also favour social matters and all Wood Pigs can look forward to attending some pleasant social occasions during the year 2000 as well as enjoying the company of friends both old and new. Any Wood Pig who may be feeling lonely or who would like additional company really should make the effort to join in more with group activities, perhaps by getting in contact with a special interest group where he will meet others with similar tastes. As with so many aspects of his life over the Dragon year, if there is something that he wants, positive action on his part really will produce results. This is a favourable year for travel and the Wood Pig should take advantage of any opportunity he gets to go away. This will be a fairly positive year for financial matters, although those Wood Pigs who move or enter into any large transaction would find it in their interests to check all the costs involved as well as the terms of any obligations that they might be entering into. Vigilance in the early stages of a transaction could prevent problems later. Wood Pigs, take note! In most respects, though, this will be very much a year for carrying out plans and ideas and, as a result, the Wood Pig can make it a fulfilling and rewarding one and will enjoy it very much.

This will be a pleasant and constructive year for the *Fire Pig*. Over the last 12 months he will have seen some important changes as well as come up with ideas that he would now like to put into practice. In the year 2000 he will be given his chance as well as have the opportunity to build on his more recent achievements. However, in order to benefit from the positive aspects that prevail, the Fire Pig should be prepared to take the initiative and make the most of what the year offers. In his work, he will impress others with his enthusiastic and willing approach and this will lead to him being given greater responsibilities as the year progresses. For those Fire Pigs who desire it, significant promotion is possible. There will also be opportunities to move to a position which will bring new and interesting challenges. For some Fire Pigs this could even involve a career change. These Fire Pigs will often feel stimulated by the tasks ahead and the chance to use their skills in a different way. During the Dragon year the decisions are very much in the Fire Pig's hands, and, as he realizes, if he is make the most of himself, he should take positive action. This also applies to the Fire Pig who is seeking work. Throughout the year he should persist in following up any openings that he sees and while there may be times when he is dispirited because of his lack of success, he should not lose heart. His enterprise and determination will ultimately be rewarded, though admittedly not always with the type of position he was originally seeking. However, a position the Fire Pig does attain will allow him to add to his skills and discover new strengths. With his many abilities, he has much to offer and the Dragon year will certainly offer some excellent opportunities to put his talents to good use. This is also a positive time for financial matters, with the Fire Pig enjoying an increase in income over the year. In view of this, he will decide to put some of this money towards buying new furnishings and equipment for his home as well as carrying out some improvements. However, if he has any money he does not immediately need, he should consider saving or investing some of it with a view to the longer term. In time this could become a useful asset. The Fire Pig could find, though, that without some control, money tends to come and go quite quickly over the year. This will also be an interesting year for personal matters and in addition to playing a full and active role in family activities, the Fire Pig will do much to assist those around him. Some family events will be a source of much pride, possibly including the birth of a grandchild, the marriage of a close relation or the success of someone dear. However, while there will be much that brings the Fire Pig contentment over the year, mixed in with this will be a few concerns and differences of opinion. Sometimes the Fire Pig's views might run counter to those of certain relatives and at such times, he would find it is better to discuss matters openly and seek some sort of agreement than let the dispute spoil what could be an otherwise pleasant time. Fire Pigs, do be mindful of this. This will also be a fairly active year socially and the Fire Pig can look forward to attending a variety of interesting events as well as enjoying many convivial times with his friends. It could also be worth him contacting those who share his hobbies and interests, either through a society or, if he is able, over the Internet. This again will not only lead to him building some new contacts but will also add a new dimension to some of his interests. The Fire Pig will enjoy the travelling that he undertakes in the year 2000 and should make sure he takes a holiday or break. He will not only benefit from the rest this brings but could also have the opportunity to visit some particularly interesting and sometimes unusual places. Generally, this will be a positive year for the Fire Pig and by making a determined effort to achieve his goals and objectives, he will obtain some worthwhile and often far-reaching results. Indeed, when the Fire Pig sets himself on a course he will let little stand in his way until he has achieved his aims, and this will be the case in the year 2000. For the most part, the aspects will support him well, making this a fulfilling and personally rewarding year.

This will be a splendid year for the *Earth Pig* and he can look forward to pleasing developments in many areas of his life. Indeed, the Earth Pig will feel more inspired than he has of late and will look on the year 2000 as a time for realizing some of his aspirations. He will not be disappointed. With his quiet, confident and determined manner, the Earth Pig knows that to secure his aims he will need to act, and this year he will not hold back. His work is particularly well aspected and in addition to completing his duties to his usual high standards, he should promote any ideas he has as well as show a willingness to make the best of any new proposals under consideration. Throughout the year his keenness and enterprise will be valued and will certainly help him to make further progress. The Earth Pig should also remain alert for promotion possibilities or for any openings that could help his career develop. For these, the months of April, May, September and October could prove an excellent time. Also, whether in work or seeking work, the Earth Pig would do well to discuss his ideas with those able to give informed advice. By being forthcoming and making the most of such opportunities, he will often be given some useful tips and sometimes a good word will be put in on his behalf. In the year 2000 the Earth Pig really does have a lot in his favour and, with determination, almost all Earth Pigs can improve on their position over the year as well as enhance their longer term prospects. The Earth Pig will also fare well in financial matters and in view of this will often be tempted to make some substantial purchases over the year, including furnishings and equipment for his home. Where applicable, he would do well to take his time in making sizeable purchases, comparing the ranges on offer as well as waiting for sales. With patience the Earth Pig can make some fine acquisitions, often at attractive prices. As far as the Earth Pig's domestic life is concerned, this will be a busy and sometimes demanding year, but one which will also bring him considerable happiness. Over the year he will spend much time helping and encouraging those around him, and his attentiveness and the active role he plays in family matters will be greatly appreciated. The Earth Pig will particularly enjoy activities which involve others. As well as mutual interests, these may involve household projects as well as any family holidays and breaks. Throughout the year the Earth Pig will truly value the rapport he has with those close to him and the many meaningful occasions his home life brings. His social life is also favourably aspected and again he can look forward to some pleasant times with friends both old and new and to attending various events. For the unattached or lonely Earth Pig, the Dragon year could see the start of a major new friendship, with the spring a favourable time for meeting others. In most respects this will be a positive and constructive year for the Earth Pig. The one thing he should avoid, though, is becoming involved in too many activities at any one time. Although he may possess a willing nature, he does need to be realistic with his level of commitments and manage his time sensibly. If not, he could find some of the free time he so values has all too easily disappeared. However, provided he bears this in mind, this is a year which holds considerable promise for the Earth Pig and with his many fine qualities he can certainly benefit from the opportunities that it will bring.

FAMOUS PIGS

Russ Abbot, Bryan Adams, Woody Allen, Julie Andrews, Fred Astaire, Sir Richard Attenborough, Lucille Ball, Hector Berlioz, David Blunkett, Humphrey Bogart, James Cagney, Maria Callas, Dr George Carey, Richard Chamberlain, Hillary Rodham Clinton, Glenn Close, David Coultard, Sir Noël Coward, Oliver Cromwell, Billy Crystal, the Dalai Lama, Ted Danson, Richard Dreyfuss, Sheena Easton, Ben Elton, Ralph Waldo Emerson, David Essex, Henry Ford, Emmylou Harris, William Randolph Hearst, Ernest Hemingway, Henry VIII, Alfred Hitchcock, Elton John, Tommy Lee Jones, C. G. Jung, Boris Karloff, Stephen King, Nastassja Kinski, Henry Kissinger, Kevin Kline, Hugh Laurie, David Letterman, Jerry Lee Lewis, Marcel Marceau, Johnny Mathis, Meat Loaf, Dudley Moore, Patrick Moore, Morrissey, John Mortimer, Wolfgang Amadeus Mozart, Camilla Parker Bowles, Michael Parkinson, Luciano Pavarotti, Prince Rainier of Monaco, Maurice Ravel, Ronald Reagan, Ginger Rogers, Nick Ross, Arthur Rubenstein, Salman Rushdie, Baroness Sue Ryder of Warsaw, François Sagan, Pete Sampras, Arantxa Sanchez, Carlos Santana, Arnold Schwarzenegger, Steven Spielberg, Ann Taylor, Emma Thompson, Tracey Ullman, Jules Verne, Jacques Villeneuve, Michael Winner, the Duchess of York.

APPENDIX

---◆◆◆---

The relationship between the 12 animal signs – both on a personal level and business level – is an important aspect of Chinese horoscopes and in this appendix the compatibility between the signs is shown in the two tables that follow.

PERSONAL RELATIONSHIPS

KEY
1 Excellent. Great rapport.
2 A successful relationship. Many interests in common.
3 Mutual respect and understanding. A good relationship.
4 Fair. Needs care and some willingness to compromise in order for the relationship to work.
5 Awkward. Possible difficulties in communication with few interests in common.
6 A clash of personalities. Very difficult.

	Rat	Ox	Tiger	Rabbit	Dragon	Snake	Horse	Goat	Monkey	Rooster	Dog	Pig
Rat	1											
Ox	1	3										
Tiger	4	6	5									
Rabbit	5	2	3	2								
Dragon	1	5	4	3	2							
Snake	3	1	6	2	1	5						
Horse	6	5	1	5	3	4	2					
Goat	5	5	3	1	4	3	2	2				
Monkey	1	3	6	3	1	3	5	3	1			
Rooster	5	1	5	6	2	1	2	5	5	5		
Dog	3	4	1	2	6	3	1	5	3	5	2	
Pig	2	3	2	2	2	6	3	2	2	3	1	2

BUSINESS RELATIONSHIPS

KEY

1 Excellent. Marvellous understanding and rapport.
2 Very good. Complement each other well.
3 A good working relationship and understanding can be developed.
4 Fair, but compromise and a common objective are often needed to make this relationship work.
5 Awkward. Unlikely to work, either through lack of trust, understanding or the competitiveness of the signs.
6 Mistrust. Difficult. To be avoided.

	Rat	Ox	Tiger	Rabbit	Dragon	Snake	Horse	Goat	Monkey	Rooster	Dog	Pig
Rat	2											
Ox	1	3										
Tiger	3	6	5									
Rabbit	4	3	3	3								
Dragon	1	4	3	3	3							
Snake	3	2	6	4	1	5						
Horse	6	5	1	5	3	4	4					
Goat	5	5	3	1	4	3	3	2				
Monkey	2	3	4	5	1	5	4	4	3			
Rooster	5	1	5	5	2	1	2	5	5	6		
Dog	4	5	2	3	6	4	2	5	3	5	4	
Pig	3	3	3	2	3	5	4	2	3	4	3	1

YOUR ASCENDANT

The ascendant has a very strong influence on your personality and, together with the information already given about your sign and the effects of the element on your sign, it will help you gain even greater insight into your true personality according to Chinese horoscopes.

The hours of the day are named after the 12 animal signs and the sign governing the time you were born is your ascendant. To find your ascendant, look up the time of your birth on the table below, bearing in mind any local time differences in the place you were born.

11 p.m.	to	1 a.m.	The hours of the Rat
1 a.m.	to	3 a.m.	The hours of the Ox
3 a.m.	to	5 a.m.	The hours of the Tiger
5 a.m.	to	7 a.m.	The hours of the Rabbit
7 a.m.	to	9 a.m.	The hours of the Dragon
9 a.m.	to	11 a.m.	The hours of the Snake
11 a.m.	to	1 p.m.	The hours of the Horse
1 p.m.	to	3 p.m.	The hours of the Goat
3 p.m.	to	5 p.m.	The hours of the Monkey
5 p.m.	to	7 p.m.	The hours of the Rooster
7 p.m.	to	9 p.m.	The hours of the Dog
9 p.m.	to	11 p.m.	The hours of the Pig

RAT: The influence of the Rat as ascendant is likely to make the sign more outgoing, more sociable and also more careful with money. A particularly beneficial influence for those born under the sign of the Rabbit, Horse, Monkey and Pig.

OX: The Ox as ascendant has a restraining, cautionary and steadying influence which many signs will benefit from. This ascendant also promotes self-confidence and will-power and is an especially good ascendant for those born under the signs of the Tiger, Rabbit and Goat.

TIGER: This ascendant is a dynamic and stirring influence which makes the sign more outgoing, more action-orientated and more impulsive. A generally favourable ascendant for the Ox, Tiger, Snake and Horse.

RABBIT: The Rabbit as ascendant has a moderating influence, making the sign more reflective, serene and discreet. A particularly beneficial influence for the Rat, Dragon, Monkey and Rooster.

DRAGON: The Dragon as ascendant gives strength, determination and an added ambition to the sign. A favourable influence for those born under the signs of the Rabbit, Goat, Monkey and Dog.

SNAKE: The Snake as ascendant can make the sign more reflective, more intuitive and more self-reliant. A good influence for the Tiger, Goat and Pig.

HORSE: The influence of the Horse will make the sign more adventurous, more daring and, on some occasions, more fickle. Generally a beneficial influence for the Rabbit, Snake, Dog and Pig.

GOAT: This ascendant will make the sign more tolerant, easy-going and receptive. The Goat could also impart some creative and artistic qualities to the sign. An especially good influence for the Ox, Dragon, Snake and Rooster.

MONKEY: The Monkey as ascendant is likely to impart a delicious sense of humour and fun to the sign. He will make the sign more enterprising and outgoing – a particularly good influence for the Rat, Ox, Snake and Goat.

ROOSTER: The Rooster as ascendant helps to give the sign a lively, outgoing and very methodical manner. Its influence will increase efficiency and is good for the Ox, Tiger, Rabbit and Horse.

DOG: The Dog as ascendant makes the sign more reasonable and fair-minded as well as giving an added sense of loyalty. A very good ascendant for the Tiger, Dragon and Goat.

PIG: The influence of the Pig can make the sign more sociable, content and self-indulgent. It is also a caring influence and one which can make the sign want to help others. A good ascendant for the Dragon and Monkey.

HOW TO GET THE BEST FROM YOUR CHINESE SIGN AND THE YEAR

To supplement the earlier chapters on the personality and horoscope of the signs, I have included in this appendix a guide on how you can get the best out of your sign and the year.

Each of the 12 Chinese signs possesses its own unique strengths and by identifying them you can use them to your advantage. Similarly, by becoming aware of possible weaknesses you can do much to rectify them and in this respect I hope the following sections will be useful. Also included are some tips on how you can get the best from the Year of the Dragon. The areas covered are general prospects, career prospects, finance and relations with others.

THE RAT

The Rat is blessed with many fine talents but his un-doubted strength lies in his ability to get on with others. He is sociable, charming and a good judge of character. He also possesses a shrewd mind and is good at spotting opportunities.

However, to make the most of himself and his abilities, the Rat does need to impose some discipline upon himself. He should resist the temptation (sometimes very great!) of getting involved in too many activities all at the same time and decide upon his priorities and objectives. By concentrating his energies on specific matters he will fare much better as a result. Also, given his personable manner, he should seek out positions where he can use his personal relations skills to good effect. For a career, sales and marketing could prove ideal.

The Rat is also astute in dealing with finance but, while often thrifty, he can sometimes give way to moments of indulgence. Although he deserves to enjoy the money he has so carefully earned, it may sometimes be in his interests to exercise more restraint when tempted to satisfy too many extravagant whims!

The Rat's family and friends are also most important to him and while he is loyal and protective towards them, he does tend to keep his worries and concerns to himself. He would be helped if he were more willing to discuss any anxieties he has. Those around the Rat think highly of him and are prepared to do much to help him, but for them to do this he does need to be less secretive and guarded.

With his sharp mind, keen imagination and sociable manner, the Rat does, however, have much in his favour. First, though, he should decide what he wants to achieve and then concentrate upon his chosen objectives. When he has commitment, the Rat can be irrepressible and, given his considerable charm, he can often be irresistible as well! Provided he channels his energies wisely he can make much of his life.

Advice for the Rat's Year Ahead

GENERAL PROSPECTS

An excellent year ahead but to make the most of it the Rat should decide upon his objectives and then set about achieving them. Positive action will lead to some beneficial and far-reaching results.

CAREER PROSPECTS

A year of opportunities. The Rat should make every attempt to improve on his present position and take advantage of any openings that occur as well as further his ideas. With determination, considerable progress is possible, with the Rat's resourceful and enterprising nature being well rewarded.

FINANCE

A considerable improvement is indicated, enabling the Rat to proceed with his ideas for his accommodation and also to undertake some travelling. Care, though, is needed if lending to others.

RELATIONS WITH OTHERS

A great year with the sociable Rat enjoying some meaningful occasions with both family and friends. Important new friendships will be formed, with the aspects being splendid for romance. This will be a year the Rat will savour.

THE OX

Strong-willed, determined and resolute, the Ox certainly has a mind of his own! He is also persistent and sets about achieving his objectives with a dogged determination. In addition, he is reliable and tenacious and is often a source of inspiration to others. The Ox is a doer and an achiever and in life he often accomplishes much. However, for him to really excel, he would do well to try and correct his weaknesses.

Being so resolute and having such a strong sense of purpose, the Ox can be inflexible and narrow-minded. He can be resistant to change and prefers to set about his activities in his own way rather than be too dependent on others. He should aim to be more outgoing and adventurous in his outlook. His dislike of change can sometimes be to his detriment and if he were prepared to be more adaptable he would find his progress both easier and smoother.

The Ox would also be helped if he were to broaden his range of interests and become more relaxed in his approach. At times he can be so preoccupied with his own activities that he is not always as mindful of others as he should be and his demeanour can sometimes be studious and serious. There are times when he would benefit from a lighter touch.

However, the Ox is true to his word and loyal to his family and friends. He is admired and respected by others and his tremendous will-power usually enables him to secure much in life.

Advice for the Ox's Year Ahead

GENERAL PROSPECTS

Although the Ox may not always feel at ease with the changes and panache that the Dragon year brings, very often its events will be instrumental in bringing about positive and far-reaching developments. A year in which to proceed carefully, adapt and make the best of new situations.

CAREER PROSPECTS

The Ox may sometimes have misgivings about the changes taking place in his work or some of the duties he is given, but often these will pave the way for new and interesting opportunities. This is a time to be watchful, to gain experience and to adapt. Considerable benefits can come from the Dragon year, setting the Ox off in new directions which can, in time, bring significant results.

FINANCE

A generally positive year. The Ox will, though, find it in his interests to take his time over major purchases and also put some money aside for recreational pursuits and a well-deserved holiday.

RELATIONS WITH OTHERS

Although this may be a challenging year for the Ox, he will draw much comfort from the support, encouragement and affection of his family and friends. His domestic and social life will bring rewarding moments and he should not be reticent about seeking advice over any matter concerning him; as he will find, a problem shared is indeed a problem halved!

THE TIGER

Lively, innovative and enterprising, the Tiger is one who enjoys an active lifestyle. He has a wide range of interests, an alert mind and a genuine liking of others. He likes to live life to the full. However, despite his enthusiastic and well-meaning ways, he does not always make the most of his considerable potential.

By being so versatile, the Tiger does have a tendency to jump from one activity to another or dissipate his energies by trying to do too much at any one time. To make the most of himself he should try to exercise a certain amount of self-discipline. Ideally, he should decide how best he can use his abilities, give himself some objectives and stick with these. If he can overcome his restless tendencies and persist in what he does, he will find he will accomplish much more.

Also, in spite of his sociable manner, the Tiger likes to retain a certain independence in his actions and while few begrudge him this, he would sometimes find life easier if he were more prepared to work in conjunction with others. His reliance upon his own judgement does sometimes mean that he excludes the views and advice of those around him, and this can be to his detriment. The Tiger may possess an independent spirit, but he must not let his independence go too far!

The Tiger does, however, have much in his favour. He is bold, original and quick-witted. If he can keep his restless nature in check he can enjoy considerable success. In addition, his engaging personality makes him one who is much admired and well-liked.

Advice for the Tiger's Year Ahead

GENERAL PROSPECTS
The coming of the new millennium will, for many Tigers, be a spur to take action and set about realizing some of their aspirations. By taking positive action, the Tiger can achieve some worthwhile and often far-reaching results. An active and fulfilling year.

CAREER PROSPECTS
Good progress is possible. By actively setting out to improve his position and following up the opportunities that become available, as well as creating or suggesting some, the Tiger will achieve some positive results. He knows he possesses many fine talents and he will be given the chance to use and develop these, and will greatly impress as a consequence.

FINANCE
The Tiger will enjoy an improvement in his financial situation, but the year still calls for care, the avoidance of risks and some control over the purse strings! The Tiger can make money but without careful management, this could be spent all too easily.

RELATIONS WITH OTHERS

A fine year, with the Tiger enjoying a full and active domestic and social life. The unattached Tiger and those seeking friends should make a real effort to go out more and meet others, perhaps by joining local societies or interest groups. New friends, romance and marriage are all possible in what will be a pleasing year for personal matters.

THE RABBIT

The Rabbit is certainly one who appreciates the finer things in life. With his good taste, companionable nature and wide range of interests, he knows how to live well – and usually does!

However, for all his finesse and style, the Rabbit does possess traits he would do well to watch. His desire for a settled lifestyle makes him err on the side of caution. He dislikes change and as a consequence can miss out on opportunities. Also, there are many Rabbits who will go to great lengths to avoid difficult and fraught situations, and again, while few may relish these, sometimes in life it is necessary to take risks or stand your ground just to get on. At times it would certainly be in the Rabbit's interests to be bolder and more assertive in going after whatever he desires.

The Rabbit also attaches great importance to his relations with others and while he has a happy knack of getting on with most, he can be sensitive to criticism. In this, difficult though it may be, he should really try to develop a thicker skin. He should recognize that criticism can provide valuable learning opportunities, as can some of the problems he strives so hard to avoid.

However, with his agreeable manner, keen intellect and shrewd judgement, the Rabbit does have much in his favour and invariably makes much of his life – and usually enjoys it too!

Advice for the Rabbit's Year Ahead

GENERAL PROSPECTS
Although the year will not always contain the stability that the Rabbit so values, it will often be instrumental in bringing positive change and long-term benefits. This is a year in which to adapt and make the best of situations. Time spent extending or taking up new interests will be especially fulfilling.

CAREER PROSPECTS
The best results will be obtained by concentrating on the types of work the Rabbit knows best. Even so, his skills will be tested and he will have challenges to surmount. This is a year in which to tread carefully and remain alert, but what the Rabbit accomplishes now will often have a positive bearing in the not too distant future.

FINANCE
By managing his finances in his usual skilful manner the Rabbit can fare reasonably well. However, this is not a year for taking undue risks or tempting luck too far. Vigilance is the order of the day – and year!

RELATIONS WITH OTHERS

The Rabbit will be truly grateful for the support he receives over the year and if he has any concerns or feels under pressure it is important that he seeks assistance. He can, though, look forward to a fulfilling domestic life, while on a social level fine times with friends both old and new are indicated.

THE DRAGON

Enthusiastic, enterprising and honourable, the Dragon possesses many admirable qualities and his life is often full and varied. He always gives of his best and even though not all his endeavours may meet with success, he is none the less resilient and hardy. As a person, he is much admired and respected.

However, for all his many qualities, the Dragon can be blunt and forthright and, through sheer strength of character, sometimes domineering. It would certainly be in his interests to listen more closely to others rather than be so self-reliant. Also, his enthusiasm can sometimes get the better of him and he can be impulsive. To make the most of his abilities, he should set himself priorities and set about his activities in a disciplined and systematic way. More tact and diplomacy might not come amiss either!

However, with his lively and outgoing manner, the Dragon is popular and well-liked. With good fortune on his side (and the Dragon is often lucky), his life is almost certain to be eventful and fulfilling. He has many talents and if he uses them wisely he will enjoy much success.

Advice for the Dragon's Year Ahead

GENERAL PROSPECTS

With an increased sense of optimism and determination, the Dragon will make a concerted effort to realize some of his ambitions. His commitment and resolve will bring significant results. A year in which to decide upon objectives and then go wholeheartedly after them.

CAREER PROSPECTS

A year of great opportunity and a chance to put ideas, skills and training to effective use. A time for the Dragon to be bold, enterprising and to make every attempt to improve on his present situation. Substantial progress can be made.

FINANCE

To gain the most benefit from the positive trends surrounding financial matters, the Dragon should decide how best to use his money, ideally saving some and setting the rest towards specific purposes. Good management will repay him handsomely.

RELATIONS WITH OTHERS

A great year, with the Dragon enjoying the company of family and friends. Both his home and social life will be active and fulfilling and he will appreciate the support he is given. Prospects are excellent for romance and new friendships, and any Dragon who finds himself in low spirits should aim to improve his social life. By taking positive steps he will achieve a great deal.

THE SNAKE

The Snake is blessed with a keen intellect. He has wide interests, an enquiring mind and good judgement. He tends to be quiet and thoughtful and plans his activities with considerable care. With his fine abilities he often does well in life, but he does possess traits which can undermine his progress.

The Snake is often guarded in his actions and sometimes loses out to those who are more action-oriented and assertive. He can also be a loner and likes to retain a certain independence in his actions, and this too can hamper his progress. It would be in his interests to be more forthcoming and involve others more readily in his plans. The Snake has many talents and possesses a warm and rich personality but there is a danger that this can remain concealed behind his often quiet and reserved manner. He would fare better by being more outgoing and showing others his true worth.

However, the Snake is very much his own master. He invariably knows what he wants in life and is often prepared to journey long and hard to achieve his objectives. He does, though, have it in his power to make that journey easier. Lose some of that reticence, Snake, be more open and assertive, and do not be afraid of the occasional risk!

Advice for the Snake's Year Ahead

GENERAL PROSPECTS

Although the Snake may have his reservations about some of what takes place this will still be a valuable year. In particular, the Snake should think about how he would like to see his life developing and should prepare for his long-term goals. Much can result from plans made now.

CAREER PROSPECTS

Consolidate recent achievements, stay alert for new developments, watch and learn. Actual progress may be modest but the year could see the start of projects, plans and even a new position which will bring considerable future success.

FINANCE

The Snake cannot afford to relax his usual vigilant nature. Avoid risks and check important documents and agreements carefully.

RELATIONS WITH OTHERS

The Snake will be thankful for the support and encouragement he receives in his many activities and will gain much from the advice of others. His domestic life will be busy but satisfying and his social life pleasurable. However, with the many demands on his time, the Snake should ensure he maintains his personal interests. Outdoor and creative activities will go particularly well.

THE HORSE

Versatile, hard-working and sociable, the Horse makes his mark wherever he goes. He has an eloquent and engaging manner and makes friends with ease. He is quick-witted, has an alert mind and is certainly not averse to taking risks or experimenting with new ideas.

The Horse possesses a strong and likeable personality but he does also have his weaknesses. With his wide interests he does not always finish everything he starts and he would do well to be more persevering. He has it within him to achieve considerable success but when he has made his plans he should stick with them. To make the most of his talents he does need to overcome his restless tendencies.

The Horse loves company and values both his family and friends. However, there will have been many a time when he has spoken in haste and regretted his words or lost his temper. Throughout his life, the Horse needs to keep his temper in check and learn to be diplomatic in tense situations. If not, he could risk jeopardizing the respect and good relations he so much values by a thoughtless remark or action.

However, the Horse has a multitude of talents and a lively and outgoing personality. If he can overcome his restless and volatile nature, he can lead a rich and highly fulfilling life.

Advice for the Horse's Year Ahead

GENERAL PROSPECTS

With high hopes and a determined attitude, the Horse will aim to make something of the year. While his achievements may not always meet his often high expectations, what he does accomplish will prove of great value, particularly in the long term.

CAREER PROSPECTS

An interesting year and one in which the Horse should make good use of his skills and strengths. What he accomplishes now will impress others and do much to enhance his future prospects. A year for making the best of the situations and opportunities that occur. A hobby or interest could, with enterprise, provide additional income.

FINANCE

A year for careful financial management. Watch spending and take time with any important documents or forms that need to be completed, as well as checking the small print of new agreements. This is not a year for risks or complacency.

RELATIONS WITH OTHERS

Some pleasing and happy times ahead with both family and friends. The Horse will greatly enjoy activities that he can share and by being forthcoming over his own hopes will benefit from the support he is given. New friends and romance will bring much happiness.

THE GOAT

The Goat has a warm, friendly and understanding manner and gets on well with most. He is generally easy-going, has a fond appreciation of the finer things in life and possesses a rich imagination. He is often artistic and enjoys the creative arts and outdoor activities.

However, despite his engaging manner, there lurks beneath his skin a sometimes tense and pessimistic nature.

The Goat can be a worrier and without the support and encouragement of others can feel insecure and be hesitant in his actions.

To make the most of himself and his abilities the Goat should aim to become more assertive and decisive as well as more at ease with himself. He has much in his favour, but he really does need to promote himself more and aim to be bolder in his actions. He would also be helped if he were to sort out his priorities and set about his activities in an organized and disciplined manner. There are some Goats who tend to be haphazard in the way they go about things and this can hamper their progress.

Although the Goat will always value the support and backing of others, it would also be in his interests to become more independent in his actions and not be so reticent about striking out on his own. He does, after all, possess many talents, as well as a sincere and likeable personality, and by always giving of his best, he can make his life rich, rewarding and enjoyable.

Advice for the Goat's Year Ahead

GENERAL PROSPECTS

A demanding year, with the Goat experiencing difficulty with some of what he wants to carry out. However this will often give him the chance to form new ideas and draw on his strengths. As a result, he will gain much of value in 2000 as well as do much to prepare the way for future success.

CAREER PROSPECTS

While the Goat should consolidate recent gains, he should also remain alert to all that is happening and be flexible in his approach. This is a year for proceeding carefully, but by giving of his best and taking advantage of any opportunities, even though they may not be ideal, the Goat can do much to enhance his prospects.

FINANCE

With large expenses likely, especially involving accommodation, the Goat should keep a close watch on his spending, avoid risks and take the time and effort to manage his financial situation.

RELATIONS WITH OTHERS

With this being a sometimes challenging year the Goat will appreciate the support he receives from those around him and should be forthcoming over any problems he might have. His domestic and social life will be busy but will bring considerable joy. Time spent on his own personal interests will prove satisfying and beneficial, particularly as these help him to relax.

THE MONKEY

Lively, enterprising and innovative, the Monkey certainly knows how to impress. He has wide interests, a good sense of fun and relates well to others. He also possesses a shrewd mind and often has a happy knack of turning events to his advantage.

However, despite his versatility and considerable gifts, the Monkey does have his weaknesses. He often lacks persistence, can get distracted easily and also places tremendous reliance upon his own judgement. While his belief in himself is a commendable asset, it would certainly be in his interests to be more mindful of the views of others. Also, while he likes to keep tabs on all that is going on around him, he can be evasive and secretive with regard to his own feelings and activities, and again a more forthcoming attitude would be to his advantage.

The Monkey also possesses a most enterprising nature, although in his desire to succeed he can sometimes be tempted to cut corners or be crafty. He should recognize that such actions can rebound on him!

However, the Monkey is resourceful and his sheer strength of character will lead him to an interesting and varied life. If he can channel his considerable energies wisely and overcome his sometimes restless tendencies, his life can be crowned with success and achievement. Added to which, with his amiable personality, he will enjoy the friendship of many.

Advice for the Monkey's Year Ahead

GENERAL PROSPECTS

Feeling inspired and motivated, the Monkey will determine to make something of the year and, with his enterprising and resourceful manner, will achieve much. However, to get the best results, he does need to give some thought to his activities, otherwise he could find he is spreading his energies just a little too widely.

CAREER PROSPECTS

A year of change and progress. To benefit and prosper from the favourable aspects the Monkey should actively pursue opportunities as well as promote his ideas and talents. There will be some excellent chances for him to advance, use and indeed extend his capabilities.

FINANCE

Although this is a positive year for financial matters, the Monkey should avoid unnecessary risks and take his time when considering major purchases.

RELATIONS WITH OTHERS

Throughout the year the Monkey will be grateful for the support he is given but should listen carefully to advice offered by family and friends. Socially, the year offers much promise, with many Monkeys making new friends. For the unattached, the prospects for romance are excellent.

THE ROOSTER

With his considerable bearing and incisive and resolute manner, the Rooster makes an impressive figure. He has a sharp mind, keeps well-informed on many matters and expresses himself clearly and convincingly. He is meticulous and efficient in his undertakings and commands much respect. He also has a genuine and caring interest in others.

The Rooster has much in his favour but there are some aspects of his character that can tell against him. He can be candid in his views and sometimes over-zealous in his actions, and without forethought he can say or do things he later regrets. His high standards also make him fussy – even pedantic – and he can get diverted onto relatively minor matters when, in truth, he could be occupying his time more profitably. This is something all Roosters would do well to watch. Also, while the Rooster is a great planner, he can sometimes be unrealistic in his expectations. In making plans – indeed, with most of his activities – he would do well to consult others rather than keep his thoughts to himself. By doing so, he will greatly benefit from their input.

The Rooster has considerable talents as well as a commendable drive and commitment, but to make the most of himself he does need to channel his energies wisely and watch his candid and sometimes volatile nature. With care, he can make a success of his life, and with his wide interests and outgoing personality will enjoy the friendship and respect of many.

Advice for the Rooster's Year Ahead

GENERAL PROSPECTS

This will be an excellent year for the Rooster, with most areas of his life being well aspected. However, to get the best from the year he should give serious thought to what he wants to achieve and then set about realizing his aims in his usual determined way. For those prepared to make the most of the opportunities, this really will be a productive and fulfilling year.

CAREER PROSPECTS

A year of great opportunities. Throughout the Rooster should seize any chance to progress, develop his skills and further his career. His prospects really are excellent and by giving of his best and making the most of his considerable talents, he can look forward to making impressive headway. A good year for promoting ideas.

FINANCE

The Rooster's success over the year will bring an improvement in his financial situation, especially in the second half of the year, but he should not allow this to tempt him into spending too readily or making hasty purchases. He would also do well to consider making some savings.

RELATIONS WITH OTHERS

An excellent year, with the Rooster enjoying and valuing both his domestic and social life. He can look forward to many meaningful occasions with those around them as well as benefit from the support and advice he is given. Romance and new friendships are well aspected and will bring much happiness.

THE DOG

Loyal, dependable and with a good understanding of human nature, the Dog is well placed to win the respect and admiration of many. He is a no-nonsense sort of person and hates any sort of hypocrisy and falsehood. With the Dog you know where you stand and, given his direct manner, where he stands on any issue. He also has a strong humanitarian nature and often champions good and just causes.

The Dog has many fine attributes, although there are certain traits that can prevent him from either enjoying or making the most of his life. He is a great worrier and can get anxious over all manner of things. Although it may not always be easy, the Dog should try to rid himself of the 'worry habit'. When tense or concerned, he should be prepared to speak to others rather than shoulder his worries all by himself. In some cases, they could even be of his own making! Also, the Dog has a tendency to look on the pessimistic side of things and he would certainly be helped if he were to look more optimistically on his undertakings. He does, after all, possess many skills and should justifiably have faith in his abilities. Another weakness is his tendency to be stubborn over certain issues. If he is not careful, this could at times undermine his position.

If the Dog can reduce the anxious and pessimistic side of his nature, then he will not only enjoy life more but also find he is achieving more. He possesses a truly admirable character and his loyalty, reliability and sincerity are appreciated by all he meets. In his life he will do much good and befriend many – and he owes it to himself to enjoy life too. Sometimes it might help him to recall the words of another Dog, Winston Churchill: 'When I look back on all these worries I remember the story of the old man who said on his deathbed that he had had a lot of trouble in his life, most of which never happened.'

Advice for the Dog's Year Ahead

GENERAL PROSPECTS

A tricky year, with the Dog facing problems and changes and having to review some of his plans. However, the Dragon year will usher in new opportunities that can have a positive bearing on the future. The Dog should remain alert and be prepared to make the most of changing situations.

CAREER PROSPECTS

A year which will see some significant changes, with the Dog taking on different duties, switching to a new job and looking closely at how he would like his future to develop. This may not be an easy year, but it will often set the Dog on a new course with interesting prospects. A good year for training and learning new skills.

FINANCE

A year for vigilance and care, especially when completing forms or taking on new commitments. If the Dog has doubts, he should seek guidance or clarification. Paperwork, receipts and guarantees need to be looked after carefully.

RELATIONS WITH OTHERS

In view of the demanding nature of some of the year, the Dog will be grateful for the support he is given and should remain mindful of any advice offered. His family and friends will prove of great value, and his personal interests and social life, including travel, will also provide many pleasurable occasions.

THE PIG

Genial, sincere and trusting, the Pig gets on well with most. He has a kind and caring nature, a dislike of discord and often possesses a good sense of humour. In addition, he has a fondness for socializing and enjoying the good life!

The Pig also possesses a shrewd mind, is particularly adept in dealing with business and financial matters, and has a robust and resilient nature. Although not all his plans in life may work out as he would like, he is tenacious and will often rise up and succeed after experiencing setbacks and difficulties. In his often active and varied life he can accomplish much, although there are certain aspects of his character that can tell against him. If he can modify or keep these areas in check then his life will certainly be easier and possibly even more successful.

In his activities the Pig can sometimes overcommit himself and while he does not want to disappoint, he would certainly be helped if he were to set about his activities in an organized and systematic manner and give himself priorities at busy times. He should also not allow others to take advantage of his good nature and it would be in his interests if he were sometimes more discerning. There will have been times when he has been gullible and naïve; fortunately, though, the Pig quickly learns from his mistakes. He also possesses a stubborn streak and if new situations do not fit in with his line of thinking, he can be inflexible. Such an attitude may not always be to his advantage.

The Pig is a great pleasure-seeker and while he should deservedly enjoy the fruits of his labours, he can sometimes be self-indulgent and extravagant. This is again something he would do well to watch.

However, though the Pig may possess some faults, those who come into contact with him are invariably impressed by his integrity, amiable manner and intelligence. If he uses his talents wisely, his life can be crowned with considerable achievement and the good-hearted Pig will also be loved and respected by many.

Advice for the Pig's Year Ahead

GENERAL PROSPECTS
A generally pleasing year, although to make the most of the favourable tends that prevail, the Pig should give some thought to what he wants to achieve and then make a determined effort to secure his aims. The year will favour the bold and enterprising.

CAREER PROSPECTS
An important year, giving the Pig the chance to take on new duties, extend his skills and show his considerable worth. The year will also bring new challenges and objectives and these will give the Pig an added incentive to give of his best. It really does rest with him to make the most of the opportunities.

FINANCE
The Pig will enjoy an improvement in his income over the year but will be tempted to make many purchases, particularly for his accommodation. It would certainly be in his

interests to keep a watchful eye on his spending and wait for sales and favourable buying opportunities rather than proceeding too hurriedly.

RELATIONS WITH OTHERS

The Pig always sets great store by his relations with others and his domestic and social life will go well. However, as with any year, some differences could arise and the Pig's skills as a master diplomat will be appreciated. There will be opportunities to extend his social circle, with one new friendship becoming important for the future.